A VERY OLD MACHINE

A VERY OLD MACHINE

The Many Origins of the Cinema in India

SUDHIR MAHADEVAN

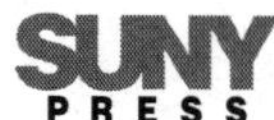

Published by
STATE UNIVERSITY OF NEW YORK PRESS
Albany

For information, contact
State University of New York Press
www.sunypress.edu

Production, Laurie D. Searl
Marketing, Kate R. Seburyamo

Library of Congress Cataloging-in-Publication Data

Mahadevan, Sudhir, [date]
    A very old machine : the many origins of the cinema in India / Sudhir Mahadevan.
        pages cm. — (SUNY series, Horizons of cinema)
    Includes bibliographical references and index.
    ISBN 978-1-4384-5829-8 (hardcover : alk. paper)
    ISBN 978-1-4384-5828-1 (pbk. : alk. paper)
    ISBN 978-1-4384-5830-4 (e-book)
    1. Motion pictures—India—History.   2. Motion picture industry—India—History.   I. Title.
    PN1993.5.I8M326 2015
    791.430954—dc23   2014045586

10 9 8 7 6 5 4 3 2 1

CONTENTS

PART III: INTERMEDIALITY

PART IV: ARCHIVES

ILLUSTRATIONS

ACKNOWLEDGMENTS

Speaking of origins, the title of this book was proposed by Murray Pomerance at a DOMITOR conference a few years ago, during a brief ten-minute break between panels. Murray has been more than a friend and Series Editor at SUNY for this project (and with the title of this book, a conceptualizer-in-chief). His guidance has been invaluable in seeing this manuscript through to book form. Thanks go also to James Peltz, co-director of SUNY Press, to Rafael Chaiken, the production and copy editors Laurie Searl and Alan Hewat, the marketing team, including Kate Seburyamo, and everyone at the Press for seeing this manuscript through to publication.

I'm grateful to my intellectual and professional homes at the University of Washington in Seattle: the Department of Comparative Literature, Cinema and Media, my current and past chairs in the department, Mìceàl Vaughan and Cynthia Steele, my colleagues in the Film Studies Program (Jennifer Bean, Eric Ames, Yomi Braester, Tamara Cooper, Cynthia Steele, James Tweedie), and my colleagues in the South Asia Studies Program in The Jackson School of International Studies. My film studies colleagues saw me through challenging moments by shouldering some of my existing teaching commitments. Particular thanks go to Jennifer Bean, James Tweedie, and to doctoral candidate Kathy Morrow in this regard. Without all of them, and the inspiration of their own scholarly work, this book is unimaginable. Marcia Feinstein-Tobey has been a pillar of administrative and logistical support, and along with Yuko Mera, an additional source of camaraderie that I have valued very much. Paul Morton copyedited early versions and also undertook some of the late research and scanning of images. I owe many of the same debts to the South Asia Program at the UW under the direction of Priti Ramamurthy and Anand Yang. Institutional support came in the form of a Society of Scholars Fellowship at the UW's Simpson Center for the Humanities. Two quarters off as part of the Junior Faculty Development Program at the UW were additionally instrumental for this project. Christian Novetzke's counsel with regard to this book as well as on more practical matters has been far more valuable and profound for me than I may have communicated to him. Michael Shapiro, as Divisional Dean of the Humanities, approved significant funds in the form of subvention for the production of this book. Priti Ramamurthy's seemingly inexhaustible source of intellectual and practical guidance has been nothing short of fundamentally enabling.

Over the years, I have relied on the staff of many research institutions and archives in India and elsewhere. I am very grateful to all of them for making this book possible. Amma (my mother Vimala Kumar) served as liaison with the Asiatic Society in acquiring scans after I had left Kolkata, and a considerable portion of chapter 5 would never have come to fruition without her intervention and extraordinary ability to patiently navigate even the most recalcitrant of bureaucracies. Her indefatigable approach to challenges is tough to live up to and easy to respect. Jessica Scarlatta provided urgently needed and timely assistance with images in the last stages of this book's production. Amit Malhotra, Prashant Kadam, Padmanabha Rao, Tim Sternberg, David McDougall, and Peeyush Sekhsaria shared their photographic and film work and thoughts on this project.

My intellectual debts are so immense that I'm not sure this brief acknowledgment will do justice. Nitin Govil is probably the most instrumental here in nudging me to think about assemblages and media archaeology for an early piece that appeared in *Bioscope*, and is dear friend and mentor rolled into one. I am also extremely grateful to Ravi Vasudevan for inviting me to share an early portion from this book for publication, as well as for his extensive feedback. The many others who read, commented, and shared ideas include Richard Allen, Eric Ames, Sareeta Amrute, Ulka Anjaria, Anustup Basu, Jennifer Bean, Ira Bhaskar, Kiko Benitez, Yomi Braester, Marshall Brown, Ranita Chatterjee, Corey Creekmur, Manishita Dass, Christof Dupin, Bishnupriya Ghosh, Stephen Hughes (whose work on early cinema in Madras is exemplary for me, and whose gentlest remonstrations on inartful formulations came weighted with insight), Priya Jaikumar, Reese Jenkins, Sonal Khullar, Antonia Lant, Brian Larkin, Anna McCarthy, Neepa Majumdar, Ranjani Mazumdar, Ivone Margulies, Anand Pandian, Christopher Pinney, Aswin Punathambekar, Ashish Rajadhyaksha, Tirthankar Roy, Bhaskar Sarkar, Girish Shambu, Ravi Sundaram, Clare Wilkinson-Weber, Kathy Woodward, Anand Yang, and Pierce Young.

Chapter 7 benefited significantly from the opportunity to give a talk at the Film and Media Studies Department at the University of California, Santa Barbara, organized by Film and Media Studies and the South Asia Studies Research Focus Group. Final versions of chapters 5 and 6 came together in the aftermath of the *Many Lives of Indian Cinema* conference at Sarai, New Delhi, in January 2014. The anonymous reviewers at SUNY have saved me from embarrassing mistakes and pointed to areas that needed more work. Acknowledging these debts must go along with my accepting full responsibility for shortcomings that are still in evidence in this book. Chapter 2 is a modified version of an article in the inaugural issue of *Bioscope: Journal of South Asian Screen Studies* (Vol. 1, No. 1. Copyright 2010 © Screen South Asia Trust. All rights reserved. Reprinted with permission of the copyright holders and the publishers, Sage Publications India Pvt. Ltd, New Delhi). I thank Sage Publications (and Neetu Kalra) for permission to reproduce that article.

Kimberly Williams-Guillèn, my partner and closest friend, has accommodated way more than she needed to while facing formidable challenges and the significant commitments of her intellectual and professional life. Destiny Mahadevan, Chance Williams-Guillèn, and Tobias Funke (and their wandering fellow-felines on Oswego Place) have made parenting (of sorts) a pleasure. With more gratitude than I can ever express in words, I dedicate this book to Appa (B. M. Iyer), from whom I inherited the passion for history.

INTRODUCTION

A Very Old Machine . . .

In 2010, walking through Hauz Khaz, a tourist "village" in Delhi that hawks "ethnic" clothing accessories and decorative objects (pashmina shawls, traditional jewelry, carpets and rugs) for tourists, I found a "Bioscope" hidden under a heavy tarpaulin cover. Bioscope was the name by which the cinema became popularly known in the early twentieth century in India. Today the Bioscope refers commonly to the traveling picture showman's apparatus that might involve still photographs, moving images, printed and painted ones, or a combination of all of these. This Bioscope was hexagonal in shape, with six peepholes. On top was an angled metal rod that served as a lever to scroll through the images. I peered into one of the peepholes and turned the lever, hoping to see something. But in order to function, the contraption still needed lighting and a roll of images that was absent (see Fig. 0.1).

Later, the friend who had accompanied me to Hauz Khas that day sent me two other photos of the same contraption, taken at an annual crafts fair in Delhi called the Dastkar Mela. This time, though, the manual Bioscope had become an electronic one, plugged in, amplified, and turned on. A mega-horn speaker was perched on top of the Bioscope, and next to it, a DVD player with DVDs, and all of this connected to a tangle of wires leading to an electrical source (see Fig. 0.2).

No technology dies a predictable death in India. Nor does it undergo an ordinary birth. Both are evident in the contraption I have just described. This book demonstrates how this axiom applies to the emergence of the cinema in South Asia. The title of the book therefore alludes to the Bioscope as an assemblage that is emblematic of film culture in India and how its

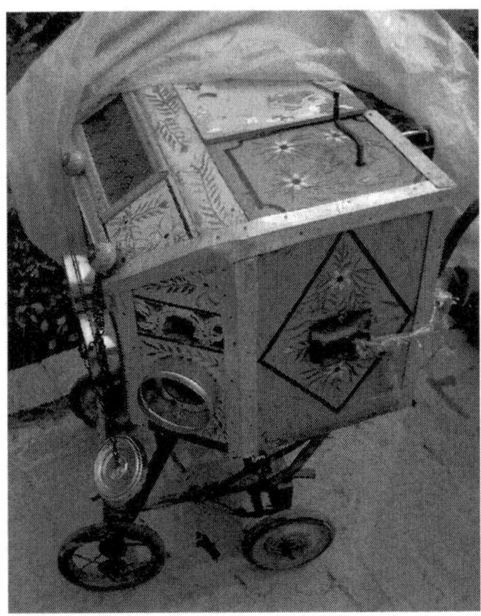

Figure 0.1. A Bioscope at Hauz Khas, New Delhi (Photo: Amit Malhotra).

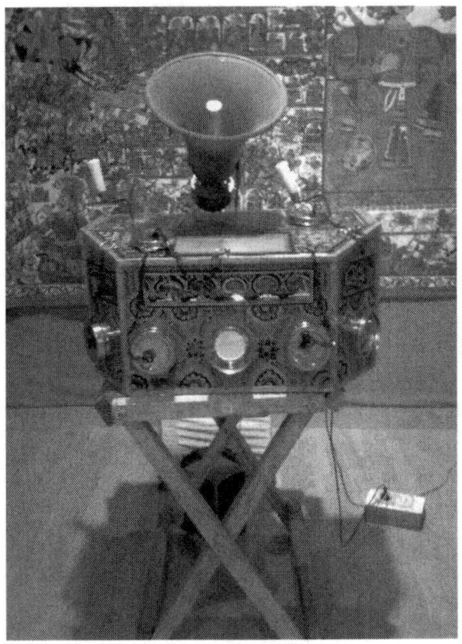

Figure 0.2. A Bioscope at the Dastkar Mela, New Delhi, 2010, with mega-horn speaker, DVD player (not visible), and electrical light source (Photo: Amit Malhotra).

history has been shaped. The Bioscope is a combination of past and present. It represents a key symbol of early cinema brushing against new and not so new media. It is the result of the refashioning of an "optical device" of still pictures well pre-dating the cinema in the nineteenth century, into a source of moving images with the help of domestic home viewing technology and digital formats. Finally the assemblage performs and demands a public space and publicity for its viability. The embedded temporalities of just a single contraption capture I think, the complexity of India's visual cultures, especially those centered on the cinema.

A Very Old Machine searches for antecedents to—or previous versions of—the imaginaries that have informed the cinema's place in everyday life and the practices that have sustained its manifestations, both mainstream and idiosyncratic, in India. I investigate the emergence of the cinema in India from a variety of perspectives: as a screen practice that became viable as much through makeshift technologies as through capital intensive practices, as mass culture whose legitimacy was won in the nexus of commerce, culture, and the global traffic in images, as hybrid media that in tandem with photography and print culture registered the experience of modern life and thus established itself as a medium of topical relevance, and finally, as a form of social and cultural memory that has been particularly suited to a cinema whose many origins have made a single archive and a singular narrative impossible to produce and sustain.

Put another way,

How did the cinema become viable?

How did it become the most prominent form of mass culture?

How has its presence come to be relevant for everyday life?

And how do the answers to these questions shape popular understandings of the cinema's legacies?

The aim of this book, therefore, is to forego a singular account of the cinema and instead to offer in its place a methodologically eclectic exploration of its past with a frequent and full embrace of the vantage point of the present. This volume draws on media archaeology, on legal and cultural histories, on contextually bound speculations over visual ephemera, and on textual analysis to offer fragments of a fissured past.

Today, outside of the movie theater, the cinema is visible and audible in India in a staggering multiplicity of ways: as billboards, as iconography for backdrops in photo studios in many Indian towns, as sources of style and fashion, and as content on television, the Internet, and other forms and platforms of new media. The cinema is also experienced in multiple ways. Alongside the single-screen theater that has dominated Indian film culture for decades and continues to exist in most parts of the country, the relatively new ritzy multiplex with its American-style concession stands and its economies of scale has created new creative and commercial opportunities for media companies, directors, and audiences alike. Meanwhile, in the illicit slum cinemas in Mumbai, one can still find a combination of action cinema and pornography on pirated DVDs and VCDs screened for migrant workers in the city. Traveling and tent cinemas continue to persist while the white cube of the art museum has seen numerous engagements with moving image media. The cinema is seen but also heard as ambient sound in rickshaws, buses, and streets in the ubiquitous film song. The accompanying intellectual infrastructures range from a desire to corporatize India's messy film industries to a pragmatic conception and production of pirate media that themselves make possible new material infrastructures for legitimate cinema as well. One could go on, but my point with the aforementioned examples is as much about the density of the cinema's presence in everyday life as it is about the staggering array of practices and conceptions, often vastly disparate in scale and size and ranging from the artisanal to the corporate, that comprise film culture in India today and characterize the entire production-exhibition-reception cycle of a film.

However, it is only more recently that this density and diversity of the cinema's presence have become the task of the discourse of film historiography. Why and how has the Bioscope in use today survived its mid-nineteenth-century origins? How old is the transnational piracy of media and how has piracy shaped conceptions of a national *Indian* cinema? What are the roots of the cinema's circulation not just on screen and other media, but also as an imaginary through photography and print cultures? And how has the cinema shaped understandings of its own history?

And it is only recently that scholars have sought an adequate critical vocabulary to answer these questions. If so much of the past has survived into the present, what constitutes an archive of the cinema? Do the embedded temporalities of the cinema demand an intensified application of the historian's toolkit—causality, the event, conjuncture—or do they demand an entirely new approach? What can South Asia teach us about the debates swirling in film and media theory around old and new media, pre- and post-cinema?

THE ARGUMENT

My central hypothesis is that even though the cinema arrived in South Asia as a form of commercial entertainment with traveling European showmen, it underwent significant reinventions in order to become culturally relevant and commercially viable. Geography is crucial here, and we need to return it to history. My inquiry begins in Bengal and its capital Calcutta (the capital of British India till 1911), where one can see a thriving consumer and entertainment culture take hold in the nineteenth century. Nevertheless, Bengal's encounter with the cinema was a simultaneous articulation of local and global circumstances, resulting in outcomes such as the coexistence of small-scale traveling cinemas with the influx of the latest foreign films. More importantly, some of these features in Bengal soon became applicable in complex ways for the rest of the subcontinent, while others did not. Enumerations—while not unimpeachable, given their official colonial origins—indicate that traveling cinemas spreading out to rural areas were far more numerous in Bengal than in other provinces of British India. At the same time, Bengal did develop a robust indigenous film production sector and urban film culture, like Bombay but perhaps not on the same scale. These nuances indicate that film culture in South Asia was neither so different as to be unrecognizable from a metropolitan European vantage point nor so similar as to prove the unimpeded transfer of Western modernity to South Asia.

In moving beyond a national cinema approach, the present work follows the lead of a number of scholars who have offered accounts of early film history in India as culturally and institutionally far too diverse to describe as the apogee of a fin-de-siècle proto-nationalist visual imaginary, or to collapse through prolepsis into the consolidation of the Indian film industry of the 1930s sound era (Govil 2005; Bhaumik 2002, 2010; Hughes 1996; Chatterjee 2011; Dass 2004, 2009; Jaikumar 2006; Schulze 2003; Majumdar 2009).

Beyond this overarching context, how do we begin to understand the cinema's emergence in India? A preliminary answer requires an attention to the cinema as a techno-material infrastructure that became viable and enduring in its presence in the subcontinent. To return to our Bioscope, an antique device from the past is still alive as a vital part of a media assemblage in the present. This book treats the "old machines" of the present as mnemonic devices that invite us to explore a historical moment when these machines were new. It contends that the obviation of obsolescence was an important survivalist tendency in film exhibition that enabled the dispersal of the cinema far and wide beyond urban areas even as the latter saw the more capital-intensive dimensions of the cinema as mass entertainment. A combination of constraints and circumstances ensured the coexistence of artisanal and commercial versions of the cinema and the possibility that old machines could be turned new and viable beyond their own historical moment. Moreover, the cinema's public life was a complex recapitulation of aspects of photography's emergence in the latter half of the nineteenth century as a ubiquitous presence in the subcontinent. Both emerged and matured and to similar ends in the interface of the spaces of imperial commerce and the places of local practices. Finally, the old machines of the cinema are not just a feature of our time; they were a feature when the cinema was itself new. Allied nineteenth-century screen practices such as the magic lantern and the diorama thrived in Calcutta prior to the cinema and deposited, for future film exhibition, vestigial devices that are in use to this day. Historians of "pre-cinema" are well aware of these screen practices. Their presence and persistence in India deepens existing histories of the hybridization and creolization of media that have characterized the cinema's indigenous and nationalist origins (Kapur 1988; Rajadhyaksa 1986; Pinney 2004; Jain 2007, Guha-Thakurta 1992). These, then, are the infrastructural components of the cinema's origins.

While the fashioning of a viable infrastructure shaped exhibition practices, the traffic in mechanically (re)produced images shaped the cinema's emergence as the dominant form of mass culture. Widely popular and reproduced lithographed images by Indian presses in the late nineteenth century became the objects of piracy. The ensuing copyright debates became as much about defining cultural value as they were about protecting commercial property. The cinema inherited these debates and, with them, the contestation between cultural identity and commercial profitability. Thus, piracy, mechanical reproduction, and the circulation of images across borders supplied the ideological and geographical matrix within which the "mechanic accents" of Indian cinema came to be situated as vernacular mass culture (Denning 1998).

Mechanical reproduction also leads us to a less frequently explored nexus between print, photography, and cinema. Quite apart from the cultural politics of mechanical reproduction, the cinema shared with photography—especially in the form of the printed photograph or the halftone—an interest in the topical event, the contemporary moment, and the sudden instant. Establishing itself as a medium of the prosaic present, in its interface with photography and print media the cinema moved beyond adopting the nationalist allegories of the aforementioned popular lithographic images. It played an active role in the temporal transformation of political protest into event, and the redefinition of public space as the space of theatrics. It recorded the spatiotemporal dynamics of a political culture, dynamics that translated into an uneven experience of modernity for Indians and Europeans alike. Its ultimate consequences and legacies are darker perhaps, more deeply entrenched in state power and certainly quite distinct from the formulations of cinematic modernity (or of the affinities between cinema and modernity) offered up in European and American metropolitan contexts.[1]

To recap, infrastructure, mechanical reproduction, and intermediality defined the cinema as, respectively, an assemblage of screen practices, as mass culture, and as a topically relevant medium in its early decades. A certain attitude to time is essential to each of these. The resilience of the old machine implies a refusal to forget. There was, however, also a refusal to remember. Mechanical reproduction's initial promise for Indians was that they could take advantage of the blurred lines between the original and the copy, the authentic and the inauthentic, in ways that would level the unequal playing field of empire to their cultural and commercial advantage. However, the ultimately beleaguered status of cinema as an inauthentic form of (mass) culture in post-independence India implied nothing short of a refusal to remember mechanical reproduction's initial promise and possibilities. Finally, the cinema's intermediality, via the photographic or moving image's ability to capture the unanticipated moment, unleashed the possibilities of reenacting and re-envisioning time. The dramatization of the medium's topical relevance at times replaced the very power of capturing unplanned moments. Reenactment, orchestrated in the service of discourses of criminality, replaced spontaneous enactment, turning the cinema into an instrument of strategic truth-telling, an evidentiary medium serving state prerogatives.

Given the multiple temporalities that have informed the emergence of the cinema in India, can we even imagine history as an appropriate discourse for understanding the cinematic imaginary in India? This is not simply a demand to parse the cinema into multiple histories. Rather, only a discursive and methodological eclecticism will serve our purpose. The coexistence of antique modes of exploitation and new multiplexes (cinema as infrastructure), the sheer behemoth size of the Indian film industry (cinema as mass culture), and the porosity of the film text, its seepage into visual culture, and other media (cinema as intermedia) are no doubt the objects of "film history" that demand research and exploration. But they are also the rhetorical tropes that have characterized populist narrations of that history. We cannot of course, separate the narrating of history from the history itself in any instance. In India, an added dimension is that a reflexive awareness and knowledge of film history is not a critical-theoretical maneuver by the knowing historian. It is an element of the practical existence of the cinema, a precondition of movies and their currency in everyday life.

So in the final analysis in this book, I take up that thing called "film history" under the heuristic of the archive (that other holy grail of historical research) and describe how it has been shaped as narrative by the very elements of the cinematic imaginary that constitute the objects of this history. The many origins of the cinema in India compel us to reimagine its archive as an open-ended and incomplete one, a condition that is a product of the history that one customarily expects an archive to enable. Precisely for this reason, the popular historical narratives that have sustained a sense of the cinema as possessing a living "history" in India are characterized by

the very tendencies that have shaped the cinema. The obviation of obsolescence refuses to consider the past to be no longer present. The inter-
play between imitation, reproduction, inspiration, and creation defines the
particular protocols that shape historical narratives of the cinema. These
popular historical narratives are significantly shaped by intermediality such
that the notable forms of popular film history I consider in this volume have
emerged at moments of the encounter with "new media" (albeit media that
never entirely supplant existing ones).

Put another way, if there is an instance where we can legitimately
conflate memory with storage, it is here in India, where the memory of the
cinema is "stored" in the present for practical recall in order to creatively
shape possible pasts and potential futures.[2] Film history in India seems the
outcome of a "counterarchive" in the sense intended by Paula Amad in her
brilliant study of Albert Kahn's *Archives de la Planète*: a memory that "is at
home, rather than at war, with forgetting" (2010: 119).

IMAGINARIES

In casting its net over more than one aspect of the cinema's emergence in
India (technology, culture, media), this book is as much about the emergence of a cinematic imaginary as it is about the cinema's history. By using
the word *imaginary* I mean the deeply embedded expectations of what the
cinema is, what its manifestations are, how it is to be put to use and experienced and how it becomes meaningful. I am using the word in the sense
that Charles Taylor (2004) elaborates in his book on modern social imaginaries: first, as a kind of embedded self-understanding held by large groups
of "ordinary people," carried in images, stories, and legends and decidedly
not theoretical in nature in the sense of an explicitly held set of formulated ideas. Taylor also proposes that imaginaries are not reducible to finite
and delimited background understandings that enable practices. Instead, he
proposes a kind of symbiosis between understanding and practice that is
especially useful in describing the cinema's manifestations in India. Taylor
notes that the background understanding may make practice possible but the
practice also "carries the understanding" (25). Background understandings
are deeply imbricated in everyday manifestations and the latter in turn are
conceptually dense. In thinking of the origins of the cinema in India and
the imaginaries it has shaped, I want to retain this sense of a conceptual
complexity that is entwined in and as practice. One sees this in the kind
of "expertise" that refashions a peephole device into a mutation of home
viewing and public broadcasting. Taylor's emphasis on the everyday and on
practice is particularly valuable for this book's consideration of the cinema
in India.

Arjun Appadurai, whose formulation precedes Taylor's, sees the imaginary as "an organized field of social practices, a form of work . . . and a form of negotiation between sites of agency (individuals) and globally defined fields of possibility" (Appadurai 1996, 31).[3] Two aspects of Appadurai's formulation are worth stressing at this stage. The conceptual move here of *situating* individual acts within *fields* of possibility points to a crucial aspect of the old machine of our opening example: its reliance on location and place, or its site-specificity. Furthermore, Appadurai's reference to a field *of possibilities*, or the "affordances" of a medium (Lister et al. 2009, 8), the things a medium enables and makes possible, will also be extremely useful here for us.

The move away from medium-specificity to the "affordances" of a medium is an acknowledgment of the cinema's diffuse place in India's media ecologies. To put it somewhat axiomatically, the cinema is less substance than agent.[4] The cinema is what the cinema does and in India, the cinema does—or appears to do—an awful lot of varied and unpredictable things. The modification of a Bioscope into a public broadcasting system is one sign that the cinema's manifestations, what it means, and how it becomes viable remain unpredictable and open to a process of reinvention and improvisation. Indeed, in excavating the Bioscope's origins, I hope this book will show that the cinematic imaginary in India has fundamentally been medium-agnostic (Tsivian 2008), less prone to an interest in pinning an answer to what is cinema or what comes next in the history of the cinema and more interested in what it is now and what affordances it makes possible at the moment. What ultimately emerges is more than a medium-specific history of the cinema (of the kind that Charles Musser proposes with his productive definition of "screen practices").[5] It is a history of media practices whose aim, in Tom Gunning's words, is to produce "multi-directional intersections" between the cinema and other media within which the cinema serves as but one key "switching point" among others (2002, 17).

Each section of the book demonstrates in one way or another, this medium-agnosticism. Exhibition practices are not restricted to the black box of the movie theater. The cinema's status as mass culture and its efficacy as a topical medium are both forged in a multimedia interface. And some of the most innovative forms of imagining the agnostic origins of the cinema draw freely on documentary and fiction, on reenactment and reportage.

If a social imaginary is normative, as Taylor proposes, it applies only with qualification to the cinema in India. The normative dimensions of the cinematic imaginary in India are very much in evidence in, for instance, the space of the dominant single-screen movie theater that enforces caste, class, and gender divisions in the manner in which seats are arranged. In the way the theater apportions relative access and proximity to the screen, the very phenomenology of the film experience is at stake. Plush multiplexes, fully aware of the sensorial stakes, have targeted precisely this experience.[6] A political economy of the cinema cannot, however, do justice to the other manifestations of the cinematic imaginary. Art historian Kajri Jain defines this popular imaginary as a "modern vernacular": the expression of mass cultural audiovisual idioms targeted to a non-Anglophone audience in India (Jain 2005). This is a tacit imaginary and its tacit nature comes into relief each time it is enlisted. The visual field of the vernacular is one that "appears to enable [artists] to generate a pure, evocative, de-narrativized charge of some sort," notes film historian Ashish Rajadhyaksha (Rajadhyaksha 2005, 162). We can take this to mean that an artist or filmmaker, for instance, need not specify or outline the semantic functions of the popular visual culture that she might utilize in her art.[7] The references to popular visual culture in contemporary art practice are "thick evocations" of texts and histories, an "elusive 'idiolect' [that] requires knowing spectators to 'get it.'" (163). The imagery and the sounds are so ubiquitous that they evoke affect without need for formal signification. In other words, the knowing spectator's knowledge is covert.

The visual culture of the cinema has emerged as an expressive vocabulary for the cinema itself. This vocabulary is now evident as self-conscious style in the work of film directors such as Dibakar Banerjee and sound designers such as Ashish Manchandani (who has worked on Banerjee's films). For example, in one of his movies, *Oye Lucky Lucky Oye!* (2008), Banerjee uses a 1970s film song on the soundtrack as an insight into the main character's compulsions (in this case, kleptomania). What is noteworthy is the sound design. In reusing a vintage tune, the soundtrack of the movie replicates the flat, echoing, monaural soundtrack of pre-stereo Hindi cinema in a film that otherwise carries digital sound. The sound design thus evokes an entire era of film music with its musical attributes (the absence of bass and the lack of dimensionality or spatial perspective to the sound). Vishal Bhardwaj in his film *Kaminey* (2006) utilizes as the musical leitmotif of the film the onomatopoeic sounds of music from action sequences of movies of the pre-Bollywood era: Dhan Te Nan! Bhardwaj's film's title translates as *Scoundrels* and is a reference to one of the most well-known clichés of hero-villain interactions in Hindi cinema: *Kuttey! Kaminey! Main tera khoon pee jaunga!* (You dog! You scoundrel! I'll drink your blood!). At their best, these invocations of the cinematic vernacular rely on the familiarity, ubiquity, and self-evident signification that govern the visual field in India. The addressee is the knowing eye and the culturally familiar public able to generate affect out of this consortium of images and sounds.[8]

This is a form of cinephilia and it is intimately connected to the everyday, a domain of experience that has with increasing frequently become a topic of interest for scholars of Indian cinema and media. Coming at the subject from a variety of critical paradigms, the focus on the everyday has involved attending to the politics of cinematic space and place, to the erotics and haptics of the image, to the banal and perverse interdictions that govern the image and cinema at large, and the dense mediation of the everyday spaces within which the cinema is one element of a visual and technologically visualized culture.[9] It is this domain of the everyday that has found figuration in contemporary cinema, multiplex as well as mainstream, as an object of cinematic representation. But more interestingly, this depicted everyday is profoundly saturated with a cinematic imaginary (or an imaginary of the cinema in and as everyday life). Thus, an embedded sensorium finds expression in innovative ways in contemporary cinema.

Do such acts of recycling carry with them a historical function? Can we see the tacit imaginary that is reproduced as formal expression, as serving as an archive of the cinema? Kajri Jain (2005) proposes that when the vernacular is invoked in self-conscious ways, it undergoes an "aura"-tization that "inserts it into the frame of historical thinking"; it is now framed "as past, as historical" (180). Jain's formulation provokes a question: Is the vernacular capable of possessing a history? Or is its historical value restricted to the effect of a deliberate discourse that frames it as belonging to a past? Can the vernacular-qua-imaginary be archived? Or is it too ephemeral, too seeped into everyday life to be formally and institutionally archivable? While the recycling of film history in contemporary popular culture suggests that there is no stable archive of the past, I also suggest that we take the ephemerality of this vernacular as itself the richest source for film history.

We must therefore distinguish between ephemerality and contingency, the latter indicating the cinema's vulnerability as medium to the ravages of time. The problems of preservation of "film" for posterity in India are rendered moot by an imaginary that sees recall rather than archiving as paramount for the preservation of the "cinema."

The possibility of the co-persistence of many imaginaries of the cinema needs to be recovered if the conflation of the obsolescence of a medium (film as celluloid) with the death of cinema is to be avoided. The claim that the obsolescence of a medium (film) may well be tantamount to the death of an institution (cinema) presumes an understanding of film history as comprised of three clear stages. According to this understanding, the contemporary digital media moment shares many features with the history of the cinema in its first decade. Both moments are characterized by uncertain futures. It was far from foretold that the cinema from 1896 to roughly between 1903 to 1908—an exhibitionist cinema more interested in showing ("views" or "attractions") than with telling (stories)—would evolve into the cinema of "narrative integration" (Gunning 1983). Furthermore, early cinema was characterized by unstable sites of presence and use. Early film exhibitions occurred as part of vaudeville, tent shows, and penny arcades, catered to diffuse audiences not imagined specifically as movie audiences, and provoked social anxieties not unlike those concerning the impact of new media. The uncertain digital present therefore mirrors a similarly open-ended period of early cinema and even pre-cinema that came to be disciplined by the "institutional mode of representation" of Hollywood (Burch 1978/79; 1990).

Situated between these two periods is the cinema as a narrative medium with exhibition venues specific to it, a consequence of the industrialization of the feature film as product in the classical Hollywood studio system of production. This classical Hollywood cinema, the paradigm through much of the twentieth century, occupies the period between early cinema and, since the 1970s, increasingly privatized modes of consumption and digitized modes of image capture and production (TV, VHS, the personal computer, and the Internet). The dominant audio-visual paradigm of the twentieth century was thus an interregnum between two historical moments (early cinema and the present moment) that mirror each other. From this perspective, it may indeed make sense to conflate the death of an institution (cinema) with the obsolescence of the medium of film in its material basis as celluloid.

Thomas Elsaesser (2008), however, cautions against seeing the digital moment as a radical break from the cinema as we have known it through much of the twentieth century, given that the cinema of the present remains tethered to long-established imperatives of production, aesthetic, and stylistic norms put in place by Hollywood in the preceding century. He also proposes, correctly I think, that we must go even farther than the "interregnum" argument and see the digital moment as the occasion for a thorough dislocation and de-linearization of film history. A media archaeological approach would reveal many cinemas emerging at many points: the cinema of screen entertainment, the cinema of science and medicine, of warfare, of interactivity and immersion. Many of these have survived through the twentieth century; they just haven't become part of the dominant narrative about the history of the cinema. That history has been dominated by an account of the containment of an unruly medium (the period of early cinema) into a business of mass entertainment (the rise and dominance of Hollywood).

I find Elsaesser's arguments persuasive and largely agree with them because they provide the most cogent and productive reformulation of the agenda for film historians. But it is still a reclamatory method—an archaeology that excavates and reclaims routes that got buried before and during the course of the twentieth century as legitimate avenues of research for the historian. This is ultimately an approach occasioned by and attempting to reckon with Hollywood as a functioning hegemonic capitalist system of image production.

But what happens when that hegemony has been absent, as in India, where Hollywood has not made significant inroads into the Indian market? Instead of one Hollywood, India possesses film industries in four major languages. The Hindi-language film industry in Mumbai has the highest output. But three major film industries in the South produce nearly as many films as Mumbai does, in the states of Tamil Nadu (in the Tamil language), Andhra Pradesh (the language of Telegu), and Karnataka (the Kannada language). More to the point, however, is the fact that many imaginaries of the cinema seem to jostle for space with each other in India. Archaeology presumes objects that need excavation. Given that obsolescence and recession have hardly been the dominant logics of the cinema in India, one might wonder if the historian would be more likely to find embedded practices and imaginations by rummaging in the present moment, than by digging into the past.

In a recent book discussing the presence of the moving image in the art gallery, Andrew Uroskie (2014) proposes that site-specificity has been at the center of critical interrogations of the cinema in the art gallery. So important is site-specificity that Uroskie proposes that if we want to understand what the moving image has meant to artists in the art gallery since the 1960s, we ought to reformulate the Bazinian question: "What is cinema?" should really become "Where is Cinema?" The cinema's location within and determination by institutional, cultural, and discursive frameworks distances us from concerns around ontology or medium-specificity.

I want to appropriate Uroskie's proposition to what is clearly a different context. I suggest a modification of Uroskie's question: Where *and when* is the cinema?[10] In using the present tense, I'm suggesting that what is and has been specific to the cinema in India is its ability to compact multiple temporalities into a simultaneous co-persistence. I am also suggesting that we take the "where" to refer not simply to site-specificity but more generally to geographical locations outside the global North.

It is for this reason that I think media archaeology sans any presumption of teleology is only one among many other approaches that illuminate film history in India. As we now know, relations between old and new media are, to paraphrase David Thoburn and Henry Jenkins, more congenial, less disruptive, and a matter of resonances between media rather than a question of precedence (Bolter and Grusin 1999; Thoburn and Jenkins 2003). Such an understanding of media history, characterized by social constructionist, new historicist, and cultural historical approaches, is justly skeptical of the modernist desire for radical newness and clean ruptures. While these new approaches serve us well in excavating the history of the cinema for media and film historians in general, in India the crucial difference is that they also seem to embody the very "operating logic" of the cinema, of how the cinema has emerged, how it operates and how it "lives" in its moment.

What do this book's findings imply for media studies in the West? Methodologically, it entails reclaiming the notion of an imaginary from its somewhat rarefied application in film studies and in art criticism.[11] The substantive conclusions are less categorical. Yes, it entails recognizing that Hollywood is not the global juggernaut it is cracked up to be. But that is no longer a pending realization. More to the point, this study suggests that a cinema can emerge and establish itself at a scale analogous to that of Hollywood through entirely different routes, devices, tendencies, and practices. The difference, however, is inseparable from the analogy, and vice versa. Perhaps more dissatisfying then, for those celebrants of Indian cinema's cultural difference, as well as for those utilizing this cultural difference as a pretext for a lack of curiosity about what happens on the other side of the world, might be this book's position that actually the cinema in India as well an *Indian* cinema's long history can invite neither a vantage point that sees radical difference, nor one that sees radical similarity.

THE STRUCTURE OF THE BOOK

This book is structured as a consideration of four logics that shaped the cinematic imaginary in India: Obsolescence, Mechanical Reproduction, Intermediality, and the Archive. The two chapters on obsolescence genealogize the cinema in relation to pre-cinematic screen practices and the history of photography. The two chapters on mechanical reproduction describe and analyze the impact of the popular lithograph's currency, on the cinema's subsequent status as mass culture. The two chapters on intermediality explore the cinema's representational interface with the newspaper image, the snapshot, and the photo-illustrated book. The last section, on the archive, examines the consequences of the cinema's eclectic origins on the popular historiography that it instigates in the present.

Reiteration and repetition emerge as processes with distinct functions through all the chapters of this book. The obviation of obsolescence is seen both in terms of apparatus and image (in chapters 1 and 2). The reformulation of creativity as an engagement with preexisting materials and the repetition of both format and iconography via mechanical reproduction (in chapters 3 and 4) become impetuses for the "culture wars" as it were. The two tendencies of reuse and reproduction—both central to the cinema's identity as a tenacious and pervasive form of mass culture—find more instrumental uses by the state in the use of stock footage in its information films and turned into a formal mechanism of reenactment. We could call this the rote pedagogy of citizenship, in which the apparatus of the cinema reveals what it has stored as potential memory from which citizens learn useful skills (chapters 5 and 6). Finally, recall and replay become essential elements in the manner in which the cinema is remembered in India.

Chapters 1 and 2 spotlight the obviation of obsolescence as an important logic that has shaped the cinema in South Asia. Both chapters prioritize the material infrastructures of the cinema, some of which continue to flourish in India. The fairground photographer and the traveling showman of today serve as invitations to excavate the origins of the cinema in the material and consumer cultures within which photography first established its roots in India. Chapter 1 shows that photography's growth as a commercial form was dependent on a combination of local and global circumstances, ranging from the smaller niche markets that characterized the uses of photography in cities such as Calcutta, to India's speedy access to the latest apparatus from Europe. The result was a photographic culture that could keep abreast of the latest European trends while continuing to sustain older practices and technologies. The reasoning here is counterfactual. Rapid obsolescence and the automation and miniaturization of camera technologies did not occur in India because of the nature of the market for photography. As a result, photography was neither democratized as it was in the United States with the emergence of the hand camera, nor was it uprooted from its personalized cultures of patronage. The latter was evident in the continued dominance of the photo studio through much of the twentieth century.

Chapter 2 argues that the cinema encountered similar circumstances as far as access to technology and the geographical relation to the imperial capitals were concerned. However, here, unlike in photography, the obviation of obsolescence is less the outcome of absent conditions and more the outcome of a capital-intensive business into which Indians had limited access and therefore drew on existing resources as much as they could. The form this "scavenging" took, drew on a long history of screen practices that ran parallel to photography, producing in effect a film culture that was capable of sustaining disparate scales of enterprise. This chapter places the figure of the Bioscopewallah and the traveling cinema at the crux and follows his presence at numerous junctures in the history of the cinema, into the late twentieth century. I'm particularly interested, in this chapter, in conceptualizing the cinema as an assemblage whose ideal form is virtual—often portrayed nostalgically in certain accounts of the cinema—but whose actual manifestation is always a process of revivification. Obsolescence and its attenuation become key to my understanding of why the cinema took the shape it did in South Asia, and how it relates to our own moment.

The difference between the two chapters can also be articulated in terms of a political economy. Chapter 1 describes the development of photography during a largely mercantilist phase of empire in India characterized by the trade in goods and commodities by petty merchants in a personalized retail-oriented consumer culture. Chapter 2 constructs a genealogy of the cinema at a moment when British India had shifted to a globalizing mode, one that was anxious of the other global empire, the United States, nipping at its heels. While photography emerges in the material cultures of Calcutta of the mid-nineteenth century, the cinema emerges in the consumer cultures of the early twentieth century.

Chapters 3 and 4 shift attention from the cinema's material infrastructures to the politics of its circulation, or to its cultural infrastructures. Both chapters are interested in the cinema's emergence as a form of mass culture whose cultural politics was defined by the circulation of images within and beyond South Asia. Chapter 3 explores a hitherto unconsulted legal archive of copyright disputes regarding the ownership and authenticity of color lithographic images, or chromolithographs. These disputes involved the most influential of the printing presses of the late nineteenth century. The images were themselves instrumental in shaping a new popular visual iconography that was nationalist in its aims, and were popular in India and abroad, as already noted above. The legal archives, however, offer an unprecedented glimpse into the circumstances and mechanisms whereby this history's key terms of reference, namely originality and cultural authenticity were defined and invoked. The copyright disputes reveal the intricate nexus between cinema and the printed image, and between commerce and culture even on the terrain of a nationalist politics. Chapter 4 follows the implications of this nexus into the film period. It reinterprets the significance of the pioneering Indian filmmaker D. G. Phalke as the founding figure of a "national cinema" in light of the international film cultures of his time. It also reinterprets his status as an originary figure and as auteur in light of the rampant piracy that characterized film culture in India at the time.

Rather than reiterating known accounts of photography as the technological basis and substrate for the cinema, chapters 5 and 6 search for a cinematic imaginary in photojournalism and the printed halftone photograph. The two chapters together demonstrate the intermediality that characterized the cinema's early decades. Chapter 5 examines amateur European photography and the manner in which new portable technologies were upending established conventions of European representation in India and setting in place new regimes of truth-telling with the aid of photography and film. I show that these new regimes influenced statist discourses on questions of development down to the postindependence period.

Chapter 6 examines continuities of form, subject matter, and context, between print, photography, and film cultures by looking at the halftone image in newspaper photojournalism, photo-illustrated books, and motion picture actualities and "topicals." The partition of Bengal in 1905 was the first major spark for mass mobilization. Chapter 6 follows this event across media. In doing so, I underscore the extent to which the cinema shared with photography and print culture the project of defining the experiential aspects of colonial modernity, including access to and the disciplining of space, and the regularization and standardization of time.

Chapter 7 moves to the present moment. If the cinematic imaginary in India has remained fundamentally agnostic with regard to questions of medium specificity and historicity, what shape have the resulting narratives of film history taken? What have been the protocols of popular movie historiography on the movies? I discuss two films that take up the history of the cinema, one a combination of documentary and reenactment, the other a found footage film. Both films discard the search for origins. *Cinema Cinema* places the documentary history of Bombay cinema in a theater where the conditions of theatrical reception are reenacted. The movie therefore goes off on a tangent from the history of and on the screen, in favor of an eccentric and occasionally hilarious pseudo-ethnographic study of reception practices. *Cinema Cinema* wants to produce a topographical engagement with the cinema's history, locating this history as a performance (to the extent that a screening can be a performance) in a specific movie theater. The audience responds to film history not in the mode of nostalgia or as a form of pedagogical address but as a provocation in their situated present to display indifference, mimetic absorption, sexual interest, selective reverie, even religious devotion as if they were watching contemporary and usual commercial fare.

Film Hi Film incorporates footage from incomplete and therefore never-seen commercial films into a story of a hapless filmmaker whose movie threatens to remain incomplete. The movie uses found footage and archives it, but not in the sense of patrimony or preservation in a museum or archive. Instead, it incorporates the found footage in a melodramatic narrative, as if it wants to restore that footage to its original context: that of the dramaturgy of commercial cinema. And as with *Cinema Cinema*, the movie filters its use of orphaned footage through its contemporary critique of the film industry, with its narrative of a beleaguered producer in a hugely disorganized film industry.

Both films, therefore, eschew a fascination with past origins in favor of contemporary usability. And contemporary usability in turn informs popular accounts of the cinematic past. As such, they also show that the miscellany, the compilation, and the collection have remained the dominant modes of writing and narrating film history in popular culture. I contrast these attempts at historiography with more sedate ones produced by the government's documentary films unit, the *Films Division*, and commercial television's recent attempts to chronicle the history of the cinema. The three examples chart a movement of popular cinema across two modalities of film history: official heritage and nonofficial historiography. These various articulations of film history attest to a more fundamental issue: that of how the cinematic imaginary in India produces an archive that, alongside the nostalgic, museological, and preservationist impulses, also embraces the cinema as social and cultural memory.

In my postscript, I juxtapose two radically distinct visions of the cinematic imaginary in the present. The first is a corporate-driven imagination of an immersive film museum that, thankfully, remains at the level of the imagination but offers a glimpse of the fantasies that remain virtual at the current moment. The second is my own experience of walking into a cinematic space that in its mise-en-scène immersed me in the quotidian imaginary of the cinema. Along with the old machines that opened this introduction, this experience of the cinematic everyday in India inspires this book's foray into India's cinematic past.

PART I

OBSOLESCENCE

1

THE NINETEENTH-CENTURY
INDIAN TECHNO-BAZAAR

Historians of the cinema in India face a dual compulsion. First, production methods of the distant past persist far longer in India than they do in the West, to the point where even as Indians attend multiplex cinemas to watch 3-D blockbusters, film exhibitions that employ technologies popular a century ago also supply alternate conduits to the moving image. So any history of the origins of the cinema must reckon with its multimedia present. Second, historians must also account for the multimedia character of the pre-cinematic era, which involved photography, print culture, and proto-cinematic screen practices. Thus, the origins of the cinema point in two directions: to a distant pre-cinematic past, and to a contemporary multimediated present.

This chapter focuses on one strand of this pre-cinematic media landscape: the history of photography in the nineteenth and early twentieth centuries. It offers material that enables us to connect the character of this photographic past to the history of cinema. While this chapter looks backward toward the emergence of photography for echoes of later aspects of film culture, the next chapter begins with the cinema but with an eye toward our present moment. The vantage point in these two chapters, however, is neither solely past nor solely present. Instead, I hope the perspective that emerges in both these chapters allows us to watch the debris of (film) history pile up, as the past transfixes us but also propels us into the future (Benjamin 1969, 2007).

Are not film and photography radically different objects? The cinema, as Michael Chanan observes, produced a distinct commodity separate from the photograph and the gramophone. In the cinema, the apparatus and film did not pass directly into the hands of the customer, whereas the individual purchase of the hand camera determined the mass consumption of photography (Chanan 1980, 27).

However, the story of these technologies in South Asia complicates and qualifies this distinction. The design-standardized hand camera never managed to replace the personalized retail culture of the photo studio centered on patronage. And permanent film exhibition never killed traveling cinemas attending to smaller audiences. Chanan's distinction between film and photography is belied therefore by the forms of enterprise that shaped both, marked by the patronage of a loyal, predictable or small-scale clientele.

Second, in both cases, the media emerged in contexts unspecific to themselves: photography emerged in the consumer and material cultures of nineteenth-century Calcutta; film emerged in a diverse set of performance venues, hardly any of which were meant specifically for movie screenings.

Finally, both were shaped by a similar confluence of opportunities and constraints afforded by the melding of what we might call today (imperial) global forces and local imperatives. It is this latter point that this chapter and the next will seek to demonstrate: that the logics that governed the history of photography and film were the same.

Two features of the life of photography in India make it quite distinct from the manner of its development in the West. First, the photo-studio dominated much of the access to photography in everyday life for most Indians throughout the twentieth century. Hand cameras simply did not achieve the density of use and popularity that they did in the West. Second, makeshift practices employing vintage methods continue to dot the photographic landscape in India.

David MacDougall's documentary film *Photowallahs* (1991) on the photo-studios in Mussoorie, the hill station and erstwhile British summer retreat in North India, depicts the confluence of both of these features. The documentary depicts a streetside commercial photographer who produces passport-sized photographs with highly ingenious methods (see Fig. 1.1). MacDougall's description in a related essay is worth quoting at length and then unpacking:

> The camera has no shutter. There is a lens cap that the photographer removes for two to four seconds to make the exposure. With the other hand (inserted through a lightproof sleeve) he manipulates the paper and a tray of developer inside the camera. Sheets of Agfa printing paper, torn into passport photo–sized rectangles, are kept in a rack or behind a piece of elastic within the camera and are moved into place on the plane of the focusing

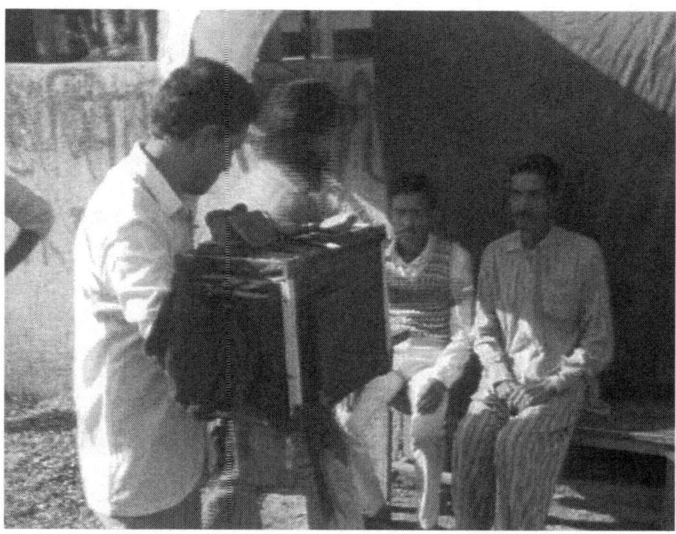

Figure 1.1. The photographer in Dehra Dun using a manual exposure "processing" camera with paper negatives (Source: David McDougall's *Photowallas* [1991]).

ground glass. After the exposure, the photographer can watch the paper developing in the tray through a hooded eyepiece, rather like that of an old stereoscope, mounted on top of the camera. The viewing light is daylight, filtered through a window of red glass that at other times is covered by a small door. Once developed, the paper is slipped through a slot in the bottom of the camera into a vertical tray of fixer. When this is slid out, like a small drawer, the print can be removed and dropped into a pail of wash water on the ground. This, of course, is only half the process. It produces a paper negative, which is usually retouched with water-color and then re-photographed on a small easel at the front of the camera to yield the final positive paper. (2006, 157–58)

MacDougall describes part of what is so singular about the life of popular technology in India: the way in which users combine extremely cheap and rapid methods with technologies of image production that stymie automation and the transformation of photography into a mass-produced commodity.

The photographer's methods also trump notions of linear historical sequence, progress, and chronology. Every element of how MacDougall's photographer produces an image comes from an earlier era of photographic history. Those elements include, as MacDougall's description makes clear, the use of a "processing camera" that allows the photographer to process images inside the body of the camera,[1] the absence of an automatic shutter mechanism, and the use of paper negatives instead of ready-to-use negative film. Innovations at various stages in the late nineteenth and early twentieth centuries rendered all these elements of camera design and photographic technology obsolete. Yet, photographers in India continued to use these cameras and this technology as late as 1991, the year MacDougall made his documentary. The work of these photographers involved a compact between the artisanal and the technical. We should note the highly ingenious "painterly" method for producing color positive prints, by which the photographer "retouches" the paper negative with watercolors and uses the same camera to re-photograph the colored negative and produce a color print.

The fairground photographer's methods seem at first glance like a throwback to an earlier era, an anachronistic vestige, quirky at best. On the other hand, his work involves the future-oriented desire for rapid-access photography, the acquisition of instantaneous prints within minutes of taking a photograph. This was, after all, the enduring function of "processing" cameras, a function even George Eastman's Kodak revolution could not adequately address. Kodak made taking a picture as easy as pressing a button, but the photographer still sent the roll film to a lab for development and printing. Photographic technology realized the dream of instantaneous pictures fitfully in Europe and the United States. The Polaroid camera is perhaps the most prominent attempt until the advent of digital photography—but our photographer in India executed this dream quite effectively.

How did the photo-studio and the fairground photographer manage to remain viable for so long? What explains the continued use of the same equipment from the nineteenth century into the late twentieth century? We may have to go back to a point where, far from being "minor" or marginal, these practices were significantly close to the norm. By exploring the emergence of the cinema and photography at an earlier moment, we are really asking the "old" and "decrepit" media of today to take us to a moment when they were new.

What would be the conceptual starting point for a genealogy of the fairground photographer? The fairground photographer's practice is a hybrid assemblage of at least three strands: the operator, his expertise, and the apparatus. Each of these strands possesses a genealogy. Of the three components of the assemblages of photography and film, I wish to begin with the apparatus, for the questions that motivated this study emerged long ago from a rather elementary empirical curiosity about the world of things: Who was selling photographic cameras in South Asia in 1840? Were any cameras manufactured locally? How much would a camera have cost, relative to other goods and commodities? Colonialism was, after all, about the traffic in objects. Material orders shape conventions of sensory perception and these conventions in turn produce social distinctions (Edwards, Gosden, and Phillips 2006, 1–34). We are reminded of this relay between colonialism, material culture, sensory perception, and social distinctions time and again, as we encounter field cameras, heavy glass plates, lantern slides, snapshots, kinetoscopes, secondhand parts, pirated and junk prints, and tents for accommodating audiences. These are not neutral objects. Film exhibitors enlisted tents in conceptions of audiences (elite, masses, poor soldiery). Junk prints testify to unequal access to capital and product. Glass slides and field cameras produced narratives about the difficulty and heroism of producing images in the tropics. Peepshow projectors and cinemas on mobile trucks created experiences that involved the management of bodies, the construction of posture, and the regulation of movement. In other words, it is fruitful to eschew a vision-centric approach to screen cultures and attend to the sensory economies surrounding them.

Linked to this material culture is the bazaar as a material, discursive, and ultimately hybrid space that was crucial for photography as well as film. In nineteenth-century Calcutta, the bazaar was one part of "a 'two-circuit' structure of local trade: one catering to the Indian population that Europeans too utilized for fresh foods and Indian-produced commodities, and a firm-based circuit in which British retailers and tradesmen supplied most imported goods and westernized services" (Furedy 1981). The European firms that supplied photographic cameras belonged to the firm-based circuit.

Culturally, urban space was indeed segregated into native and European quarters (or the Black Town), mirroring the two-circuit trade networks (Sinha 1990, 33). The Black Town was populated by an English-educated Indian middle class from whose ranks emerged the first stirrings of nationalist thought, as well as "lower orders" of traditional artisans, craftsmen, domestic servants, and the like; all those who were part of the service economy for the Bengali elites (Banerjee 1989, 23). The Black Town possessed a distinct popular urban visual culture derived from rural visual forms. Scroll paintings, wood and copper engravings, and countless cheap books illustrated from these engravings flourished in the bazaar (Guha-Thakurta 1992). Photographic expertise, too, branched off, as we will see, into distinct European and Indian strands, of which the latter flourished in the bazaar.

According to Swati Chattopadhyay, despite racial and cultural distinctions, Calcutta was in practice a mixed city. In the so-called White Town, larger European stores were interspersed with smaller petty shops and dwellings occupied by Indians and Europeans. European businesses spilled from the White Town into areas considered notorious for their gambling houses and taverns that catered to poorer Europeans. The bazaars mirrored such mixed use and "clearly blurred the lines among the classes, ethnic groups and races, contradicting the fundamental basis of a colonial culture. Both Bengali and English commentaries noted the cosmopolitan nature of the main bazaars" (Chattopadhyay 2005, 85).

Cultural tastes crossed the racial divide as well. Elite Bengalis consumed cheap German lithographs of classical European paintings, just as poorer Bengalis and poor Europeans shared the taste for the cheapest kinds of direct-positive photographic images produced on japanned glass or tin plates that were relatively inexpensive to produce.

Even in an economic sense, the bazaar was hardly a space of small transactions, clumsy and un-analytical accounting, and a structure incapable of creating effective networks for exploiting untapped market possibilities (Ray 1995).[2] On the contrary, the indigenous money market that financed the long-distance inland trades of the bazaar economy in India was vital to the colonial banks for setting currency rates. By the early twentieth century, bazaar networks had facilitated the emergence of indigenous merchant capital that would invest in industrial projects but also in the culture industry itself. As Kajri Jain observes, it is little remarked that the culture industry was one of the early domains of sustained indigenous economic activity (in the production of chromolithographic calendar images) and then became a site of investment by cotton and jute merchants wishing to branch out into the capital-intensive film business (2007, 78–82). It is for this reason that the bazaar has had analytical purchase as well. For example, in Kaushik Bhaumik's account of film culture in Bombay, the bazaar emerges both as a source of indigenous financing for film and as the location for the appeal of those genres that capitalized on sensation, technology, and affect, such as stunt, crime, and adventure films. These were directly aimed at the social and physical space of the bazaar, unlike the more respectable mythologicals (and precisely for these reasons as well the bazaar was a target of opprobrium by Indian educated elites). The mobilization of capital for early Indian film enterprises often occurred in the bazaar. But they occurred *as* an attempt by Indians to ensure the circulation of that capital, and its translation into images, on a wider scale beyond the bazaar itself. The material cultures of mid-nineteenth-century India captured a particular form of globalization, one governed by a mercantile form of capitalism that by the end of the century would mutate into something more territorially self-conscious and imperializing in its aims (Goswami 2004, 32). In either form of capitalism, the bazaar remains a useful discursive and spatial frame of reference for us, both for its place in everyday life in British India and its links to wider circuits of capital flow.

FROM NOVELTY TO APPARATUS: PHOTOGRAPHY'S MATERIAL CULTURES

Photography's material cultures serve as a precursor to the spaces and materials of the fairground photographer's livelihood, and an important precursor to the Bioscopewallah's ability to provide a tokenistic, transactional, and haptic access to the very apparatus of the cinema. Newspapers in Calcutta and Bombay first announced the sales of photographic cameras in 1840, less than a year after Louis Daguerre's announcement of the daguerreotype process. Calcutta bookseller Thacker, Spink, and Company announced their first cameras in 1840. A Thacker notice from January 25, 1841, in the *Bengal Hurkaru* listed books and periodicals, printed images, watercolors and maps, optical toys (including views of the Egyptian pyramids, touted as an "interesting toy for children"), Mordan's Pistol Pencil Cases, and of course, the daguerreotype, the camera obscura, and "photogenic boxes." The announcement referred to the daguerreotype cameras as "the new art of sun drawing" and photogenic boxes, the ad noted, "for copying objects by means of the sun."[3] All in all, this was an alluring combination of "languorous oriental baubles and honest utilitarian labor" (Schaffer 1996, 57).

It was a measure of the labile nature of photography and the materiality of its emergence that it arrived in India with books, jewelry, fine chemicals, and imported champagne and that trades as diverse as apothecaries and furniture makers sold it. In today's terms, it is as if the dollar store guy stocked the latest interactive 3-D gaming technology along with towels, crockery, detergent, and plastic flowers. Extending that analogy, we could suppose that the imaginations that invented 3-D interactive gaming incubated within the bric-a-brac of the dollar store and the everyday habits of touch and use these inculcated, rather than within any disembodied epistemology that sought to reshape perception. This fertile incongruity of circumstances characterized early photography in South Asia and found distant echoes in the fairground photographer of our times.

The European in Calcutta depended in part on "Europe shops" for the latest goods. The shops provided emporia of every conceivable luxury good. They hawked and displayed prints along with cheese, the latest magazines, imported veal, alcohol, a cornucopia of things that, by 1840, for the first time included the daguerreotype camera.[4] The operative word here is "things." The heading of one of Calcutta importer R. C. Lepage & Company's notices read "MISCELLANEOUS ARTICLES just received." What were these articles? "Photographic copies" of popular prints, Williamson sectional paper, cutlery made of the best Sheffield Steel, Gentleman's Shooting Pocket Knife, "emigrant's knife for the colonies," Ladies' Writing Desk, and innumerable other items. One day, Lewis Stewart and Company hawked magic lanterns and photographic and other slides. Another day, a full broadsheet notice from the same company touted silverware of every possible kind.

Only the elite could afford photographic cameras, and they had various motivations for purchasing them. Conspicuous consumption by "non-official Europeans" in India and a desire to keep up with European fashion, and sometimes to be ahead of it, provided the major impetus for the purchase of cameras.[5] From the perspective of those who sold photographic goods, novel items provided an edge over competitors in a trading world perpetually in flux from new and temporary entrants.[6]

Why should a bookseller have imported pricey new gadgets such as cameras? Thacker's bookstore held pride of place in 1830s Calcutta. "Next to the jeweler's shops, the most magnificent establishment in the city is that of the principal bookseller, Thacker & Co," wrote Emma Roberts, a travel writer, in 1835 (Joshi 2002, 93). For Roberts, books were proximate to jewelry in value because, like the latter, they were scarce, expensive, and in high demand in India.

Booksellers were not, however, the only vendors selling cameras. Apothecaries such as Smith, Stanistreet and Company (established in 1810) were also suppliers, given that, till the1870s, methods of fixing and developing the image required the supply of fine chemicals.[7] In these two companies, we find two contexts for the availability of photographic materials. While one dealt with a cultural commodity in high demand (books) and could therefore easily expand the line of products it offered to include photographic materials, the other supplied fine chemicals, the essential ingredients of the photographic trade.[8] Shoe and furniture makers,[9] watchmakers, and opticians[10] too supplied photo materials and can be grouped with apothecaries as artisan retailers. Photo-studios would belong in this category. Even notable confectioners such as Federico Peliti[11] entered the business of photography.

Other venues where photographs and photographic materials were available defy easy categorization by the historian[12] but they included traveling showmen. J. W. Newland, a visiting entertainer and showman, announced that he had more than two hundred miniature colored daguerreotype views of South America, Sydney and Hobart Town, Queen Pomare of Tahiti and her entire family, and much more to fascinate "the Ladies and Gentlemen of Calcutta." Visitors could also get a colored likeness of themselves complete in a Morocco case for twelve rupees.[13] By 1855, Mr. Newland announced, "Amateurs and the trade supplied with plates, chemicals, and paper."[14] Newland also produced the phantasmagoria shows popular at the time, making him, at once, a retailer, photographer, and showman. Inquiries about the new medium published in local newspapers confirm a culture of public display for its technology, one quite distinct from the privatized and individualized consumption of images that ensued by the end of the nineteenth century with the Kodak camera in the West, or the client-centered form of the photo-studio in India. One letter writer[15] to the *Bengal Hurkaru* offered details—while requesting further information—of the new daguerreotype process. The two short notes appended in response by the newspaper's editor are more revealing of the local habitus of photography than the drily informative letter: "Mr. J.L. Belnos,[16] the portrait painter residing at No. 6 Writer's Buildings has obtained some excellent pictures in daguerreotypes!" and, "It has fully answered the most sanguine expectations. No limner could have drawn such exquisitely correct landscapes as those shown to us by Mr. Belnos."[17]

The varying prices track not only the increasing popularity of photography, but also its expense as a hobby or vocation relative to other pursuits and indulgences.[18] Historian Siddhartha Ghosh notes that a daguerreotype portrait in the 1860s was cheaper at twelve rupees than a painted portrait at one hundred rupees. Ghosh qualifies this fact by noting that imported champagne was even cheaper, at forty rupees per dozen bottles, than the daguerreotype. Cameras and lenses were expensive as well, with prices comparable to those for entire magic lantern and phantasmagoria kits, and expensive watches. The cheap and affordable ambrotypes and tintype/ferrotypes (direct positive images on tin or black-lacquered glass) served as alternatives to the expensive daguerreotypes. These turned out to be enormously popular with Bengalis and poorer Europeans in nineteenth-century Calcutta (Ghosh 1988, 4).[19] Adeshwar Ghatak, author of the first Bangla-handbook on photography for amateurs, *Photography Shikha*, published in 1906, reminisced about the touts of photo-studios who roamed Calcutta's Chinabazaar and Rajabazaar localities, luring rustic gentlemen with cheap "glass-images" for as little as eight annas. (Sixteen annas made a rupee). By the end of the century, when Ghatak could see a few aging photographers still in business from his childhood days, these tintypes and ambrotypes cost only four and two annas respectively (36).

On the other end of the spectrum, by the turn of the century, high-end photo-studios catering to the wealthy could supply their clients with extraordinary, elaborately painted photographs, photographs on silk, photographs that utilized platinum in the emulsion, and photographers who would visit the homes of wealthy clients for their portraits.

Cameras made in India were distinguished by their quality and design compared to their English versions. Photo historian John Jenkins observes that tropical cameras were

> specifically designed and produced in small quantities for the British RAJ, [and] were, by necessity, exceptionally well-made and finished. They were more expensive than the standard models,

> often being made to order and to certain specifications, hence
> their rarity. If you consider the extra work entailed; cutting-in the
> brass bindings, the strong gluing, the generous lacquering, together
> with the special care and attention required on a Tropical, the
> small additional charge they made . . . was very good value in
> those days for the administrators of our [*sic*] Empire. (1981, 73)

Railway transportation rates three decades after the arrival of photography
show that photographic equipment cost far more to transport, as was the
case with books ("writings") and images, compared to the materials of empire
building (red earth, maps, tents, surveying instruments).[20] Other sources,
such as postal rates and directions published by the postal service, show how
difficult it may have been to transport photographic images since, by the
1850s, photographic images were produced on heavy glass plates, as opposed
to the copper plates of the preceding daguerreotype process:

> Contents of book packets can contain any number of books,
> newspapers—printed or lithographed letters, photographs (when
> not on glass or in cases containing glass), prints or maps—may
> be printed, written, lithographed, engraved or plan or admixture
> of these. Only paper, parchment or vellum allowed, but printed
> books, publications, maps, prints etc. can be on canvas or cloth.[21]

Vendors sold the camera, the chemicals, slides, and sometimes images as
well, as a single unit.[22] They often sold cameras for differing photographic
methods together.[23] In contemporary notices, we can find a relationship
between the marketing of photography as a complete kit and frequent
descriptions of it as a toy. The relationship implies a process that is manual
and interactive, involving an object whose "inner" workings were not yet
central to its identity, an object black-boxed through sheer novelty rather
than through a process of scientific experimentation that established the
transparency of its workings. If we accept this premise, the dexterity and
manual skills of the showman-photographer at this early moment must seem
less like "expertise"—a formalized knowledge—than an enticing skill. The
fairground photographer's performance of his manual dexterity in the 1990s
contained traces of this logic of display, just as vendors displayed the images
themselves as curious objects in those early years.

My aim in describing this world of material goods and consumer culture is to emphasize the elasticity and openness of photography's uses and
meanings in the first decade or so after its arrival in South Asia, reflected
in the variety of circumstances in which it is available, circumstances that
situate it in a crowded world of goods. In these early years, photography

emerged as a novelty, a toy, a showpiece, and was for the most part blissfully disconnected from the complex multicontinental history of experimentation and invention that resulted in the daguerreotype and the calotype in France and the UK, respectively.[24] This openness would soon make way for a formalization of knowledge, but not uniformly for European and Indian practitioners of photography, and with mixed long-term results. The history of the shaping of "know-how"—which I will distinguish from formalized expertise—supplies one conspicuous link to the fairground photographer's technical ingenuity. I turn now therefore to expertise, the second element of the photographic assemblage.

FORMAL EXPERTISE AND INFORMAL KNOW-HOW

Starting from around 1855, we witness the emergence of the photographic apparatus as a singular technological object with discrete parts, rather than a self-contained toy. The first notice devoted solely to photographic goods, with each component of the photographic apparatus listed singly—as opposed to a random cornucopia of unrelated consumer goods—appeared in 1855. One can also see the expanding market for photographic practice in the increased variety of prices and sizes of available instruments. By the second decade (1850–1860), vendors provided daguerreotype cameras in three different sizes at staggered prices of 120, 150, and 220 rupees; exposure slides were available singly; calotype cameras came with prices listed separately for the camera, chemicals, and paper; and in many instances, retailers threw in daguerreotype and calotype cameras together as one deal, again at different sizes.

If in the first decade the consumer was the curious dilettante, the showman, the painter, and the commercial photographer, by the second decade, the serious amateur and the official photographer had become prominent. The incorporation of photography into official documentation policy in 1854 was an important milestone. The East India Company decided to replace its reliance on the draughtsman in 1854 for archeological and topographical surveying purposes with the photographer. Soon after, the 1857 Sepoy Mutiny (an insurrection in the East India Company's army by Indian soldiers) constituted one major threat to the British presence in South Asia. The mutiny spread through much of North India and nearly ended the Company's presence in the subcontinent. It was quelled and eventually resulted in the transfer of administrative power from the East India Company to an administration overseen directly by the Crown, thus properly inaugurating the British Empire. Given this tense context, the "official" photography that emerged was marked by two paradigms of knowledge. The Orientalizing "salvage paradigm" documented South Asia's ancient and seemingly timeless past as evidenced in her architecture, now under threat from the modernizing aims of the colonial agenda. The other paradigm was driven by paranoia and surveillance in the wake of the mutiny, a "detective" paradigm that produced in commissioned works a body of knowledge about India's castes and tribes that intersected with and serviced the colonial state's discourses of criminology, forensics, race, and genetics.[25]

The second development was the formation of photographic societies in Calcutta, Bombay, and Madras, the three major "presidencies"—or provinces—of British government in South Asia, in 1855 and 1856. In addition to the curious customer, there were now two other constituencies: the government photographer, and the Victorian gentleman-scientist of the photographic society interested in optics and chemistry[26] and in photography as an experimental process.[27]

Caught at the intersection of amateur science (the photographic society) and governmentality (official photography), the photographic apparatus was as material and heavy to transport as it was prone to breakage. The apparatus was as tangible as the shards of a broken light bulb or the pieces of a shattered gramophone record. The photographer carried the heavy glass plates on which the image would be exposed, the various chemicals required for the exposure, as well as the large camera that was quite unlike the hand camera that would emerge decades later. The equipment, as well as its vulnerability to breakage, resulted in a rhetoric of against-all-odds heroism, which pervaded colonial photographic practice, quite unlike the survivalist, practical, and vocational mode of the contemporary fairground photographer. The famous British photographer Samuel Bourne's accounts noted the numerous negatives he lost as he trekked up the Himalayas with his retinue of recalcitrant coolies who occasionally had to be whipped into submission (Ollman 1983). The following is an extract from 1877 from a contemporary amateur photography handbook by John Blees:

> [W]henever you call at Kamptee, have a look not only at the Kanhan bridge, but also at its photograph as taken by me, for they will both repay the sight. . . . I am very sorry to say I cannot sell you any more copies. Fancy me carrying a negative safely all over the continent and England for the purpose of getting it printed in carbon; fancy me carrying it over the Atlantic and Indian oceans, over the Mediterranean and Red Seas, and then to get it smashed in Bombay harbour by the carelessness of coolies when transferring the case which contained it from the P. and O. steamer to the launch. Misfortunes such as these, my friend, you must bear like a man, like a true philosopher, for if you don't, you won't be fit for a travelling photographer. (1877, 170–71)

Blees's implied photographer is the European amateur photographer. What about Indians? In 1857, the commandeered expulsion of Dr. Rajendralal Mitra, a learned scholar and treasurer of the Bengal Photographic Society over political differences—the issue had to do with whether Indian judges ought to have the right to try Europeans in criminal cases in *mofussil* courts—led to the en masse resignation of other Bengalis from the society in protest. Indian membership dropped precipitously as a result. If in 1857 the Bengal Photographic Society boasted thirty Indian members out of one hundred, in 1861 only seven of 267 members were Indian. The number of Bengali photographers increased, however, at a much faster rate than the number of European photographers. Judith Gutman estimates that "by 1860, there were probably one hundred and thirty Bengali photographers in Calcutta (four times the thirty in 1857, a faster rate of growth than European photographers, of whom there were seventy in 1857 and two hundred in 1860)" (1982: 99).

An Indian public for photography developed, and photography spread as a force in the bazaars, not in the learned societies and government art schools and amateur exhibitions. Subsequent to Mitra's expulsion most Indians, Gutman speculates, were possibly learning the craft from their fathers, running studios ensconced within the structures of family business practices, such as the three generations of Lala Deen Dayal's photo-studio,[28] and peddling their portraits in bazaars. The location of the fairground photographer's practice—the fairground, the bazaar—situates him far from the history of serious amateur European photography discussed in the halls of learned societies. He emerges from an Indian photographic culture that skipped the formalization and institutionalization of the medium. However, there is also no denying his distant affinity to this history of official photographers and gentlemen-scientists. To them, the fairground photographer owes his origins as a *bricoleur* and tinkerer. Finally, he inherits the early flexibility of photography's form and appearance in European consumer culture in Calcutta, and that flexibility was/is evident in the makeshift nature of the camera and its use in Indian bazaars and fairgrounds. Ultimately, the assemblage of photography was partly tangible and material (the equipment), partly intangible and conceptual (the expertise), and partly performed and gestural (the enactment of the expertise). This assemblage emerged out of the material and consumer cultures of mid-nineteenth-century Calcutta.

But how did this assemblage—or the practices associated with it—survive into the second half of the twentieth century? The answer to this question is as essential for what happens after the arrival of the cinema, as it is for the subsequent history of photography. Here, the localized, site-specific, and tangible assemblage encounters the varying scales and spaces of the proto-global geographies crafted by imperialism. This encounter was one of the major determinants in the shaping of photographic cultures in South Asia, and in the longevity of the practices of the nineteenth century.

PROTO-GLOBAL INFLUENCES:
THE SCALAR AND SPATIAL LOGIC OF EMPIRE

If the retail and material cultures of nineteenth-century Calcutta can be considered one set of precursors to the contemporary fairground photographer, Bengal's position in the networks of imperial commerce constitutes another important determinant in the continuing use of antique techniques. The emergence of the gelatin dry plate in the 1870s, three decades after the arrival of photography, was an important turning point in the history of photography. The dry plate replaced the cumbersome wet-collodion process, in which everything from the coating of the collodion and emulsion onto the glass plate, to the exposure of the glass plate, to the fixing and developing of the image, had to be done on the spot before the collodion dried. Unlike its precursors in the photographic process, the gelatin dry plate was therefore also durable and portable across long distances. Finally, the ease of use ultimately resulted in the transference of expertise from the hands of the photographer to the developing lab of the photo-studio, and this became the dominant economic and technological model for subsequent innovations in photography such as the Kodak camera (see Jenkins 1975).

As a new mass-manufactured product from Britain that could be transported to India with ease, the gelatin plate's first major effect was the emergence of a "colonial market" for ready-made and mass-manufactured photographic goods (unlike the vagaries of taste, trends, and novelty that had governed the importation of photographic materials in the preceding period). Its second effect, however, is one that results in a counterfactual explanation. Mass-manufactured in Britain, and easily transportable, the gelatin plate made local mass-manufacture unnecessary in India. There was therefore little pressure on older methods and technologies of photographic image production to recede into obsolescence. These methods included the daguerreotype with its copper direct-positive plates, the calotype with its paper negatives, and the wet-collodion process with its glass negatives and its albumen-coated positive paper. Transformations in photography from the 1870s onward (the dry plate, the hand camera, new kinds of photographic paper) constituted additions to an already existing repertoire of possible methods of image production rather than transforming the face of picture production in any dramatic way, as it had done in the United States or in Europe. The preeminence of import in this case sustained a diversity of practices that local mass-manufacture might have extinguished. Together, the older and newer methods of image production and technical infrastructures ensured the coexistence of dissonant and sometimes overlapping scales of production, consumption, and commercial exploitation.

More generally, the culture of photography had developed in a manner suited to the persistence of old with new. Calcutta had witnessed segmented if somewhat overlapping constituencies of users and consumers since the earliest years, intersecting race, expertise, and wealth. Calcutta's complex social structure comprised elite and poor Europeans, amateur and commercial photographers, and elite and poorer Indians. What practices and methods dominated in each of these segments?[29]

Photographic image production occurred in four identifiable and sometimes overlapping worlds—the commercial European photo-studios, the commercial Bengali photo-studios catering to elite and middle-class Bengalis, the Bengali bazaar photographers whose clienteles consisted of the poorer sections of Bengali society, and the largely European serious-amateur photographic community, which had its own subcultures of use and preference.

The European photo-studios catered mainly to a European population and export market for images. Accordingly, they exhibited a clear preference for labor-intensive and expensive methods. Almost all of the photographs of the famed photo-studio Bourne & Shepherd were albumen prints taken from glass wet-collodion negatives, which Bourne produced from his travels in the Himalayas in the 1860s. A perusal of contemporary exhibition checklists reveals that the firm sold albumen prints[30] well into the 1920s, and eventually added images from considerably more expensive methods, such as platinum prints, as well.[31]

Urban Bengali photo-studios, likewise, catered to a section of the population that could afford expensive processes as well as personalized services. Most Calcutta-based Bengali photo-studios offered personal visits to households for family portraiture, as well as in-studio photography. However, unlike the European studios, they were keenly aware of the need to cater to the widest possible set of demands. In 1864, Gangadhar Dey, a "portrait and landscape painter in the English and Foreign styles," announced that he "paints from life or from photos….To prevent disappointment, please make an engagement by correspondence. Will wait upon respectable parties at their places when called" (Ghosh, 306). Another such studio, Mitter and Company, announced that it "executes orders of every description with artistic neatness and elegance at a moderate rate. Ladies are photographed by accomplished Female artists either in our studio or at their own houses. Out-door and Mofussil orders are undertaken" (311).

Other Bengali studios, such as the Mahila Art Studio and Photographic Store, included platinotypes (another name for platinum prints) and photographs on silk. These studios depended on and ensured the continuity of patron-client relationships attuned to the social and cultural mores of the Calcutta *bhadralok* (gentry).

Particularly noteworthy is the survival of variations of the daguerreotype, the earliest viable photographic process announced by Louis Daguerre in 1839, into the early twentieth century. Where the expensive European and elite Bengali studios had given up on the daguerreotype by the 1860s in favor of the wet-plate process, at least up to the first decade of the twentieth century, the lower-end Bengali studios sold ambrotypes and tintypes (also called ferrotypes) in Calcutta for four and two annas apiece (3).[32] These were direct positive images that were much cheaper to produce than the daguerreotype. In the second edition of his amateur handbook for India, George Ewing observed that ferrotypes were "in great vogue at English watering places and in the bazaars of Indian towns" (Ewing 1895, 176). One also finds, around 1903 or 1905, ferrotypes *and* collodion among the exhaustive list of photographic materials that a Bengali supply firm such as the Photographic Stores and Agency Company sold (Ghosh, 309).[33]

The arrival of dry plates in the late 1870s, did, however, result in an overall shift away from wet-plate photography, among both amateur photographers as well as commercial European and Bengali photo-studios. The dry plates also brought with them other transformations. Since the plates were portable, they enabled the use of smaller "hand" cameras instead of the bulkier, large "field" cameras. Photographic paper underwent further transformations by the 1890s, when developers no longer needed to sensitize it on the spot and could obtain it factory-produced and presensitized.

These changes did not happen overnight, and more importantly, none of the changes meant the certain death of an earlier product and method. Film studios, such as New Theaters in Calcutta, utilized large-sized dry plates and bulky field cameras to produce publicity stills for their productions until the late 1950s, in part because enlargements from smaller roll film negatives lacked the fine grain quality and tonal contrasts required for publicity brochures, handbills, and posters (Mukherjee 2007).

A report on a photographic exhibition in *The Englishman* newspaper of Calcutta from 1895 summed up the serious-amateur preferences for a combination of expensive varieties of photographic paper and labor-intensive methods of photographic image production:

> Among the many general impressions a photographer will receive in the course of an inspection of the pictures, perhaps the most important is that the ordinary albumenized paper silver print is practically a thing of the past. Platinotype [or platinum paper] is certainly first favorite among printing processes, and gelatino-chloride papers [or POP], toned to a variety of different

shades, and often with a matt, instead of the usual highly-glazed surface, rank next. A very effective printing method called "Mezzotype" has been adopted by several English exhibitors, which consists in using plain salted paper, with a rough surface, and fixing the print without any toning process. Bromide papers are still popular, especially for enlargements.[34]

What about the Kodak camera? The Kodak set itself apart from its predecessors by separating the tasks of developing and printing from the task of taking the photograph. Eastman's strategy also devised a roll film as a replacement for the dry plate. The Kodak camera was released in 1888 and became wildly successful in the United States almost instantly. The roll film it utilized, combined with the fact that printing and developing were removed from the hands of the photographer, constituted in essence a technological system. That system addressed three functions: the production of photosensitive papers, the taking of a picture, and the developing and printing of the picture. By removing the first and last functions from the hands of the photographer, Eastman created a vast new set of photographers who had to do nothing but "press the button" to produce a photographic image. As Reese Jenkins notes, the Kodak marked crucial change, a change "in conception of who was to practice photography . . . one of the most revolutionary ideas in the history of photography" (Jenkins 1975, 13).

Who adopted the Kodak in Bengal? Bathgate and Company, Smith, Stanistreet and Company, and John Blees and Company all offered printing, enlarging, and developing services to the "snapshotter," a type serious amateur circles particularly reviled. For a measure of the derision attached to the Kodak, one needs look no farther than George Ewing's handbook for amateur photographers in India:

> And if you want a picture, do not attempt photographs of horse races, they are not really difficult, but the unaccustomed attitude of riders and horses make them more curious then beautiful. Photographing men and women in unwonted situations may appear very funny, but it is the sort of fun that appeals to 'Arry and 'Arriet, and classes you with them. And do not yield to the impertinent demands of friends to "take them"; they really do not care a brass farthing for your efforts, and you should always try to maintain the dignity of the art, although you may own a Kodak. (Ewing 1895, 337–38)

If the target consumer for the Kodak camera was the Indian with no prior experience in photography, that person could not afford the Kodak camera in India. A glance at the advertisements in Calcutta newspapers such as

The Statesman reveals that well into the second decade of the twentieth century, in 1915, the Kodak camera was marketed largely to the elite European or Indian who could afford to vacation abroad rather than the average middle-class Indian who probably could not afford the varieties of available Kodak cameras. The cameras cost as much as fourteen pounds. A folding pocket Kodak cost five pounds and the cheapest, the Kodak Brownie, cost between five and fifty rupees.[35] Even a secondhand pocket-folding Kodak was an expensive fifty rupees.[36] In addition to the prices, per capita income levels in India, when compared with those of the UK and the United States, suggest that far fewer people in India had the elasticity of income to afford hand cameras (Maddison et al. 2003, 60–62, 87–88, 180–82).[37] Literacy was an implied prerequisite for camera users as they needed to read the manuals that came with the Kodak. And an 1881 census suggests that only 6.6 percent of Indian males—corresponding statistics aren't available for women—were fully literate, or thirty-five individuals out of a thousand (Joshi, 43–45).

Let me venture, however, that the absence or presence of literacy is irrelevant here. Indians did not learn to operate cameras in the discursive terrain of the photographic society where optics and chemistry ruled as disciplinary frames of reference. Nor did they have access to written manuals. Instead, they acquired the expertise at stake here through access to the camera itself and the operatively embedded technical knowledge the camera materially embodied, in the specific configurations of parts that constituted its *dispositif*. This techno-epistemology disrupts the project of a media history in favor of a media archaeology, because what occurs when the 1990s *photowallah* operates an 1870s manual processing camera is "a media archeological short-circuit between otherwise clearly separated times," in Wolfgang Ernst's superb characterization (2011, 240). More importantly, one expertise did not cancel out the other, so that multiple conceptions of photography coexisted. This was, if any, the superseding logic. Thus, apothecaries such as Smith, Stanistreet and Company that supplied photo-chemicals in the earliest days could by the end of the nineteenth century possess sizeable research and development wings, replicating the Kodak logic. Meanwhile, the photo-studio and the commercial photographer operated in a very different mode and world at the same time.

To what extent can we verify the claims made here, at least the ones that involve some empirical measure? Colonial records of sea-borne trade list, in a scattered and uneven fashion, photographic materials among the goods imported, but do not break down this broad category further so that we can isolate cameras. It is difficult to verify empirically the ubiquity of the photo-studios in the colonial period as they were not required to register, and when they were, no one preserved the records. The city directories for the preindependence and postindependence era reveal increasing numbers of Indian photo-studios as the nineteenth century comes to a close, but studio names appear and disappear from year to year, and for much of the nineteenth century, city directories rarely mentioned Bengali photographers and photo-studios. For the same reasons, rural areas and small towns pose a further challenge. While the supremacy of photo-studios is anecdotally and visibly evident in India, the constraints and limitations of empirical verification suggest the importance of ethnography, of the kind practiced by David MacDougall.

How exceptional are the outcomes in Bengal in relation to Europe? My point here is not to make an overarching claim that all the methods employed in late-nineteenth-century Calcutta were already "obsolete" in Europe. Rather, I have sought to illustrate the diversity of preferences for early and newer methods of producing images. The availability of collodion for sale in the 1920s gave a distinctive character to photographic culture in India, since the wet-collodion process had indeed fallen out of favor in Europe and the United States by the 1880s. Likewise, photographic culture in Bengal, surprisingly, included ambrotypes and tintypes. In Europe, these processes quickly ran out of favor as the daguerreotype itself receded in use. In the United States, however, they were extremely popular as late as the 1860s during the Civil War years (Mace 1999, 20). These direct-positive images, it seems, were popular in Bengal later than in the United States, into the 1920s. The popularity of albumen prints declined at the same rate in South Asia as it did in Europe, in the period between 1890 and 1910 (103). Nevertheless, elite photo-studios in India, such as Bourne & Shepherd, continued to produce these prints off their existing store of wet-collodion negatives until the end of and beyond this period. The Kodak—and hand cameras in general—did not catch on, but they certainly ushered new genres of representation, as we will see in subsequent chapters. A complex combination of forces ultimately shaped photography in Bengal: technological shifts, new routes of access to and importation of the latest materials in Europe through improvements in communications and transportations, and a striated and varied colonial society.

These aspects call into question the scalar and spatial categories of the global and the local in globalization theory. The simultaneous coexistence of older and newer photographic methods and technologies, and the obviation of obsolescence, was partly intrinsic to the peculiarities of the photographic trade within South Asia (the lack of local manufacture of materials that might, through sheer scale, pressure older methods to recede), but these peculiarities were also a symptom of South Asia's place within a broader imperial space (Bengal's proximity to British manufacturing sources). Here, I find Aihwa Ong and Stephen Collier's discussion of the relation between the global and the local useful. Ong and Collier, drawing on work of Deleuze and Guattari and Bruno Latour, juxtapose global forms that are open to abstraction, dynamic, immutable, and in circulation, with an understanding of assemblages as multiply determined, unstable configurations of elements. Ong and Collier expressly note that these immutable ideal/typical "global" forms are not to be counterposed with assemblages conceived as local mutations. Instead, they argue that assemblages are irreducible to a single logic (2007, 3–21). From this perspective the task is not to come up with a grand narrative of the globalization of culture, but to look at the circulation of quite specific global forms and the process of their de- and re-territorialization within mutable assemblages.[38] For example, we can consider the fairground photographer as an instantly recognizable figure not restricted to South Asia. In this sense, he is an ideal/typical and "global" character. When, however, we speak of the fairground photographer in the 1990s in India, we are speaking of a specific, historically contingent re-territorialization of the ideal character in the Indian context. We are no longer thinking of the global and local as scalar or spatial categories. Instead, the two terms point to a much more contingent congealment and dispersal of practices, technologies, and expertise. The textured history of photography's imbrication in consumer culture, state initiatives, scientific interest, and commercial exploitation, and the changing meanings and uses of the apparatus (from toy to science to commercial service) show the periodic reinvention and recalibration of the technology itself, as well as its meanings. The cinema, the next chapter will contend, needs to be understood along similar lines.

What postscripts may we add to this early-twentieth-century history of photography? One can reasonably surmise that the hand camera did little in overall terms to curtail the power of the photo-studio in catering to the need for vernacular and domestic photographs.[39] Over the past decade, "cybercafés" set up with refurbished personal computers armed with web cameras, and cell phones also armed with cameras, have, in varied ways, made possible personalized practices of image production and circulation. It seems that photographic history in colonial and postcolonial India bypassed an entire stage, that of the Kodak camera and the personal snapshot, in favor of a continuation of a patronage-based culture of image production and consumption, at the center of which lies the photo-studio, from which it frog-leapt to the age of the smart phone.

But such an account misses the complexity of photography's engagement with other media. In chapter 4, I want to propose that we do pay some attention to the late-nineteenth- and early-twentieth-century hand camera if only because the hand camera intersects both with developments in print culture and with the cinema in the genre of photojournalism. Nearer to our moment, Chris Pinney (1997) demonstrates the photographic medium's overlap with videocassettes and local cable TV networks in 1990s India. While video became *de rigueur* as medium of record for important occasions such as weddings, the absence of Video Cassette Players in most houses resulted in a reliance on the local cable TV operator to air the wedding for occasional family gatherings. Only on such occasions would the videocassette, dusted off its place in a cabinet, realize its efficacy, since the video technology was not at hand. At the same time, the aesthetic of video recordings remained profoundly photographic—the video program comprised superimpositions and dissolves of hieratic poses for the video camera including photomontages of still images of the wedded couple. In such an instance of a new technological interface, people continued to rely on the local and linked expertise of the photo-studio, the videographer and the cable TV operator. As Nishtha Jain's 2005 documentary *City of Photos* similarly reveals, the availability of digital cameras and new imaging software such as Photoshop reinforced the dominance of photo-studios, as studios replaced actual painted backdrops with digital ones customized for clients' needs on the personal computer. In both McDougall's and Jain's documentaries, we find that it is popular cinema that provides the most enduring and popular tropes and imaginations of performing identity for clients in photo-studios, as backdrops (painted or Photoshopped) mimic the mise-en-scène of a Hindi film song and clients dress in movie costumes and the studio cameraman accordingly obliges them.

We could update the fairground photographer's techniques to the digital age with one last example. Ellora, one of India's protected archeological sites of caves containing rock-cut architecture from between the fifth and tenth centuries, located in the western state of Maharashtra, is today a major tourist attraction. The site reveals the deep involvement of corporations in local economies of image production, as photographer Peeyush Sekhrasia and Shiva Avhad document through their interview with Ajay Chowdhury, a local photographer. Polaroid and Kodak convince local photographers to adopt their products by sending sales representatives to the tourist site. Polaroid's decision to increase the price of its cassettes of photo paper cuts into the photographers' profits, ending the use of its products among dissatisfied photographers. With Kodak, the company's proposal that local photographers adopt their digital cameras and printers hits a basic stumbling block: the absence of electricity. Battery-operated printers solve the problem of electricity. Furthermore, in an echo of the nineteenth century, a state development institution, the National Bank for Agriculture and Rural Development (henceforth NABARD) offers a one-month course in commercial photography held on the premises of the local school. As Sekhsaria puts it, the net result is that currently seventy cameramen operate in the Ellora area, carrying, for instance, a kit that could comprise the

Canon digital camera, an Epson battery-operated printer with two battery sets (the additional one for backup), and a set of "150 sheets (4" x 6") [of photo paper] on which one can also take passport size photographs." Hawkers switch professions to become photographers. While a photographer can earn four hundred to five hundred rupees a day (approximately seven to nine dollars at current exchange rates), those who cannot afford the equipment can themselves hire it for one hundred rupees a day.[40]

CONCLUSION

While this chapter focuses for the most part on photography and the next one attends to cinema, such a demarcation is forced. We find that, as with photography, early filmmakers and exhibitors had to translate constraints that were transcontinental in nature and origins into localized and spatially dispersed forms of enterprise. Photography was shaped within the material cultures of 1840s Calcutta and was dominated by personalized retail practices in the long run. These circumstances are antecedents to the early years of the cinema, its often itinerant and clientist forms of enterprise, and its ability to sustain those forms in the long run despite becoming a highly commercialized enterprise with vast scales of production by the 1930s, the decade that marked the arrival of sound cinema and with it, regional film industries. As much as we can see the cinema in photography's nineteenth-century emergence, we can also see photography's continuing intermedial futures in the twentieth century, as it intersected with the cinema and print culture (through photojournalism), with video and cable television, with the arrival of digital cameras, and in the survival of the digitally updated photo-studio.

2

TRAVELING SHOWMEN, MAKESHIFT CINEMAS

· ❖ ·———· ❖ ·

The Bioscopewallah and Early Cinema

> What we familiarly refer to, for example, as film, photography, and television are transient elements within an accelerating sequence of displacements and obsolescences, part of the delirious operations of modernizations.
>
> —Jonathan Crary, *Suspensions of Perception*

A considerable proportion of film exhibition in India occurs in itinerant form and in makeshift and often temporary establishments, rather than in permanent theaters. Traveling showmen—familiarly known as Bioscopewallah or the Bioscope man—put together many of these exhibitions and in doing so transform the quotidian spaces of thoroughfares into theatrical spaces, exhibiting moving images through a combination of vintage and obsolete projection equipment and film scraps from established studios.

Showmen such as Mohammed Salim in Calcutta and Feroze and Hanif Bhai in Ahmedabad retrofit their hand-cranked silent-era projectors[1] for sound with additional roll mechanisms, secondhand optical readers and photocells, and handmade speaker boxes. Astrologers use two-rupee lenses to read palms. Light bulbs originally meant for autorickshaws replace more expensive firsthand light bulbs in these projectors and suffice just as well. The showmen install their projectors in large wooden boxes fashioned with peepholes for individualized viewing, and cart them from locality to locality, where their exhibitions cater to both children and adults (Biswas 2004; Sternberg 2007; Lakhani 2006). Such methods take on the dimensions of an "autographic" art, an art of the signature like painting, defined by action in the form of the projectionist's hand and "a certain telos," to borrow D. N. Rodowick's words. The exhibition concludes when the projectionist stops cranking the projector and the film ceases to unwind before the lens. The *dispositif*, or entire arrangement, by incorporating the live performance and transforming the quotidian spaces of thoroughfares into theatrical spaces, also undermines distinctions between film as a semiotic and textual fact and the cinema in all of its institutional, logistical, and spatial dimensions. At the same time, if we stay with Rodowick and pursue the similarities between the Bioscope and the traditional arts, we see that the former retains, however compromised, a spatial and temporal separation between production (of the movie) and its performance (as a screening). This quality characterizes "two-stage" arts, such as music and cinema (Rodowick 2007, 14–15). Thus, the Bioscope is not an unambiguous manifestation of the cinema. It is both a live performance by man and machine that varies in each instance, and a more conventional screening of a film in the form of compiled footage that is in principal standardized across multiple instances (see Fig. 2.1).

Whereas Salim provides a traveling show, Sikandar Gul Muhammed Khan, aka Raja Filmwala, is sedentary. He transforms the ground level and first floor of his living quarters in the slums of Bombay into, respectively, a cinema hall and projection booth, while the third level remains his living

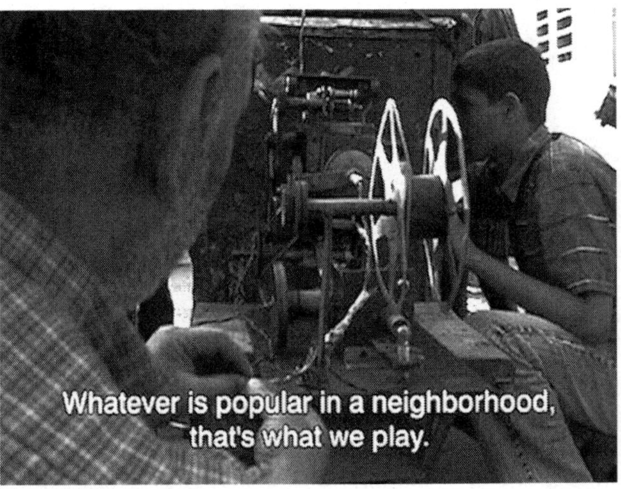

Figure 2.1. Salim and his son conduct film showings for children in the neighborhoods of Kolkata, with a refurbished and retrofitted movie projector ensconced in a rolling wooden cart (Source: Tim Sternberg's *Salim Baba* [USA: HBO, 2007]).

quarters. As with the previous examples, Raja's "films" comprise "scrap" or junk reels discarded by film studios, which raddiwalas (garbage/rag-pickers) and bangle makers pick up.[2] The exhibitors purchase the reels at ten rupees per kilo, a price likely cheaper than any pirate economy could foster as a startup cost for a print. The exhibitors edit and string together the "scrap" reels to create movie-collages of scenes, songs, and dances for entertainment at a price cheaper than the cheapest movie ticket. All these showmen escape licensing regimes and entertainment taxes by operating below the lowest category of movie theaters in the Indian state's regulatory and classificatory schemes, staying invisible (Grimaud 2002). Some showmen, such as Rau Waghmare, a Bioscopewallah on the outskirts of Pune, work with even older instruments. He operates a hand-cranked projector that features still images of Bombay film stars in an exhibition spectators view through peepholes (Kadam 2007).

The showmen's own assessments of their future include references to transformations in India's media ecologies since the 1980s. Feroze and Hanif Bhai recall how they survived the challenge to their livelihoods posed by television programs such as *Ramayan*, and *Chitrahaar*,[3] but they profess skepticism that they will survive the onslaught of DVDs and VCDs. The Bhais' situation is not a battle between old and new media. Rather, the vintage apparatus of the peripatetic showman whirrs and hums; it contains within it shards of both the past and the future. It binds other media forms in shared affinities with the cinema. The Bioscopewallah offers a film-on-demand in the craft mode of production. He conflates the media of precapitalism with the media of late capitalism. His work renders speculations on the death of film in the age of digital media either supremely outdated or supremely premature. This chapter therefore follows the Bioscopewallah in history as he weaves in and out of private and public, official and nonofficial, commercial and artisanal worlds over the span of more than a century. Its aim, of course, is to ask a question quite similar to the one posed in the previous chapter. How has this Bioscope survived? The comparison with photography is instructive. The dominance of the photo-studio can be traced to the survival of a personalized retail culture that in the long run won out over the mass-manufactured hand camera in defining access to photography. By contrast, the comparable emergence and survival of itinerant and small-scale cinema constituted only a portion of the overall film enterprise in South Asia. In the early twentieth century this enterprise involved the thriving global traffic in films and film technologies that set up networks between numerous locations in the British Empire and also to what was the dominant source of films in South Asia until the 1930s, the United States. In the decades after independence, we can see the resilience of itinerant cinema as such only in the shadow of India's behemoth film industries.

This difference reminds us, of course, that we cannot entirely discard the way Michael Chanan differentiates between photography and film as commodity forms: that one passes into the hands of the customer, as Chanan put it, while the other is experienced through the purchase of a ticket. The "idiosyncratic" film and photographic cultures of South Asia are unavoidably tethered as ambivalent departures to their corresponding norms outlined by Chanan. The dominant photo-studio will always remind us of the hand camera that failed to supplant it, while traveling cinemas will always remind us of the capital-intensive and mass-cultural dimensions of the preponderant mainstream film exhibition.

There is no unbroken line that links the contemporary makeshift projector with its vintage counterparts, a fact that qualifies the search for the origins of the traveling cinema. An example will make this clear. Mohammed Salim, one of many itinerant Bioscopewallahs operating in the by-lanes of Calcutta, is the subject of a beautifully shot and scored documentary, *Salim Baba* (2007), by the filmmaker Tim Sternberg. Salim's approach to film history demonstrates how traveling film exhibition practices in the present trump notions of linear historical sequence, progress, and chronology, and complicate any reflexive sense that the practices testify to "the lost past of cinematic virginity" (Armitage 2008, 41). Sternberg's reflections in an interview bear this out:

> We had all of these ideas of the death of cinema, and he's going to have some great Buster Keaton or John Ford one-reel film that's been waiting since the teens. We had these fantasies that he was the living link to the age of Lumière and the origins of cinema—how cinematic technology was distributed through the colonial paths. When we got there and we tried to talk to him about Satyajit Ray and the history of cinema, he was very practical. He was like, "I remember those movies vaguely from years ago; they were in black and white. I think I have one black-and-white film left; the rest I just threw away." What he had was from 1989. He was like, "The kids don't want to see that!" He has to make a living. So we all had to recalibrate. He kind of humbled us. (Sternberg 2008)

Salim's eschewal of the past frustrates Sternberg's desire for a colonial path that would lead from past to present. That stance should discourage any romantic idea concerning the recovery of lost origins. That said, regardless of Mohammed Salim's disregard for the past, there were indeed colonial paths to the contemporary Bioscopewallah. They just weren't linear. Mapping them leads us to a fuller account of the history of early motion picture exhibition practices and the extent to which those circumstances resonate and persist in changed circumstances in the present.

PHANTASMAGORIA SHOWS

What movie exhibition genealogies can we construct, relying, it would seem at first glance, only on the "memory of living men," the projectionists, and the workings of their hands?[4] We could begin with the optical amusements that could be found in in Calcutta in the mid-nineteenth century, even as photographic cameras were first appearing in importers' inventories. These instruments served as early precedents for the traveling cinema—and indeed the cinema itself—both in practice and as technology. Some of the contraptions endure in today's Bioscope shows as viable remains of those that constituted nineteenth-century amusements. In the city's venerable Sans Souci Theatre, Messrs C. and J. Trood from London advertised in early 1845 a packed program featuring the new "oxy-hydrogen" microscope followed by a "Biscenascope" showing with the help of Drummond's light, which was followed in turn by "MAGNIFICENT Transparent Dissolving Views!"[5] The terms indicate innovations in the technology of magic lantern entertainment, and at the time overlapped with each other. Dissolving views, perfected in 1818, enabled audiences to see one image "dissolve" into the subsequent one, with the aid of a metallic shutter that closed upon one image while at the same time opening another image up for projection. The Biscenascope further improved on the method of presenting dissolving views since it involved a magic lantern with at least two optical units, each with its own lens and light source so that as one image replaced another, the light sources correspondingly dimmed and brightened, creating again a sense of continuity across images. Oxy-hydrogen and Drummond's light utilized limelight, a form of illumination that transformed the possibilities of visual entertainment, making the "dissolves" between images much smoother, enabling with its brighter and steadier light the projection of microscopic views of the subvisible world. Limelight became the key method of illuminating buildings until the arrival of electricity. All of these improvements were ultimately proto-cinematic, nascent illusions of movement incorporating a narrative development in time and space. The more loosely applied name for such theatrical and spectacular presentations of the magic lantern was the phantasmagoria show (Altick 1978, 219–20).[6] The Troods' show in Calcutta therefore condensed a variety of recent technological breakthroughs in visual entertainment into one show.

The Sans Souci show's content included twenty-one views, of which five were clearly meant to present a sense of temporal and spatial continuity: "Cornhill, with the old Royal Exchange," the Exchange up in flames, the ruins of the Exchange after the fire, Prince Albert laying the foundation stone ("embracing many excellent portraits"), and the new Royal Exchange. The solitary "local" view was "Gungatree—the sacred source of the Ganges," sharing its place in the lineup of slides with views of Constantinople and the Rhine, "Last Interview of Louis XVI with family," Dieppe Harbor, and "Byron's Dream."[7]

The tickets in 1845 could not have been cheap, at five rupees for the boxes, four rupees for the stalls, and two rupees for the "pits," the latter possibly affordable only for the poorer soldiery. They could be purchased at prominent European hotels in Calcutta. The *Bengal Hurkaru* reviewed one of these shows later in the year:

> The apparatus, which is on the principle of an enormous triple magic lantern, lit by the Drummond or Limelight was placed behind the governor-general's box and threw its pictures upon a screen occupying the whole front of the stage. In many instances, these pictures, which were beautifully executed and brilliantly coloured, covered the entire surface of the screen, and had a most illusive effect, which was much heightened by the performance of appropriate music during the period of their exhibition. In most cases, the melting of one scene into another was perfection itself, and seemed like the effect of magic. . . . A series of folk dancers provided much amusement. Not the least interesting part of the exhibition was the very curious and beautiful Chinese fire-works the formation of which was certainly a Chinese puzzle to the spectators; even as regards their appearance only, they must be seen to be understood. . . .
>
> This exhibition will assuredly become a very popular one. . . . It is pleasant to be enabled to say that there was no row last night, nor was any advantage taken of the twilight which prevailed for the perpetration of practical or other jokes, but all went off in a most orderly and decorous manner.[8]

The review illuminates the variety entertainment format, the novelty of watching images projected on a screen, the remarkable illusion of watching images dissolve into one another, as well as a hint of the social composition of the audience, suggesting that the dimmed lights may have occasioned rowdy behavior by those in the "pits." These shows continued into the 1850s with one commercial photographer, J. W. Newland, coming to prominence and receiving favorable reviews in the local press.[9]

Along with the vast variety of photographic goods now advertised for sale in the Calcutta newspapers, retailers also advertised phantasmagoria lanterns, complete with sets of dissolving views, moveable slides, astronomical slide sets, and the "lucernal microscope," which came with a slide set for projection.[10] Advertisements described in detail some instruments such as the "panoramic machine or print examiner" advertised by prominent booksellers Thacker, Spink and Company:

> This is an entirely new invention for the purpose of showing off small pictures, sketches, drawings or paintings. When a series of Views are exhibited, they are tacked on to a piece of calico to any length, and wound round two rollers, which are inserted horizontally inside the machine. On looking through the lens at the back the view is reflected, magnified in front with such vividness and the perspective so perfectly thrown out that it appears as if the real object were looked at. By turning a handle at the back the views may be moved so as to be seen from end to end. Single Prints and Paintings may also be put in for inspection. Persons fond of drawing and painting will find an endless source of amusement in this instrument, while for families where there are juveniles, its attractions are immense. They are made to accommodate pictures, 6 inches, 9 inches and 12 inches in height and are very handsome in appearance[11] (see Fig 2.2).

While the advertised contraption was similar to a zoetrope or praxinoscope as it employed a roll-mechanism as image holder—in this case a piece of

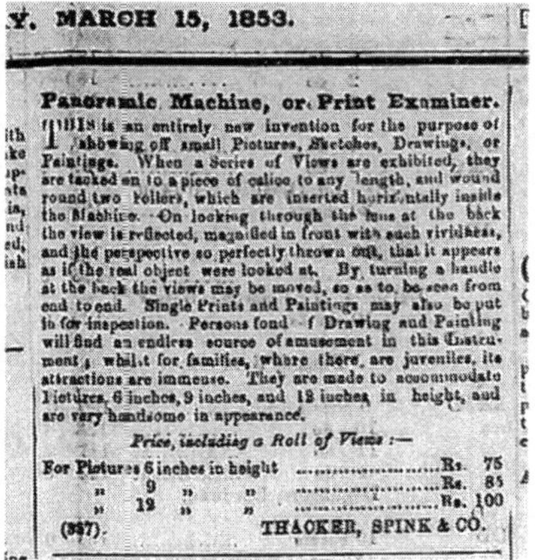

Figure 2.2. Thacker, Spink, and Company advertises an optical viewing device called a Panoramic Examiner (Source: *Bengal Hurkaru*, March 15, 1853).

cloth[12]—it differed from the other two since it included a magnifying lens and a viewfinder fitted on a box that held the roll of images inside.

The panoramic machine Thacker, Spink and Company advertised found its equivalent partly in the indigenous *pats* or scroll paintings. These paintings accompanied the oral narration of the *patua* as the images painted with gouache and fruit dyes illustrating the narrative progressively unrolled. Art historians have discussed in some detail the impact of mechanical reproduction on these pats, noting that by the 1860s, the images of scroll painting began to be sold as mass-produced single pictures. The consumers of these pictures constituted an early form of the cinema's mass audience (Guha-Thakurta, 1992). In the subsequent decade, these single pictures would find an entirely different expression, this time as color lithographs of mythic subject matter from India's religious epics presented as historical images of a classical past, in the tradition of realism in British oil painting. These lithographs, too, majorly influenced the cinema, not just generally in iconography, but even more specifically in the case of the iconic Indian filmmaker D. G. Phalke (1870–1944), whose first films—the earliest extant Indian narrative films—were mythologicals. Phalke drew on the currency of the chromolithographs and their "traditional" subject matter.

I have digressed into a discussion of these indigenous precursors to the early years of Indian cinema in order to underscore another surprising source for the cinema in India: offshoots of the European devices that catered to European life in Calcutta and which lasted well past the European presence. Variants of the Thacker, Spink and Company's imported panoramic examiner still exist in India today, as we see in Prashant Kadam's documentary on Rau Waghmare, the travelling Bioscopewallah in Pune, a city close to Bombay. Here the Bioscope does not refer to moving pictures. Waghmare's Bioscope is remarkably similar to the Panoramic Examiner of an earlier century: an octagonal tin box with viewfinders all around, a handle for hand-cranking the roll mechanism, and the roll mechanism itself within the box for holding photographs—this time, views of Bombay's teeming urban life, as well as images of major film stars. Waghmare's Bioscope instantiates (along with music CDs and cassettes, billboards, pirated VCDs and DVDs) the transformation of Bombay's cinema into new media and renewed content. With its similarities to the Thacker panoramic examiner, Waghmare's apparatus also emblematizes the diverse strands of screen practices, of European and indigenous pedigree, that preceded the cinema: the mechanical pictures, magic lanterns, phantasmagorias, scroll paintings, chromolithographed images, dissolving dioramas, panoramas, Parsi theater, and photography. For our purposes, the proto-cinematic optical entertainments of European life in Calcutta are therefore the first set of screen practices that anticipate the

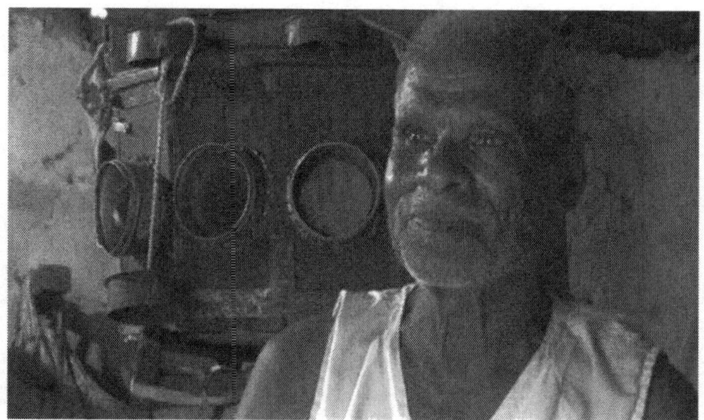

Figure 2.3. On the outskirts of Pune, Rau Waghmare's livelihood depends on a viewing device similar to Thacker, Spink, and Company's Panoramic Examiner, and catering to children. See Prashant Kadam, *The Bioscopewallah*, 2007 (Source: www. visualcultures.com).

emergence of cinema in South Asia, its Indian industries as well as the contemporary Bioscopewallah of the slums of Calcutta (see Fig 2.3).

The surprising European pedigree of contemporary Indian screen practices speaks to the complexity of the spaces of commerce that characterized South Asia's encounter with the British Empire. The Bioscopes and panoramic examiners of today, rusty or not, celluloid or still image-based or "juiced up" with electricity and VCRs and loudspeakers, nevertheless remind us of mongrel cultural spaces and practices from a different time. Wanda Strauven's (2011) argument that the world of "pre-cinema" contained two potential directions for the cinema is relevant here. Those two directions were: that of embodied participation, which many optical toys of the nineteenth century (the stereoscope, kaleidoscope, zoopraxinoscope) demand, and that of distanced contemplation. The latter became the norm and defined the cinema that emerged, but embodied participation is the cinema's repressed past that is evident in contemporary gaming and its kinesthetic and interactive modes, argues Strauven. Like Strauven, I see an embodied culture of practices around film and photography that predated the cinema, characterizes a large portion of ongoing photographic and film cultures, and persists well past its expiration date. However, the fact that these embodied and interactive cultures emerged in radically different contexts in Europe and South Asia and led to significantly variant outcomes, provincializes Strauven's discussion of pre-cinema in Europe, to Europe and the West. At the same time, it paradoxically reminds us that pre-cinema in South Asia cannot be entirely provincialized because film history under colonialism cannot escape a comparative frame of reference, as colonialism produces difference that encompasses the distance between geographical spaces, between metropole and the colony.

LANTERN SLIDES, KINETOSCOPES, AND JUNK FILMS

The traveling Lumière cameraman Marius Sestier conducted the first projected film screening in India in Bombay's Watson's Hotel. Early accounts in India, as elsewhere, framed the cinema as the latest stage of a preceding set of optical devices and screen practices, such as the magic lantern. The *Times of India*'s review of the screening at Watson's on July 7, 1896, is well known: as an "advanced stage" of "the art of photography and the magic lantern . . . something like seven or eight hundred photographs being thrown on the screen within the space of a minute" (Barnouw and Krishnaswamy 1980, 5).

Photography served as a point of reference for narrating film history in more ways than one. Retrospections by serious amateur photographers at this time claimed the dry gelatin plate of the 1870s had transformed photography and taken it downhill, leading eventually to the Kodak and the snapshot craze. In a 1905 address delivered in London and published by the *Photographic Journal*, James Waterhouse, now retired from half a century of civil service in India and an accomplished photographer himself, reminisced fondly about the old days of collodion wet-plate photography, when "we had to coat our own plates, prepare chemical solutions, sensitize printing papers, and, not infrequently, make our own collodion, silver nitrate, gold chloride, albumenized and salted papers." Waterhouse, however, went on to add the following:

> At the same time it must be allowed that to these ready made gelatin emulsion dry plates and papers is mainly due the enormous development of photographic work in its specially pictorial aspects and its applications to the graphic arts and book illustration as well as to scientific investigation in all branches of science, which would have been impossible under the old conditions. They have even made it possible by means of the cinematograph to record the successive phases of movement with the utmost rapidity and again reproduce them with life-like verisimilitude.[13]

Waterhouse delivered his address not more than three decades after transformations in technology and materials fundamentally altered photography. To recap from the previous chapter, these transformations included the shift from wet plates to dry plates in the 1870s, the shift to the roll film and Kodak camera in the 1880s,[14] as well as the availability that same decade of new methods of photographic illustration that enabled the mass publication of images along with printed text. All had transformed the nature of photographic expertise, ushered in a democratization of image production unlike any instance before, resulted in the prominence of the photographic mass-image, and transformed the functions of photography.

Waterhouse's nostalgia was not an exception among photographic circles around the world. If modernity is the historical confluence of circumstances and events engendering a sense of clear rupture from the past, the dry plates, the Kodak revolution, and halftone processes all delivered the fix of modernity. The changes seemed to clarify the narratives of photographic history, providing a singular and stable identity to the "good old days" when everything had to be done by hand. This rhetoric had a pervasive presence in photographic journals across the world, and with more or less contentious consequences for photographic institutions and camaraderie. In Britain and India, the nostalgia took the form of longing for the days of gentlemanly science, whereas in the United States the debates were much more furious, with Alfred Stieglitz at the forefront of efforts to give institutional legitimacy to photography as an art (Sternberger 2001).

The cinema only reinforced the place of photography as an enduring frame of reference. The section quoted above ends, after all, with a mention of the cinema as the latest stage of improvement in photographic science. Where photographic methods made a quantum leap in the 1880s that left all preceding practices as obsolete remnants of a bygone era, the cinematograph was itself seen as only the most recent development in a history of far more significant transformations that had already transpired with photography. It would be correct to conclude that in 1905, for someone such as Waterhouse, deeply immersed in photographic history including the writing of it, the dry plates were without precedent, a transformative event, but not so the cinematograph, which owed its origins, lineage, and patrimony as it were to the dry plates.

The first mention of the cinema in the *Journal of the Photographic Society of India* in 1896 likewise rejected the idea that the magic lantern was in its "decadence" or decline. "The latest phase of the lantern at home is the moving picture," wrote the editor.[15] He then went on to describe Lumière's *L'Arrivée d'un train en la Gare de la Ciotat* (1896), and *Le Débarquement du Congrès de Photographie à Lyon* (1895), although it is not clear where or when he saw these movies. A review of his experience watching Edison's kinetoscope in Calcutta followed his description. The kinetoscope scenes described resemble scenes from the Edwin Porter–photographed *Life of an American*

Fireman (1903) made for Edison, although the journal issue itself is dated July 1896.[16] I reproduce an extended section of the article, for it captures, I think, a template of "first encounters" with the cinema that appears, over and over again in contemporary documentary and fictionalized accounts, including in Tim Sternberg's work and elsewhere: the conspicuous work of the "decrepit" apparatus that hums to life, the bewitching nature of the images that apparatus nevertheless affords, the visual pleasure interrupted and then resumed by the operator's tasks of hand-cranking and reloading the film, and the "performance" of man and machine that binds all this together.

> I had an opportunity last cold weather of viewing Edison's Kinetoscope in Calcutta. It was certainly extraordinary because it depicted what I have just been describing. But the pictures were too small and the duration of the scene too short, to altogether satisfy me. Looking down through an object glass into a breast-high box one was first conscious of a whirring sound, then a sparkling light, and presently a picture about 2 in. square appeared. It was a supposed scene at a fire: a fireman in glistening helmet clambers up a very short ladder, and limp female forms appear above him and are handed down over his shoulder one after the other with a rapidity only more startling than the decorous adjustment of their garments. Having caught the hang of it, I was about to settle down comfortably to a good view when the whirring suddenly ceased, out when the lamp, and I appealed to the showman. There's nothing gone wrong—that's all he said. Oh! That's all is it? It looks very indistinct, and the movements are too rapid to be grasped with advantage. Mayn't I have it all over again? The operator was very obliging, and I had a second performance. When I had taken breath I began to ask questions. There was an absence of smoke, bustle, crowd, &c., about the fire which was more suggestive of a carefully planned performance in a well-lighted studio than a scene taken at a real fire—and then I bethought me of a description I had read of Edison's works where there was a studio for acting of these pieces. Be this as it may, the scene was stirring enough in all conscience, and I gathered that it took a continuous chain or band of 1400 celluloid positives to represent it. This band ran under an illuminated screen below which was an electric lamp— and to bring out the scene required a special camera invented by Edison. But the large moving pictures I have described is, I take it, an advance on this Kinetoscope idea of Edison's—and a very remarkable advance it seemingly is. Seeing that all kinds of scenes

from life and from Nature may be so reproduced, no one will care to aver that the lantern is showing signs of a decrepit age.[17]

The repetitive nature of hand-cranking the apparatus, of proffering repeat "performances," quite apart from merging man and machine as co-implicated and equal elements of an assemblage, is crucial to the logic of commodity production at stake here and becomes a feature ultimately of the slum cinema of the late twentieth century, as we will see shortly.

By the 1920s, magic lanterns were indeed far from decline. The deputy instructor of visual instruction of Bombay presidency testified before the government-constituted Cinematograph Committee that his department had been utilizing lantern slide shows for educational purposes from around 1910 and that the department owned 110 lantern apparatuses. Asked if the cinema would be useful for educational purposes, he argued that the cinema would be a useful "adjunct" to the lantern slide show especially where still image slides would be unable to give a "concrete idea" of the movements of glaciers, earthquakes, and volcanoes.[18]

If these institutional engagements link the cinema to nineteenth-century optical devices and screen practices, other deep-rooted and multifarious connections tie the cinema and photography into a pragmatic alliance. Cinematic practice prior to and after Phalke often depended on the enabling expertise in and familiarity with photography and photomechanical processes. Photographic expertise may have been the *sine qua non* for many of the early Indian filmmakers, a basic qualification for making moving pictures. D. G. Phalke, whose *Raja Harishchandra* (1912) stands as the earliest extant feature-length movie, was an acclaimed photographer (in addition to being a magician, a draftsman, and a lithographer in Ravi Varma's press situated in Western India). So was Calcutta's Hiralal Sen (1866–1917), who was one of the first Indian filmmakers, and who started the Royal Bioscope Company in 1899. Sen had begun his career as a photographer before turning to filmed actualities in 1898. He opened a commercial photo-studio, H. L. Sen & Brothers, on or about 1890 in his village of Bogjury in the Manikganj district of Bengal and spent a considerable sum of money, fourteen or fifteen thousand rupees, to learn photography (Ghosh, 138). Dhiren Ganguly (1893–1978), another prominent early Calcutta filmmaker, trained in the Government Art School in Calcutta in photomechanical processes and had an early interest in photography. Harishchandra Bhatavadekar (b. 1868), Sen's contemporary in the Western Bombay/Poona region, began his career as a photo-studio owner in the 1880s and ventured into filmmaking after the Lumière films "hypnotized" him. One of the earliest known touring film exhibitors before 1910, R. Venkaya Naidu had been one of the leading photographers in Madras and had a prestigious studio in the elite Mount Road section of the city before he moved to film exhibition. His contemporary touring film exhibitor S. Vincent had been a draughtsman for South Indian Railways before he turned to films (Hughes, 41–42).

Where did early cinema equipment come from? The "colonial market" that had emerged during the 1880s gelatin dry plate years, became one source. Many established photographic supply firms updated their inventories to supply motion picture equipment as well. By 1907, for instance, the French firm Pathé had opened its own office in Calcutta for supplying film titles as well as equipment and established an early dominance in the film import and supply business that would last until World War I.[19] Other companies in Calcutta that supplied equipment included the Coronation Bioscope Electric Company, which claimed in an advertisement in 1915, to be "the largest dealers in cinema machines, films of every description viz. exclusive, feature, dramatic, comic, present war topicals, etc. Sole agent for Kinetophone (Talking Motion Pictures) for India, Burma, Ceylon."[20]

Nevertheless, before 1910, access to the apparatus for interested Indians often occurred through less institutionally organized routes. Mail order catalogs, secondhand purchase from traveling foreign showmen, and borrowed equipment characterized their entry. Hiralal Sen may have purchased his first "cinematograph" projector from John Range and Sons, London, for five thousand rupees (Banerjee 1989, 294). Sen saw the earliest motion picture exhibitions in Calcutta, and may have made his first film with equipment borrowed from the traveling showman who put them on, Professor Stevenson (Rajadhyaksha and Willemen 1994, 210). When Sen's company folded in 1911 under competition from Madan Theaters, he sold his cameras to the men who started the Aurora Cinema Company, another Calcutta-based film producing firm (Banerjee 1989).[21]

Exhibition venues in the first decade were diverse. Variety shows in bazaars and fairgrounds incorporated films, sandwiching them between theatrical productions, snake dances, and opera shows. Sen screened his early films at the homes of wealthy landlords in Bengal, at the All India Industrial Exhibition of 1900, and at private societies and clubs such as The Dalhousie Institute. Later, as he turned to commercial exhibition, he screened his shorts during the intermissions of staged Bengali plays before he started screening films as exclusive programs (Banerjee 1989, 293). Other film exhibitors announced that they could hold screenings at "weddings, garden parties, or other entertainments, at moderate charges" (Chaudhury 1996, 119, fn.14). Magic shows were equally important in Bombay and in Calcutta as venues (Chaudhury 1996, 103; Garga 1996, 12). At least in these initial years, the Lumière screenings at Bombay's Watson's Hotel in 1896 were therefore exceptional, and not the norm, in that they seem to have been stand-alone shows comprising only the cinema as their main attraction.

It is, however, the persistence of these diverse venues, and their dispersal into wider nonurban domains into the 1930s and beyond, that separates Bengal from Britain or the United States, and even perhaps from Bombay province.[22] Ranita Chatterjee's recent work sheds light for the first time on a robust film culture in the city of Calcutta (2012). What nevertheless seems to make Bengal stand out in comparison with other provinces is its profusion of traveling cinemas.

Between 1922 and 1927, Bengal had many more touring cinemas than Bombay for each of the five years, with thirty-six touring cinemas in Bengal in 1927, compared to only five in Bombay.[23] In 1927, permanent cinemas amounted to approximately 275 (including seasonal cinemas, but excluding Burmese permanent and seasonal cinemas).[24] In comparison, licensed traveling cinemas amounted to 354 in number (again excluding Burmese cinemas).[25] How had this come about? Indigenous exhibitors could not be availed of financial capital from imperial institutions, unlike their foreign counterparts. Until the advent of sound, 90 percent of all films screened in India were of foreign origin. For Indian film producers, by the 1920s, the reinvestment of profits from film exhibition into film production served as a major source of capital; the other source centered in the indigenous merchant communities, which invested in film from other lines of trade. However, acquiring capital for initiating film production and access to exhibition venues were barriers to entry for those without easy access to startup funds from other enterprises.[26]

Bengal and Bombay underwent somewhat different trajectories in this regard. Bombay in the nineteenth century was central to the cotton and opium trades, in which a number of indigenous merchant communities—the Bhatias, Parsis, Gujarati merchants, as well as the immigrant Baghdadi Jews—played important roles, including during the cotton boom of the 1860s spurred by events related to the American Civil War. These merchants played a significant role by investing in the film business subsequent to the wartime boom of the World War I years that also marked the entry of indigenous capital into the circuits of imperial trade and commerce. In Bengal, on the other hand, European agency houses controlled major trade and manufacture, although there were exceptions. By the time of World War I, educated Bengalis enthused by what one historian refers to as a "strident technocratic nationalism" had ventured into advanced lines of manufacture (newspapers, pharmaceuticals, electric bulbs, and consumer goods such as hair oil and cosmetics), and indeed into film (Goswami 1992, 249–50).[27] Nevertheless, they were often dependent on imperial and institutional sources for capital that proved unavailable. The imperial banks would only lend to Europeans and by the second decade of the twentieth century, with the steady onslaught of foreign films whose costs were already paid for in the foreign home markets and the comparatively high cost of Indian film production, Indian film companies found it difficult to make a profit that would enable them to stay in business. The disparities between the tariffs of imported exposed films ready for exhibition and tariffs for raw film stock ensured that it was about ten times as expensive to produce an Indian film as it was to import a foreign one.[28] The Indian firms such as Madan Theaters, which dominated the film business in the pre-1931 or pre-sound era, were those that not only had access to the supply networks for foreign films, but also possessed enough theaters to be able to set the terms for hiring other producers' films and the terms for renting out their own productions to outside exhibitors.

Faced with the difficulty of recouping the costs of production through exhibition venues in Calcutta, competing with the vast varieties of French, British, and American films that dominated Indian screens, and unable to obtain institutional sources of financing and capital, many film producers and exhibitors preferred touring cinemas, setting in place the distinctive character of film exhibition in Bengal. S. N. Guha of the Bengal Educational Film Company observed that as tents were expensive, canopies and open-air exhibition were the predominant locations for touring cinemas. The cinema could be as cheap or as expensive as resources would permit, as the following exchange reveals:

> CHAIRMAN: What about the poverty of the people? Do you think they can afford it?

> S. N. GUHA: This is a country where one can feed thousands of people, where rich European countries can't. We will make them sit on the grass and see it in the open air. We will make it cheaper.[29]

Put negatively, neither the cinema nor photography in India hewed entirely to the contours of a rationalized consumer culture and commodity production. To recall Chanan's distinction, the apparatus of the cinema may not have passed on to the hands of the consumer in Bengal. But far longer than in Britain and the United States, the commodity-logics of itinerant movie exhibition in India were predicated upon a revivification of the material base of the cinematic apparatus—the recycling of secondhand kinetoscopes and projectors. Exhibitors, crucially, took the cinema to its scattered audiences, rather than build theaters and expect the masses to flock to the cinema.

It is in this last respect that the cinema's emergence in Bengal departed from Britain or the United States and emulated the personalized retail patterns of consumer culture of the early industrial era, as outlined by Jean-Christophe Agnew and others (1993). Bengal was paradoxically both proximate and distant from the European metropolis. Its rapid access to the machines of mechanical reproduction from Europe—print, photography, cinema—was offset by other factors within South Asia, which I have outlined in this chapter.

What about the films themselves? With capital accumulation the primary barrier to entry into the film business, itinerant cinema exhibitors in turn became one of the key consumers of pirated and "junk" films (films deemed unfit for exhibition because they were degraded or damaged), since they could not afford the expensive first-run or new prints for exhibition. In 1910, an American consul general assessing the market for American producers suggested that the used films dealer would do well in India (Thompson 1985, 48).[30]

Where did the junk films come from? London was at the center of the film trade until World War I, an entrepôt for film reels to be shipped to the rest of the world. Imperialism itself provided the infrastructure for London's supremacy as well as for the lubrication of networks for pirated films, of which the junk film was perhaps the most degraded version. As a *Moving Picture World* article put it, looking back in 1919 at London's centrality in the prewar years:

> London, with a well-oiled organization, established primarily for the purpose of carrying on trade in all lines with the many English colonies which in turn were local distribution centers, was the logical city in which to sell anything intended for the foreign trade by the "job lot" process. (Thompson 1985, 31)

MOBILE CINEMA AND VISUAL EDUCATION

The use of wornout or deteriorated junk prints marked the intersection of illicit circulation and state regulation within India, embodied in the discursive realization of audiences by exhibitors and government officials alike. Questioners linked the quality of the film experience to that of junk films, and in turn directed attention to public health concerns. They issued recommendations to "re-censor" films on "medical grounds," either because the damage in the film was so great or the use of old machinery with inexperienced projectionists resulted in a "flicker" effect harmful to the eyes. The discussion revealed the extent to which the state sought to regulate the cinema and the assumptions regarding audiences and tastes.[31] One official wondered if additional legislation was necessary to control the use of old machines, beyond the licensing system already in place. Distributors' responses, however, revealed that policing the use of junk films faced a far more intractable problem. How did one identify a junk film? "I know travelling showmen who purchase condemned films from our stocks. Of course we are not selling. They purchased condemned stock and they show it by cutting pieces here and there."[32] As Ravi Vasudevan notes, the anxiety over junk films was particularly so when it came to the complex of efforts that defined the government's engagement with film for development-related educational films, because decrepit prints "would reflect poorly on government" (Vasudevan 2011, 76).

The infantilization of audiences by the state in these discussions is noteworthy, especially in light of the importance of children for the contemporary itinerant Bioscope show. Indeed, by the 1940s, reports on the need for visual education posited homologies between technology, demographics, territory, and infrastructure. In 1938, for instance, a committee appointed to explore visual education in the Central Provinces proposed four schemes: two for rural and two for urban areas. Mobile cinema vans targeting adults would serve rural, motorized roads. Magic lantern and film slides meant mainly for children would service rural, nonmotorized roads.[33] Middle and high school children in "Anglo-vernacular" schools in urban areas would watch 16 mm films, while urban commercial theaters would show educational films for adults on a compulsory basis.[34] Given that, until 1994, the postindependence Indian state did indeed require that educational shorts be screened prior to the main feature in commercial theaters, the legacy of such initiatives was far-reaching (Roy 2007, 34). These elements of the longer history of itinerant practices insert the contemporary Bioscopewallah's materials into a labile history. For instance, Tim Sternberg's documentary subject, Salim Baba, emulates the strategies of visual education outlined above and likewise customizes his screening program to locality, as he screens songs or trailers depending on local preferences. The demographics of itinerant or traveling exhibition practices ensure that the cinematic or proto-cinematic apparatus veers between adult optical curiosity or toy, an apparatus of commercial entertainment, a pedagogical tool for children, or a bit of all of these, depending on context and period.

The paucity of permanent movie theaters has been a persistent backdrop to the history of movie exhibition. The colonial government did make attempts at government subventions such as by providing loans for the construction of movie theaters, primarily conceived for utilizing the cinema as a tool for public education. Theater construction remained marginal, however, to the postindependence Indian government's developmental, "nation-building" objectives. A moratorium on "non-essential building" in the 1950s restricted the construction of new movie theaters, a circumstance whose effects remain with us today (Govil 2005, 426). Given the size of its annual moviegoing public, and despite its status as the largest film industry in the world in terms of the number of films produced each year (approximately eight hundred), India has one of the lowest ratios of screens to population: thirteen screens per one million people.[35] Available figures suggest that not only has there been an increase of touring cinemas *every year* from 1950 to 1986, the proportion of traveling cinemas to the total number of cinemas in India has also increased.[36]

The most recent developments, such as the multiplexes designed to coordinate with high-budget releases and rationalize the release of prints across screens in such a way as to maximize capacity utilization, also, however, reshape urban life as an aspiration toward a globalized consumer culture, this time with support from the posteconomic liberalization Indian state. More pertinently for us here, just as the traveling cinemas of the early twentieth century remind us that the film experience was hardly tethered to urban spaces, the multiplex "deploys new forms of differentiation between urban and rural spaces within India" (Govil 2005, 457), recalling official attempts in the preindependence period that I cited above. Multiplex and mall developers now target smaller cities. Related digital cinema initiatives have particularly targeted theaters in smaller towns, as a way of short circuiting the exhibition time lag that results not just in severely degraded celluloid prints reaching the lowest-class theaters in the exhibition food chain, but also in pirated DVDs and VCDs. Multiplexes also update colonial homologies technologically but without a substantive change in the hierarchies that tie media consumption to the management of populations. They offer a rationale for imagining digital film delivery methods (in short, "new media" formats) for exhibitors in the smaller towns that would render decrepit and pirated media obsolete. Thus, the relation between film-as-commodity and the exhibition contexts within which it realizes value through a recouping of its production costs, depends on conspicuous but unstable relations between licit, illicit, and decrepit prints, each category of which demarcates distinct sets of assemblages.

A RECYCLED MODERNITY

Analogies between present and past don't, however, always square up. In scale and method, we cannot see showmen such as Salim Baba and Raja Filmwala as comparable to the present-day traveling tent show exhibitor, the more obvious successor to the traveling cinema of the early twentieth century, and who, easily enumerable and licensed by the state, can rapidly rustle up the infrastructure for serving many hundreds if not thousands of spectators by drawing on local workmen and contractors at every stop.[37] By contrast, the Bioscopewallah is an instance of the working of a logic that results in the obviation of obsolescence. I'm using the word *obsolescence* not as if it were a state of being, immanent to and inevitable in the process of technological change, nor so that it serves as old-fashioned ethnographic fodder for theories of slow-moving societies where cultural inertia transforms vestigial modes into aesthetic practices. Instead, I suggest we see the negation of obsolescence as a historically and geographically varied strategy for film exhibition, one conceived as a calculated and deliberate mode of commodity production and consumption.

Giles Slade observes that the strategies of advertising, branding and packaging, and planned obsolescence (whether through technological innovation or stylistic product updates, as in the case of automobiles) were ways of tackling the problem of the overproduction of commodities by ensuring a process of repetitive consumption through the invention of disposability (2006). The description of the Kinetoscope showing in Calcutta that I quoted at length earlier, while no doubt attesting to what Neil Harris has famously called the "operational aesthetic" (1981, 57) or a technical fascination with how machines worked, also puts on frontal display the repetitive consumption instigated by this "film performance" and by the centrality of the apparatus itself: "Mayn't I have it all over again? The operator was very obliging, and I had a second performance."[38]

Seen as a tactic, planned obsolescence is central to the history of early cinema as well. The authors of a recent volume on the economics of film argue that the evolution of a system of film rentals or exchanges rather than outright sales, the international expansion of film distribution networks, and the creation of secondhand markets, ensured a working system that would carry a film print from first release to eventual detritus, finding audiences at every stage of its life. A steady stream of new films would draw more audiences meanwhile to the theaters under the lure of novelty, even as the existing ones would be managed through the hierarchical chain of exhibition practices (Sedgwick 2004, 13–14). Such a schematization highlights a paradoxical economy of thrift (every print must be utilized, production must keep pace with consumption, especially given that the natural life of a reel of film rarely keeps pace with its itinerary through the exhibition cycle) and excess (in repetitive consumption practices and the integration of disposability—albeit a managed one—into the film print's itinerary).

The tactics of Raja Filmwalla, the slum dweller who turns his slum into a makeshift movie hall, however, mark a radical departure from this economy. Even as he incorporates repetitive consumption into the screening cycles of a normal day of business, his practice depends on circumventing obsolescence. By not having the luxury of acquiring access to the legitimate chains of the film enterprise, he extracts value from the film reel even in its death throes, discarding the unusable portions of the scraps purchased from the *raddiwalla* and fashioning the usable ones into a concatenation of action sequence, song and dance, and drama.[39] As Grimaud notes, in order to avoid entertainment taxes that even a C-class theater would be charged, as well as to escape the legal action he would face for conducting film screenings in his residential dwelling, Raja Filmwala charges the very minimum possible for a ticket: ten paisa for every ten minutes of screening, which is followed by a brief enforced break, for a total of fourteen hours of screening time, thus avoiding the semblance of a regular three-hour film screening. The result is that not only do his audiences consume a moviegoing experience in fragments (Grimaud notes the constant movement, and hustle of people in and out of the tiny hall) but Raja also makes far more money than he would if he held a regular three-hour screening. In a perfect corollary to the reanimated film scraps, what would normally be a three-hour screening is itself extended into fourteen hours of projection, and thus is magnified in overall value even if Raja keeps the price of admission absurdly low. Grimaud reminds us that Raja's pricing strategy "has no equivalent in the legal sphere" and that in the process, Raja earns "repeat audiences," a much-valued demographic for established film producers as well. Waghmare, Salim Baba, Hanif Bhai, and others discussed and described here likewise replicate the pragmatic calculus that predicates every show on such one-to-one transactional values.

At the same time, however, the behemoth film industries in India themselves offer an inescapable frame of reference for the Bioscopewallah, including in the use of words such as "house-full" to describe a good day of business (Sternberg 2007). The screening "program" mimics the circulation of films in and through Indian permanent theaters: snippets of *Jurassic Park* (Steven Spielberg 1993) dubbed in Hindi, Gujarati mythologicals, longstanding box-office successes such as *Sholay* (Ramesh Sippy 1975), and more recent fare featuring stars such as Govinda and Shah Rukh Khan (Sternberg 2007). Given the social class and caste hierarchies and exclusions enacted in permanent movie theaters (Srinivas 2000), perhaps the traveling and makeshift cinema shows, open in principle to anyone willing to fork over the low ticket price, enact literally tokenistic and piecemeal departures from such hierarchies. Perhaps too, as an assemblage, we can think of ancillary exhibition practices as akin to Deleuze and Guattari's understanding of minor literature, defined not as being written in a minor language, but as minority constructions within the major language of the commercial film industry (Deleuze and Guattari 1986, 16).

Ravi Sundaram's discussion of urban techno-cultures in Delhi and Bangalore as forms of "recycled modernity," in stark contrast to the elite cyber cultures of IT corporations, offers a descriptive vocabulary that particularly resonates with the material presented here. Relying on used or junk hardware foraged from long-standing single-commodity markets for computer parts, and pirated software, the urban techno-culture of India draws its energies from a culture of "innovation" as a survival strategy, "ad hoc discovery" and informally acquired technological knowledge. As with the practices discussed in this essay, this techno-culture has no discrete spaces of its own and no self-defined oppositional political stance, and has scant regard, Sundaram writes, for the modernist premium on originality. It is not future oriented either, unlike the grand technological plans of the erstwhile Nehruvian developmental state. (Recall my discussion earlier of emergent temporalities.) But perhaps most importantly, it takes place in the rather quotidian domains of the everyday, amid the striking retreat of the state from this domain, a feature that finds its corollary in the invisibility of makeshift cinema for the state's classificatory gaze (Sundaram 2001). Elsewhere, Sundaram has argued similarly for two layers in the contemporary media landscape: that of elite media empires and "a dynamic, informal and often illegal media space of urban India, which has, for all practical purposes, retailed the new cultural constellation to the mass of citizens" (Sundaram 2005, 57).

Junk prints, vintage and obsolete projectors, and makeshift cinemas, inserted as they are into the folds of a wider set of contemporaneous developments and arguments regarding the politics and logic of media transformations in South Asia, enable us to outline micropolitical and varying scales of film enterprise provoked by differential access to the mainstays of the film business that has characterized the history of the cinema in India. Beyond this, the Bioscopewallah provokes a closer examination of the practices that preceded the emergence of the cinema in India, a media archaeology that is far more historiographically inclusive than has hitherto been the case. As Brian Larkin has argued, different epistemic structures and different genealogies of practices mark the ontology of the cinema as highly contingent upon location (2008, 79, 81). Indeed, the genealogies I have offered here sought to theorize not just in time (the distinction between "early cinema" and "late cinema") but also, as Larkin proposed, across space by foregrounding provisional distinctions between Bengal and Bombay, between urban, small town, and rural spaces, and by situating developments in Bengal as a consequence of its status as a node in a network of locations.

PART II

MECHANICAL REPRODUCTION
AND MASS CULTURE

3

COPYRIGHT AND CULTURAL AUTHENTICITY

The Politics of Mechanical Reproduction in South Asia

INTRODUCTION

This chapter and the next move away from the media archaeology of the preceding section to explore a radically different archive, one that underscores the extent to which the circulation, mechanical reproduction, and piracy of images between South Asia and Europe, as well as within South Asia, shaped the cinematic imaginary. These flows and counterflows of images instigated copyright disputes. Drawing on a legal archive, this chapter discusses those disputes as they pertained to mass-produced and enormously popular images and as they ultimately had a bearing on the cinema's place in postcolonial India as the preeminent form of mass culture. Indian producers of these images constructed a complementary relationship between culture and commerce. Driven by nationalist sentiment, they sought to convince British authorities that the cultural importance and authenticity of these images necessitated a protection of their profits from piracy (and therefore necessitated protection under copyright law). On the other hand—and this may seem odd from our vantage point in the present—the British administrations in India were hardly eager to update copyright laws to include new classes of works, even when, by the 1920s, India was awash in French, American, Italian, and British films, many of which were pirated and of dubious probity.[1] The free dissemination of Western knowledge would necessarily suffer under more stringent intellectual property laws.

These opposing views on the circulation of cultural commodities held by the producers of images and the state constituted a basic chessboard of positions. What was really at stake in these debates? They enable us to witness the circumstances under which the cinema acquired its status as mass culture, and the legitimacy crises this form of mass culture encountered. The legacies of the copyright debates were deep. The invocation of cultural identity and authenticity, its relation to profit, and the desire of a popular culture for state sanction only to be met with suspicion and surveillance, became part and parcel of the cinema and its encounters with the state in the postcolonial era. Was the cinema a legitimate form of popular culture, or was it a commerce-driven enterprise produced at scales at which claims to authenticity, originality, and authorship made little sense?

The scale implicit in the phrase "mass culture" is important. Where the absence of obsolescence speaks to the frequently artisanal forms of cinema's presence, the widespread circulation of images takes us ultimately to India's behemoth film industries. Put another way, the preceding chapters described the material infrastructures that shaped and continue to shape the cinema's deep percolation into the spheres of everyday life. Here, I outline the intellectual infrastructures that define another aspect of the cinema, its status as mass culture. I'm interested now in the commercial "viability" of images as opposed to my interest in the previous chapters in the viability of the machines that produced them. The practices of film showmanship we considered earlier are site specific and emplaced. In contrast, the circulation and reproduction of images occurs across and through sites. The trope of obsolescence enabled us to figure the practical infrastructures of cultural production. The trope of reproduction will be the optic that enables us to recognize what Charles Ackland defines as the "intellectual production that occurs within industrial ranks" or the "episteme of popular entertainment" (2003, 32, 14).

Few have researched the copyright disputes I found in a law library and subsequently in other legal archives. As with the previous chapters, I do not, however, want to begin with the cinema. In fact, the archive at hand in this chapter mostly comprises legal disputes around the copyright and piracy of chromolithographs, or color lithographic images, of popular gods and goddesses, or renderings of scenes from religious and classical epics.[2]

While Indians sought to construct value for the images they produced, so did the British enthusiasts of Indian culture. It would be fruitful to consider the British arguments in favor of copyright, because these arguments bore traces of a more literal kind of piracy, that of the conquest and collection of objects so central to colonialism. I begin, then, with a petition to update copyright law that I found in the same files that contained the Indian printing presses' petitions.

EMPIRE AND THE IMPOSSIBILITY OF ORIGINALITY

Imitation was an organizing principle, a precondition for any debate on copyright law. Lara Kriegel notes the "impossibility of originality in an industrial and trading nation such as Britain whose cosmopolitan commercialism reigned supreme" (2004, 264).[3] By the late nineteenth century, South Asia was well sutured into a commercialism that caused George Birdwood, the Anglo-Indian naturalist, author of the *Industrial Arts of India* (1880) and a central figure in defining British perspectives on Indian art, to petition the government to update copyright law. Birdwood wrote in October 1883 to complain that an importer of Indian wares had copied and registered in England patterns from his book on Indian art and from the Prince of Wales and India Museum collections. Furthermore, the same importer used the copied patterns for full-size reproductions made by the very potters in Mooltan (Multan, now in Pakistan) who had made the originals for Birdwood. Birdwood hastened to add that "this was alright and proper." What bothered him, however, was the fact that the importer also wanted to register the designs in India, so that the same potters who had been making these vases would no longer do so freely. Noting that the copied designs were "strictly traditional" and of the "highest antiquity," Birdwood concluded, "I should be very glad, if when the Indian government may undertake any improvement of the law of copyright, they would carefully guard against such a monstrous abuse of the protection it is meant to give only to genuine inventors."[4]

The official memo on Birdwood's letter noted his confusion between copyright and patents and was terse and dismissive of the complaint. First, his was an issue for patent and not copyright law since it involved designs and patterns, not photographs or pictures. Second, if the designs had already been published in a book, they could not now retroactively be covered by any of the existing patent acts since the design was already in the public domain. Third, if the designs were of the highest antiquity, as Birdwood claimed, they would not be eligible material for patents anyway.[5] One could extend the government's reasoning with an additional question. Who needed this protection from piracy—the potters of Mooltan or Birdwood, since the latter was concerned about the designs that he had already appropriated and reproduced in his book? Setting aside this rhetorical question, Birdwood's confusion between patents and copyrights, between inventions and designs on the one hand, and pictures and illustrations on the other, was part of the broader dilemma faced by those seeking an extension of copyright law to new classes of works, as we will see shortly.[6]

Birdwood's interest in protecting India's cultural heritage was of a piece with British initiatives in India through much of the nineteenth century that deemed colonial modernity a threat to Indian artisanal manufacture and indeed much else, including its ethnographic tribes and its architectural ruins. British Orientalists therefore encouraged the protection, cataloguing, and documentation of such indigenous features. This perceived need for cultural preservation and dissemination motivated Birdwood's concern for the continuing rights of Indian artisans to produce arts and crafts freely. But it motivated as well his sanguine attitude to the equally free imitation and duplication of those vases in England. Copyright law was considered fundamentally antithetical to these projects. Birdwood took no offense to the theft of designs and their transplantation to Britain where they could be freely copied, but took umbrage at the thought that laws should restrict the talents of Indian producers of these designs. These were the parameters of what constituted permissible and unacceptable piracy. They demonstrate that for the project of cultural patrimony, copyright was an obstruction and a hindrance. The implicit ethics of Birdwood's position informed the administration's stance toward copyright in the colonies.

The desire to frame the debate on mechanical reproduction as concerning a national style—as Birdwood had done—cut across subsequent references to copyright, whether these references came from Indian, Anglo-Indian, or British sources. Several figures used the "national style" argument to naturalize colonial appropriation (as in the Birdwood example), to demand an extension and enforcement of copyright law (as was the case with Indian printers we will encounter shortly), and to reinforce the responsibility of the British toward the education of their Indian subjects (as was the case with the colonial state's position with regard to copyright). It also eventually found its way into debates pertaining to the relation between Hollywood and the Indian film industry, both in the early twentieth century and in our time, when the problem pertains to policing "Bollywood" appropriations of Hollywood storylines as well as enforcing the copyright of Hollywood films in India.

FROM GENIUS TO GENUS

The legislative department received two other petitions the same year (1883) it received George Birdwood's. In these petitions, the desire to legitimize the mass image as culturally important needed to coexist with recognition of the marketplace. The petitions came from two printing presses, the Calcutta Art Studio in Calcutta and the Chitrashala Steam Press in Pune, a city close to Bombay where a thriving film culture would later take hold. We know far less about the outcome of the Chitrashala Steam Press petition than we do of the Calcutta Art Studio dispute. However, I include a description of the Chitrashala petition because that press resurfaces quite dramatically in a subsequent and separate dispute over the infringement of copyright, which I discuss at length.

The chromolithographs produced by these two presses directly affected the cinema. A number of developments in painting, print culture, and urban theater coincided by the late nineteenth century. Printing presses in Calcutta (on the eastern side of the subcontinent) and Pune (on the western end) were at the very forefront of the mass production of printed images. This was a period of rising nationalist sentiment that very shortly in the first decades of the twentieth century became a full-fledged mass mobilization against the British. The iconography influenced nationalist imaginary. From the 1870s on, the presses churned out chromolithographs that visualized themes and iconography from classical Hindu texts and epics. Given the emerging nationalist context, however, these images were increasingly marked by a semantic subterfuge of barely concealed, politically incendiary meaning that sought to evade colonial censorship and surveillance. Chitrashala Steam Press printed some of these images. Images of caged and uncaged parrots, which appeared as postcards, of mythological figures who embodied kingly renunciation and exile, and of the cow as a mythic symbol of national community "could be sent freely," as Christopher Pinney observes in his detailed study of the chromolithograph's history in South Asia,

> through the public mails as a sign whose intent was quite clear to sender and receiver. Slipping through the gaze of the anxious colonial state, decorative images . . . were given a wake-up call by Chiplunkar's journalism: he supplied the remaining half of an allegory whose pictorial infrastructure was easily disseminated. (2004, 56)

Chiplunkar founded the Chitrashala Steam Press. On the eastern side of the subcontinent, in Calcutta, the Calcutta Art Studio produced images that owed their popularity to a form of middle-class Hindu spirituality that critiqued colonial morality.[7] Religion was becoming a principal vehicle for nationalist imaginaries. In Pinney's words, the colonial censorship policies formulated in response to such visual representations were in turn "iatrogenic," that is to say, they gave rise to the very threats they sought to contain (2009, 30). "Authorized religion becomes the vehicle for a fugitive politics" and served as allegory for a newly assertive sense of cultural identity and authenticity at a nationalist moment (30).

Aside from these two presses, still other printers, such as Raja Ravi Varma (1848–1906), belonged to the second but decisive generation of British art school–trained oil painters turned printmakers. Varma trained in the art schools the British established to inculcate practices of naturalistic painting in Indian artisans. This training resulted in a form of realism uprooted from its original European contexts and representational aims that was put to new unexpected uses. Ravi Varma's oil paintings drew from classical Hindu epics. His choice of medium (oil), technique (perspectival), and aims (*trompe l'oeil*) were derivative and reflective of British academicism and colonial art school training, but they bestowed historical palpability to mythological figures, transforming myth into a history marked by photorealism. Varma capitalized on the popularity of his paintings by transforming them into chromolithographs and then mass-produced oleographs[8] through his printing press.[9]

Meanwhile, popular urban theater in Calcutta as well as in Pune drew on the subject matter of these images, thereby amplifying their resonance. From the vantage point of the early twentieth century, the cinema was only the most recent entrant to this inter-ocularity (Pinney 2004, 34). Common personnel moved across print, photography, film, and performance cultures, aligning the separate media with shared preoccupations and politics. D. G. Phalke (1870–1944), whose mythological film *Raja Harishchandra* (1913) ushered an indigenous film practice, is considered the most significant of these figures. Phalke trained as a draftsman in painter Ravi Varma's chromolithograph press, before he moved into the movie business. *Raja Harishchandra* and other early Phalke films drew on the mythic iconography of gods and goddesses from ancient Hindu epics such as the *Ramayan* and *Mahabharat* popularized by the printed image as well as in popular urban theater.

The output of the two presses I singled out above was enormously consequential therefore in linking mechanical reproduction to the emergent Indian public sphere and its visual cultures. Art historian Tapati Guha-Thakurta (1988) situates the output of these presses at a midpoint in nineteenth-century South Asian visual culture when they impacted the viability of earlier forms of visual culture, which catered to an indigenous clientele, such as the woodcuts, engravings and scroll paintings, while also anticipating the mass audiences for the cinema that would emerge later. In Bengal, writes Guha-Thakurta, the printed image enlarged local and non-Westernized clienteles into a "wider undifferentiated mass clientele that spanned many layers of education and literacy . . . almost the same amorphous mass audience that would later be drawn in by the radio or the Hindi movie" (5–6).

The disputes over the images produced by these printing presses are therefore significant for how they link picture production to the subsequent cultural politics of the cinema. The intersection of the vagaries of commercial trafficking in images and the cultural politics of nationalism shaped cinema's role. These disputes enable us to trace, as Patrick Geary puts it, the "cultural parameters of commodity flow," the mutually constitutive nature of culture and commerce with technology as an important and hardly neutral determinant (1986, 169). In the absence of legal protections against piracy, plaintiffs on piracy issues had to do much more than establish their own authorship over the images and prove those images' originality. They had to establish the value and importance of the images they produced. It is here that a legal discourse spills over and becomes a political and cultural one. The result of these disputes conflated two models of cultural production. One pertained to copyright and control over authenticity and authorship. The other pertained to trademark and the control trademark conferred over reproducibility and exhibition value. Put another way, the image conceived as intangible representation and index of originality and cultural genius encountered the demands of the image as material property whose ownership and reproduction involved profits.

Originality is a key frame of reference. In the first of the petitions I discuss here, originality emerges as authorship, conceived much like Birdwood conceived of the potters of Multan as an instance of successful cultural creativity and identity. At the same time, the aesthetic discourse of authorship as originality and creative genius rubbed unavoidably against a commercial discourse. A much more limited conception of the author as commercial proprietor emerges in these debates as a result.[10]

What was the Calcutta Art Studio's gripe? Baboo Kristo Chunder Pal, the proprietor of the press, complained that a man named Shib Chunder Mullick was producing piracies of his chromolithographs of "works illustrative of the mythology of the Hindu religion" in England and selling them at a cheaper rate in the Calcutta market. The petition argued that the existing copyright law ought to be amended to enable the registration of copyright in pictures and works of art. The High Court in Calcutta issued an injunction against the further sale of the pictures until the suit was heard, but only because the studio's pictures were bound up in the format of a book of which the studio was the registered author. "No means exist in this country," the studio went on to note in its letter, "for the registration of copyright in pictures and works of art, except as part of a book." Just as the studio was beginning to "reap the rewards of [its] labours," the piracy of its pictures ensured that "the sale of [its] pictures was seriously interfered with."[11]

Pal asserted his credentials by invoking "creative genius." In his petition, he reminded government that the Calcutta Art Studio artists belonged to "respectable families" and were "formerly students of the Government School of Art in Calcutta."[12] To bolster his case, he appended press reviews. The reviews spoke repeatedly of originality. For example, the Calcutta newspaper *The Indian Mirror* wrote:

If native artists wish to excel and prove their real talent for the arts they embrace, they should avoid confining themselves to the work of mere copyists. It should be their ambition to be original. . . . It is to the credit of the Hindu artists of the Calcutta Art Studio that they are already making efforts in this direction. Their Hindu mythological pictures . . . are infinitely superior to the old artistic pictures of Hindu gods and goddesses, which are devoid of artistic beauty and independent of scientific principles.[13]

Likewise the *Banga-Bashi*, detected sublimity in the Art Studio's pictures, filtering mythology through a Romanticist lens: "In the eyes of the public, the Art Studio pictures are very beautiful. The forest scene of *Nala Damayanti* is imposing deep, dark, silent and lonely forest."[14]

Here, we find an early indication of the impact of colonial art education on demarcations of a popular aesthetic. These reviews contrast the implicit (and scientific) *trompe l'oeil* naturalism detected in the chromolithograph with an earlier indigenous aesthetic that is patently and deplorably not realist in nature. The petitioners for their part believed their training had conferred on them the status of artists, explicitly differentiated from the lowly artisans of the bazaar that produced woodcuts and engravings. In other words, they extricated themselves from artisan picture production, instead aligning their training in *trompe l'oeil* as part of their proximity with the Western art institutions in the city. They could not afford to be relegated to "drawing masters, draughtsman, engravers and lithographers" (Guha 1998, 11). The British art academy placed the fine arts and naturalistic depictions at a higher evolutionary scale than the decorative and industrial arts (Dewan 2001). India, however, was considered superior in the industrial and decorative arts. The schools of industrial art in India sought to reverse their perceived decline. Conversely, in the realm of fine art production, in paintings, engravings, and picture production, the Indian artisan was considered an excellent copyist but not an artist. The colonial art education system sought to train Indians in naturalism and the rules of Western art so that they might produce original art. And the Calcutta Art Studio trumpeted this originality.

The Romanticist, even Expressionist, language of the *Banga-Bashi* review—"the deep, dark, silent and lonely forest"—cannot be isolated from the other tendency that informs the Calcutta Art Studio petition, the tendency to confer on authorship a significant proprietary aspect. The Art Studio's attempt to bolster its social reputation—a press founded by *artists*—was reminiscent of developments in England that culminated in the ambiguous emergence of the modern author as both proprietor and originator of the work. Mark Rose (1988) lists three developments in England also in place in nineteenth-century Bengal: a commercial market for the work that ends older forms of patronage, an aesthetic discourse of authorship as creative genius, and a rhetoric of property based on Lockean possessive individualism, and its attendant implication of proprietorship. The studio's description of its images as "the fruits of our labours" reveals this possessive individualism as a perspective that blended with, and at the same time, attenuated the originality and artistic skill implied in authorship.

The offending party, Shib Chunder Mullick, offered a defense that reveals a still further displacement of authorship as a claim to national belonging in favor of circulation, provenance, and format. Mullick was himself a prominent Calcutta printer. His lawyer claimed that he had purchased the Art Studio's pictures from other picture sellers and then sent them to England to be chromolithographed so that "they were got up in a style which got them a ready sale in the streets of a city like this," and that "they were framed to render them serviceable for hanging up in the rooms."[15]

From Mullick's perspective, however, copyright law in India did not afford protection to pictures and The Art Studio had already sold the images singly prior to binding the images into book form and registering the book in London at Stationer's Hall. In the absence of a law that protected the copyright of pictures as individual objects, the very act of dissemination, diffusion, and sale could leave the pictures vulnerable to imitation and exploitation.

Mullick's second argument bore on the "nationality of the work," its provenance. The Art Studio, he offered, could not claim the protection of British copyright law, that is, the Fine Arts Copyright Act of 1862 that extended to the dominions and the East Indies. The colony lacked a legal machinery to enforce copyright protections.[16] In this instance, the legal protection of an English copyright law for categories and classes of objects yet to be recognized in India was available in theory, but not implementable.

By emphasizing provenance, circulation, and format, the defense lawyer for Mullick echoed the concerns of the second petition from the same year from Chitrashala Steam Press, the other major petitioner. Indeed, Chitrashala's petition marks a still greater distance from the Art Studio's ambivalent recourse to the value of genius. The case here was occupied with the control of the contexts of mechanical reproduction and circulation rather than with the assertion of the image's originality or, for that matter, its authorship. Chitrashala's concern for *genus*, a class of works the legal statutes did not recognize, represented a departure from the Calcutta Art Studio's claims of authorship as *genius*.[17] Mr. Vasudeo G. Goshi, Chitrashala's manager, wrote in his petition that it engaged in chromolithography, black lithography, and colored lithography. The press employed a number of skilled artists and "in the last 4 years, the press has printed nearly 25 pictures, with each edition containing about 3000 copies. Some pictures have undergone 3 or 4 editions," a testament to the sheer scale of production involved here.

Chitrashala was founded to encourage "scientific painting" and the printing of pictures, but some people were exploiting its good fortunes "by taking photos of our pictures and offering them for sale at almost a trifle." Goshi went on to note that

> the practice of taking photos of our pictures and selling them at an extraordinarily low price has of late assumed such extensive dimensions, that the Chitrashala has suffered a heavy loss during the last two years. Our pictures cannot be registered under the laws at present in force, and thus copyright respecting them is without any protection.[18]

These arguments are noteworthy as they freely move back and forth between the author and the proprietor. By doing so, they counter the aims of colonial art education. They are also strikingly contemporary in nature. Lionel Bently argues that far from conceding entirely to a Romantic conception of the author as a creative originator, contemporary copyright law goes by a standard of "minimal creativity" and that authorship is "a point of attachment—a point at which to ascribe a property right and by which that right can be determined" (1994, 980). The petitions we are considering seem to have invoked creative authorship as no more and no less than what Bently calls "a point of origination" (980).

We know no more about the outcome of the Chitrashala petition, but as I have noted above, the Chitrashala Press resurfaces later, and I will return to it. In the intervening years, and subsequent to the Art Studio's and the Chitrashala Steam Press's petitions, demands to update copyright law increased in frequency. By 1910, the Books and Publications wing of the Home Department of the Government of India estimated seventeen cases of hardship due to piracy, including nationwide coordinated petitions and letters from the Rangoon, Calcutta, Madras, and Punjab trade associations.[19] For instance in 1903, the German Fritz Schleizer wrote to the government requesting copyright protection for the printed images produced by the Ravi Varma Fine Arts Lithographic Press, which he managed.[20] However, by this time the name "Ravi Varma Press" was itself up for grabs among several competing lithography presses in the region. By 1906, Ravi Varma had transferred proprietorship of the press to his brother Raja Raja Varma who sold the press to Fritz Schliezer. As Guha-Tkahurta writes elsewhere:

> From this point begins a new unauthorized and unbounded history
> of the Ravi Varma image in the picture trade of modern India.
> It is a history that leaves the founding figure and his maiden

press far behind. . . . In the explosion of Ravi Varma presses
and prints that burst upon the market in the first decades of
the 20th century, it seems fairly futile to search for an original
Ravi Varma product . . . The names Ravi Varma Fine Art
Lithographic Press, Ravi-Uday, Ravi-Vaibhav and Ravi-Vijay
Press keep coming up with changing addresses. . . . Even more
mind-boggling are the images that spill into the market, some
of which flaunt Ravi Varma signatures and teasingly refer to a
known painting of the master, while most others fully take off
on their own course. (2006, 23)

The sheer number of requests and cases are an index of the profusion
of visual images by the turn of the century, and a mark of the arrival of a
visual culture that seemed truly pan-Indian.[21] By this time as well, pirated
images were mainly disseminated as postcards. The Calcutta Trades Association petition cited the album of photographs of the Viceregal Tour to
Cashmere (taken by the famed Calcutta photo-studio Bourne & Shepherd)
that found their way almost instantaneously after the release of the album
into Calcutta's New Market, where they were unbound and sold singly as
postcards. The Calcutta Trades Association quoted an Indian photographer
in its petition to government to reform copyright law:

An enormous number of pictorial prints in colours is annually
brought to India, which may be seen at railway stations, on walls,
and in public vehicles, all of them produced in countries where
the work of the artist is thoroughly safeguarded, whilst in India,
where useful industries should receive every legitimate protection and encouragement, the best work of a colour printer made
with great labour and expense for machinery, when published, is
simply an invitation to the piratical speculator.[22]

The official response reveals an inability to comprehend the utterly
transcontinental dimensions of piracy: "But this swindling in photographs
is almost entirely an Indian affair . . . and an Indian remedy is sufficient."[23]
What do these disputes say about the function of mechanical reproduction
in Indian society? The presses considered fair use to mean the right to profit
off images copyright law invested with singularity. But this singularity was
not about restoring aura to the mechanically reproduced image. Indeed,
the balancing authorship with proprietorship implied recognition that, in
classic anthropological terms, the distinction between gift and commodity
was not tenable because objects could slip in and out of commodity status
(Appadurai 1986).

The distinction between the singularly authentic and the technologically reproducible is undermined by the powerful efficacy of the reproduced image in the contexts of faith and social significance (Mitter 2003; Inglis 1999; Jain 2007). This has consequences indicative of the specificity of South Asia's encounter with modernity. Today, mechanically reproduced oleographed images of gods and goddesses circulate far and wide in India as ritual and cult objects. Their reproducibility only seems to reinforce rather than work against their status as cult objects. These images circulate both as part of calendars and as single framing pictures that adorn the walls of family prayer rooms, shops, and offices. These aspects of the printed image's ubiquity and the seeming inapplicability of Benjamin's distinction between the authentic and the reproducible prove, in Kajri Jain's words, the "inadequacy of the [Indian] nation's claim to a normative, post-sacred modernity." The calendar image "circulates publicly like the work of art, but as an icon its value is still that of the cult and ritual" (2001, 54). For Jain, the bazaar is central to the intensification of the ritual values of the image. The purchase, sale, and exchange of these images between merchants especially during auspicious occasions confer a strong ethical dimension to the neutral space of the bazaar by lubricating social ties. She notes that "while bourgeois Europe seeks to privatize the affective and ritual engagement with the divine and, in the public sphere, to supersede it with the aesthetic, the bazaar is happy to perpetuate, orchestrate and indeed to intensify this engagement" (54). While for Benjamin, technological reproducibility removes art from ritual and ushers it into the realm of politics, for Jain and others, reproducibility intensifies the ritual functions of art even as it also politicizes it, as the experience of nationalism in South Asia as well as the more recent forces of Hindutva revealed.[24]

Ultimately, as Christopher Steiner contends, the ritualization and politicization of the printed image indicates that the authority of the mass image originates from its *mass-produced nature*, not from its differences from unique traditional art (Steiner 1999, 89). The ability of the nineteenth-century presses to claim genius as a cultural attribute precisely in order to protect it as a source of profit, suggests a canny recognition that the mass image comes with its own "canons of authenticity—a self-referential discourse of cultural reality that generates an internal measure of truth-value" (Steiner, 95). This measure is internal, that is to say, with the qualities a mass-produced image shares with *other* mass-produced objects and commodities. While the producers of the printed images were entirely cognizant of the commercial value of these images, buyers introduced the mass-produced images within sacred contexts of worship and transformed them into singular objects. This does not mean that the producers and consumers were blind to each other's conception of the viability of the mass image. They arrived at the same point—an awareness of the interchangeability of the original and the copy in the age of technical reproducibility—from different directions.

TURNING THE TABLES: THE NATIONALITY OF THE IMAGE

Could the absence of an enforceable copyright law in India, the same condition bemoaned by Indian printers, have enabled Indians to engage in the unauthorized duplication of British images? And was it possible that this absence could both expose piracy and protect it from further litigation? These contradictions were present in a dispute that anticipated the relations between Hollywood and the Indian film industries in much of the twentieth century.

In 1912, an Indian printer entered into an agreement with an Indian customer that involved printing twenty thousand copies of a picture produced and registered in the UK by the famed British producer of prints and postcards Vivian Mansell & Co. The picture showed the coronation of King George V in India at the grand Delhi Durbar of 1911/1912. This time, the pirated picture in question was a British image insofar as the negative belonged to a British firm. The location of replication had also switched. The pirates replicated the image in India, not the UK. Finally, the party that complained of a possible loss now was not an Indian but a British producer.

Three things had shifted: the "nationality of the work," the location of replication, and the "victim" of the piracy. And yet, the enabling condition remained the same. The absence of machinery for copyright enforcement in India left British images in India as vulnerable to piracy as it did Indian images in Britain. There was no machinery to enforce British copyright law in India, for images of Indian or British provenance.

The story only gets more interesting from here. The 1912 pirate seems to have been none other than the manager of the Chitrashala Steam Press, Vasudeo G. Goshi, whom we have already met as the author of a petition from 1884. The case in the Appellate Civil Court in Bombay[25] comes to light only because Goshi's contract with his buyer fell through on a rather minor point of incomplete payment and ended up in litigation. At the hearing, Goshi[26] contended that under the contract the buyer should have signed a letter of indemnity taking all responsibility for any future action Vivian Mansell & Company might bring for the unauthorized reproduction of their images. Was this a routine and habitual requirement in all such transactions? We do not know, but the requirement itself exposes the weakness of copyright enforcement. Pinney writes that producers of pictures with allegorical political content had a "clear sense of the deliberate misrecognition that the image was seeking to provoke" (2009, 42). In the realm of transaction, however, it was not misrecognition but hyper-recognition that mattered. All the parties knew that the images were pirated. Covert meaning may have offered a conduit to politics. But in this case, it was the overt and acknowledged action in the form of piracy that carried political implications. When the judge ruled in favor of the buyer and ordered Goshi to pay damages, Goshi appealed on an even more audacious ground. He contended that since the contract infringed on existing copyright belonging to someone else, Vivian Mansell & Company, it was fraudulent on its face and therefore Travedi had no claim on the material he had purchased. The appeals judge dismissed this case too, as there was no way to enforce Mansell's copyright in India. Technically therefore, no infringement of piracy had occurred. The contract was far from fraudulent. The judge's elaboration of his reasons for denying Goshi's appeal makes his reasoning clear: the pictures were produced in Goshi's press; the pictures were to bear the name of their buyer, Travedi; and they were to be marked by the phrase "Made in India." All three of these facts meant that the process had a self-evident transparency.[27] Setting aside the problem of absent legal machinery, the judge reasoned that there was nothing fraudulent when ownership and authorship were so clearly and self-evidently marked. In retrospect, then, the colony was in a legal twilight, neither able to enforce Britain's laws in a distant location, nor able to deny that this inability itself afforded privileges, namely, the ability to engage in piracy with impunity, which would otherwise be prohibited.

CULTURAL PATRIMONY MEETS "POPULAR" CULTURE

The legal hurdles here anticipate the state's peculiar place in relation to mass culture and to these disputes. They also reveal the extent to which the traffic in literature and information both influenced the retardation of copyright law. The Calcutta Art Studio's understanding of its own quandary was correct: there was indeed no provision to register pictures or photographs in India for copyright purposes.[28] The history of legislative initiatives, however, included numerous bills, memos, and reports urging an update of copyright law,[29] including a bill in 1886[30] and another one in 1910.[31] The Indian government finally recognized the fine arts, which included photography, as worthy of copyright protection in 1914. The 1914 Act essentially adopted without modification the 1911 Imperial Copyright Act.[32]

Intellectual property law imagines and posits a private secret as its core justification. It assumes that the invention, the work of art, or the work of literary genius would remain a private affair if not for the law, which encouraged and provided a temporary monopoly to the creator so that he or she may share the creation with the public. The state instituted copyright law to regulate the move of cultural commodities from the private to the public domain, but it was always a few steps behind the technological and commercial contexts that befuddled and trumped the law's regulatory functions.

These instances also revealed the shift in the state's role from enthusiastic patron and commissioner, as was the case with the official photographic projects of the mid-nineteenth century, to the role of a reluctant regulator and arbitrator of the global flows of cultural commodity production. Yet, how was the state to successfully arbitrate these flows when the empire's bureaucracy itself was so fractious and fragmented? Copyright law[33] languished in part because the provincial governments in India, the government of India in Delhi (henceforth GOI), the India Office in London that oversaw Indian affairs, and the British government, as well as numerous producers, publishers, and printers, could not reach an agreement. Furthermore, London could override actors' decisions in India, which were expected to follow legislation in Britain rather than set their own precedents.

In addition, three sets of laws had to be synchronized: the imperial, colonial, and international copyright regimes. Colonial copyright regimes were specific to the colony where the law was passed (India, Canada, and Australia, for instance). The imperial copyright regime conferred copyright throughout the empire. International copyright regimes followed the Berne and Berlin conventions of 1886 and 1908, were bound by signatories to the conventions and conferred copyright in British dominions to foreign countries party to the convention's agreements.

Copyright debates at the height of empire are therefore structurally similar to contemporary discussions of Hollywood and its policies vis-à-vis the piracy of its productions in the global South. As with contemporary efforts by Hollywood to control the piracy of its products well beyond the United States through international trade agreements that seek to harmonize copyright law, then too, several parties sought to harmonize laws in bureaucracies spread across India, the UK, and other nation-states (Miller 2005).

From the state's perspective, the more important concerns shadowed printed matter and not visual images. Copyright of printed matter impacted the international book trade and the profitability of translations, which was especially pertinent to India since numerous English texts were translated into the vernacular for educational purposes. The Government of India insisted that copyright law ought to protect translation rights minimally since the translation of English-language books into the vernacular was perceived as the most useful way of disseminating useful knowledge. Respectable British publishers, such as Macmillan, Murray, Routledge, and Cassells, that had ventured into the business of producing vernacular textbooks for the various boards of education in India, obviously disagreed for commercial reasons. Here, as in so many other arenas of trade and commerce, an official free-trade policy clashed with the development-oriented agenda of the colonial state. The British government in India, eager to develop an imperial and educational literary patrimony, saw copyright law as a threat to such priorities of governance (Bently 2006).

If the dissemination of free and useful knowledge was one policy deterrent against the extension of copyright provisions, the dissemination of information was another. Reuters had in fact tried in 1878 to acquire copyright protection for its telegrams in India. It claimed that its telegrams' information constituted "a peculiar kind of property."[34] The government of India's response trotted out the standard argument: that it followed London, not a dominion's parliament's decisions.[35] But it also stated that

> all copyright laws are in the nature of restraints on the general usefulness of things protected. In the case of works of literature and art there is a distinct public advantage in granting protection; but no sufficient public advantage has been shown for similarly protecting telegrams, newspapers or oral tiding. Indeed, perhaps the public advantage is the other way.[36]

In these responses, the government's approach to information-as-commodity was similar to its approach to translations and literary copyright. In fact, it used its policy of restricting literary copyright as a justification for a similar approach to Reuters's telegrams.

Even as the government sought to create an English literary patrimony in the vernacular and saw images as information commodities, Indian images were transforming the mass politics of the subcontinent in lucrative ways for the producers of these images and in ways that compelled these producers to plead for government intervention, as the disputes between the two presses in the subcontinent and the subsequent chromolithographic influx, attest.

Furthermore, the basic picture of a state eager to establish an appropriate educational and civilizing mission, and a popular culture that sought state patronage but received in return some combination of indifference, surveillance and censorship, appeared again in postcolonial India with popular cinema. To recap, the questions motivating this chapter are as follows: What were the standards of authenticity that sustained conceptions of an appropriate national culture in the postindependence context? What meanings did the very possibility of mechanical reproduction possess for cultural guardians? And what was the role of the marketplace as an arbiter of this appropriateness? Popular cinema seemed on the wrong side of all of these issues: unabashedly commercial, part of a disorganized and informal economy, and able to achieve a breadth of address and audiences the state could never achieve. The next chapter explores the consequences of this complex history as they bore on the cinema.

4

THE CINEMA AS MASS CULTURE

· ◆ ———— ◆ ·

The Melodramas of Mechanical Reproduction

Mechanical reproduction and mass culture become the implicit objects of critique in Guru Dutt's *Pyaasa* (*Thirst*, 1957), one of the iconic allegories of the first decade of postindependence Indian cinema. Made exactly ten years after independence in 1947, the movie is justifiably viewed as an indictment of the failed idealism of the postindependence years. In the movie, the poet-protagonist's claims to his own identity and work are in an inverse relation to the publication and dissemination of his creative work.

Guru Dutt's film tells the story of Vijay (Guru Dutt), a sensitive poet suffering the world's indifference to his art. Vijay is a flâneur roaming Calcutta's red light districts, mourning the apathy and hypocrisy of a materialistic world that leaves nothing untouched, including the closest of family relations. The plot traces a series of fateful losses that underscore the cosmic ethical and Manichean forces of a melodramatic universe over which our protagonist has little control. First, Vijay loses his poetry (his uncaring brothers, who have expelled him from the house, sell the poetry as waste paper), the very poetry for which he seeks a wider audience. Then he runs into a college sweetheart who had left him for a man of better means, a noteworthy publisher. Intimated of the past relation between his wife and Vijay, the publisher employs a desperately unemployed Vijay as a menial help without guarantee of ever publishing his poems. In the third major loss of the movie, Vijay finds out belatedly that his mother has died. Finally, in the cruelest twist of fate in the film, his suicide attempt at the railroad track fails as he tries to rescue a beggar—to whom he has just given away his blazer—who is caught on the tracks of an oncoming train. The rescue attempt fails too, and the beggar, wearing Vijay's blazer, is crushed under an oncoming train. However, it is Vijay who is assumed to have died on the tracks. His poetry is published; he achieves posthumous fame; his manipulative friends and relatives claim him as their own for a while, as he languishes in a lunatic asylum unable to convince others of his real identity. When he succeeds in escaping the lunatic asylum and witnesses the hypocrisy of those who are now eager to embrace him at a gathering that includes his stone bust (covered in a cloth, and ceremonially uncovered at the event), he renounces his fame, leaving Calcutta and walking away into the sunset with the one soul who loves him for his poetry: the prostitute Gulabo.

Many motifs establish themselves in this rich, beautifully shot and enacted melodrama. Among those, the repeated images of papers foreshadow Vijay's eventual loss of access to his poems and through that loss to his voice, his body, and his identity. When the movie opens, Vijay retrieves his poems, shown consigned to a waste paper basket by a petty publisher. Then he finds out the rest of his work was sold to the waste paper dealer/recycler by his uncaring and contemptuous brothers. The recycler sells the papers to the streetwalker Gulabo who encounters Vijay precisely as she sings his poetry in order to lure him to her brothel. Leaving the brothel, Vijay drops a sheet of his poem, allowing Gulabo to recognize that the man she has lured is the poet whose work she admires. Later, at his former fiancée's house he stands Christ-like in the center of two intersecting planes of books with his hands outstretched, prefiguring the poetry's eventual publication and Vijay's concomitant marginalization. When he is assumed to have died, the stunned Gulabo, whose love for Vijay is a combination of devotion and erotic affection, stands collecting the papers of his manuscript flying in the wind in her room, airborne by the breeze sweeping through open doorways and billowing curtains. Gulabo then takes the papers to Vijay's former fiancée, to whom the poems are dedicated. The fiancée's publisher husband publishes the poems. This is indicated with a montage of a printing press and the thousands of sheets of his manuscript rolling off the press. One of the final images of the film, as Vijay renounces his fame and takes leave of his fiancée, is once again a bird's eye view of a windswept room in which papers fly in the wind (see Figs. 4.1, 4.2, and 4.3).

So what are we to make of this melodrama, and how does it respond to the histories of print and film cultures mapped so far in the preceding chapter?

There are, first, the travails of authorship. The loss of identity as the author of his poems is anticipated twice, first in Gulabo's discovery that she had been seducing Vijay with a song whose words were penned by him. Abdul Sattar, the movie's comic character, street masseur and Vijay's friend, also sings a song that is penned by Vijay while entreating passersby to enjoy

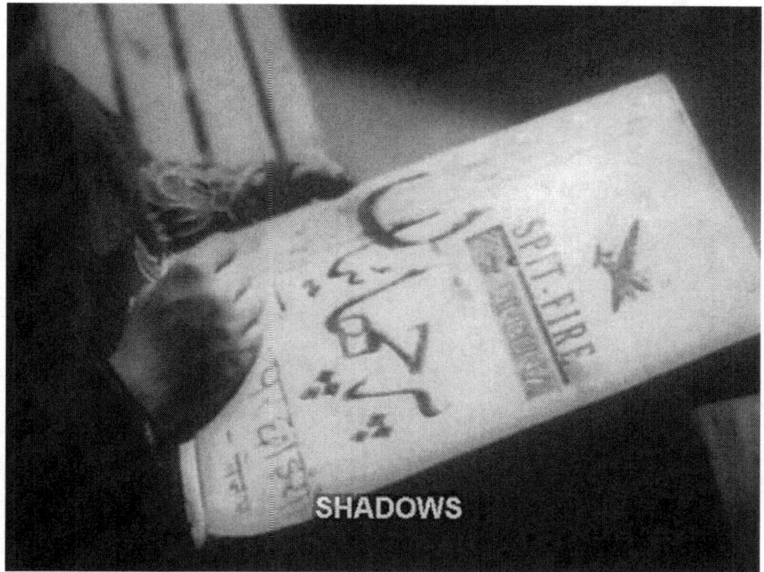

Figure 4.1. A manuscript of poems (Source: *Pyaasa*, Guru Dutt, 1957).

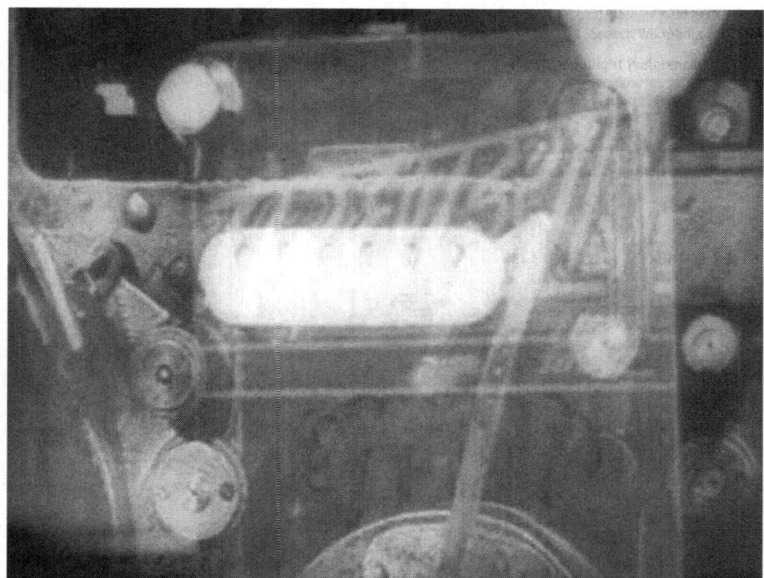

Figure 4.2. Printed and sold in the hundreds like hot cakes (Source: *Pyaasa*, Guru Dutt, 1957).

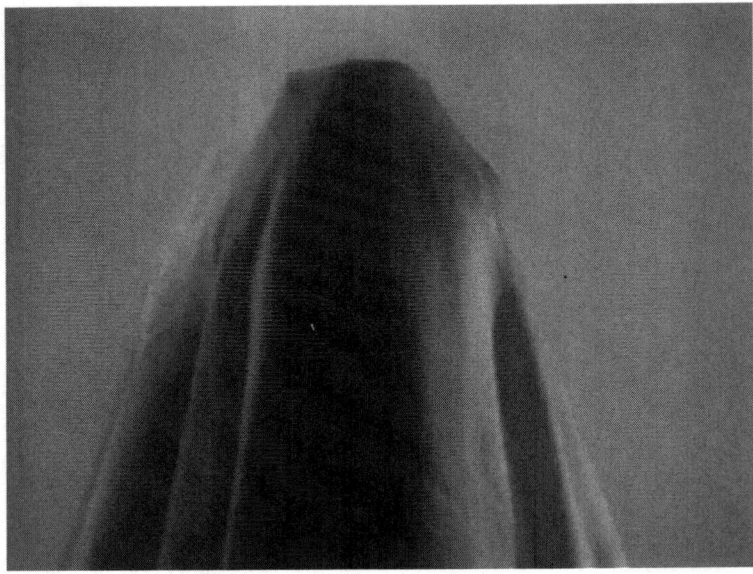

Figure 4.3. The poet petrified into a bust of stone (Source: *Pyaasa*, Guru Dutt, 1957).

a head massage. Indeed, Sattar's character duplicates that of Vijay and is the movie's comic foil to Vijay's pessimism. He sings Vijay's song and like Vijay he is in love with a woman who will not appreciate him because he does not hold a promising future.

Also unremarked in discussions of this movie is the journey of his poetry from a looseleaf sheaf of paper to its stitched and bound provisional copy or manuscript to finally its mass-produced printed form. This process signposts and eventually parallels Vijay's move into forced anonymity. Put formulaically, to mechanically reproduce the poetry is to destroy its aura, to destroy the aura is to lose one's (Vijay's) voice and body, and to lose one's voice and body is to lose one's identity, petrified into a cloth-covered stone bust even while one is alive.[1] How did print and the mechanical dissemination of art into mass culture become so pernicious a force? Vijay's rejection of his fame, motivated in the plot by the hypocrisy and greed of those once close to him, obfuscates a more important development in this movie—that the very poetry that he saw as being underappreciated by a mercenary culture *does in fact sell like hot cakes once printed*. Could it be that Vijay's rejection of the success of his poetry underscores the extent to which art can be effortlessly mass-produced and commodified? The movie does not give us any conclusive sense of this possibility, or even that this is a realization that Vijay experiences. Nevertheless, the plot compels us to consider precisely this issue.

Indeed, the movie's stance toward popular culture, articulated as a rejection of the mass-reproduced commodity, runs counter to the history of print culture in South Asia that we have encountered in the preceding chapter. The long-term impact of lithography in Bengal on print culture is hard to underestimate. While typefaces for print in many languages were still in infancy, lithography was a technological breakthrough. It made possible the mass-produced manuscript, which "met the criteria of cultural authority that the type-set text could not" (Shaw 1998, 89). While in Europe lithography remained on the periphery of book production, in India it established itself in the mainstream. Yet, *Pyaasa* seems to want to valorize the hand-written and bound manuscript, not the mass produced and mechanically reproduced book.

Two contexts from the political and cultural history of South Asia can explain the movie's pessimism about mass culture. Together, these contexts overdetermine the plot of *Pyaasa*. First, the long arm of Romanticism and its rejection of the conditions of cultural production in a moment of industrialized modernity cast a shadow over this movie. Guru Dutt's *Pyaasa*, like his other masterpiece *Kaagaz Ke Phool* (*Paper Flowers*, 1959), draws on an enormously influential character in Indian cinema: the self-destructive and dissolute tragic hero, fundamentally unable to reconcile the passing of an established order and the emergence of modernity with his own place in the world. This figure arrives in Indian cinema via the adaptation of an iconic 1901 Bengali language novella, *Devdas*, by Sarat Chandra Chatterjee. In it the eponymous hero is the son of a rural landholder unable to defy his father's refusal to allow him to marry a childhood sweetheart who is of a lower caste than he. A failure in love but Westernized in education, appearance, vice (alcohol), and bohemian in practice (he haunts brothels), Devdas retreats to the city, travels the length and breadth of the country by train in drunken sorrow and ultimately dies at the doorstep of his childhood village sweetheart. As Corey Creekmur puts it with some wit in discussing the novella's numerous cinematic adaptations, "The now-iconic figure of Devdas also might be read as the ritual sacrifice of the young Bengali brahmin to European romantic aestheticism, transporting the sorrows of young Werther-*ji* into the subcontinent" (Creekmur nd).[2] At the center of the Romanticist sensibility, writes Dipesh Chakrabarty (2004), "was a perceived connection between identity and aesthetic activity in the realms of art, music, literature, and language." This romanticism, according to Chakrabarty, was as much a nationalist as a literary project.[3] Self-expression and sublimity were of vital importance in discovering a national spirit (658–59). Vijay's romanticism forges just such a connection between his identity and self-expression. More to the point, his excoriating critiques of the bazaar around him in one of the movie's masterpieces of choreographed songs links the project of self-expression to the fate of the nation. In an inebriated state where tears blend into alcohol, Vijay walks the red light districts of Calcutta. The cadences and rhythms of the song he sings diagnose and expose the moral occult (Brooks 1978, 1995) of the world around him:

> Yeh kooche ye nilaam ghar dilkashi ke
> Yeh lute hue kaarawaan zindagii ke
> Kahaan hain, kahaan hain muhaafiz khudi ke?
> Jinhe naaz hai hind par vo kahaan hain?

> These streets, these auction houses of the heart
> These ravaged caravans of life
> Where are they, the protectors of pride?
> Where are they, those with pride for Hind?[4]

Vijay sees his creative endeavors as intrinsically allegorical, as vital to his idealist conceptions of an ideal India. Perhaps this idealism then also explains why the plot of *Pyaasa* should prefer that the project of creative self-expression lead to an outcome other than its dispersal via mechanical reproduction into the domain of mass culture.

Pyaasa's disenchantment with mechanical reproduction could also be seen as a defensive posture at a historical moment when the film industry was rapidly falling out of favor in the priorities of the newly independent nation-state. Through *Pyaasa*, we can see the cinema establishing its own importance and salience, reflexively—a visionary medium that like its protagonist offers privileged insight into the debased world of mass culture from which it sets itself apart by virtue of its representation of that mass culture.

There is a third and different kind of archive we have explored that might determine *Pyaasa*'s rhetorical maneuvers. The copyright disputes around printed, cinematic, and photographic images troubled the implicit stability of conceptions of national culture and authenticity underlying the Romanticist and classicist conceptions of Indian culture outlined above. The auratic potential of art that Vijay mourns in *Pyaasa* was itself negotiated, as we have seen with the 1880s disputes, against the backdrop of imperial commerce and trade and in the bazaar, as it were. This is a feature Vijay does not seem to recognize. It is as if the maturation of nationalism resulted in a willed historical amnesia, a forgetting of the fact that so many of the nationalist initiatives of the independence movement, rather than abjuring the marketplace, in fact depended on and fostered alternative routes of commodity consumption that were not dictated by the unfair terms of imperial finance. The disputes from the legal archives encountered in the preceding chapter belie the conceptions of auratic art sustained and mourned by *Pyaasa.*

In the rest of this chapter, I want to extend the implications of the last chapter into reconsideration of filmmaker D. G. Phalke's place not as an isolated pioneer but as someone situated within the nexus of art and commerce. Phalke, this chapter shows, inherited the disputes around the printed image that we discussed in the previous chapter and embraced the implications of those disputes in how he conceptualized himself as a filmmaker. Put more simply, just as the printers of the nineteenth century deemed it necessary to assert authorship as the production of commercial property, so did Phalke. Recognizing this aspect of Phalke's career might more easily connect the dots that lead from the printing presses' embrace of the profit imperative to *Pyaasa's* rejection of the same.

PHALKE THE CRAFTSMAN

Official hagiographies associated with Indian cinema single out founding figures such as D. G. Phalke as exemplary originators. Troubling this understanding of origination seems the first order of business if we want to situate culture in a wider matrix and explore how it becomes *mass* culture.

Phalke did not seem to consider himself an author in the literary sense. In this he was aligned with the presses we have encountered, in so far as their understanding of author as proprietor bound them to other mass cultural forms of entertainment of the time such as music and theater. It also differentiated all these forms of popular culture from the "authors" of serious literary genres in print culture. So that while the writer of a biography was an author, the writer/director of a theatrical play was an impresario (Dharwadkar 2005).

Parsi theater (so called because the theater companies were started by Parsis or Zoroastrians) is one example of creative authorship reformulated as the skill of showmanship. Parsi theater companies had emerged in the 1850s, modeling themselves on British amateur theatricals catering to the European population. By the 1890s, these companies were the most popular sources of urban, commercial theater, catering to a diverse audience and offering an eclectic mishmash of Indo-Muslim fairy romances, bourgeois social dramas, Hindu mythologicals, as well as translations of Shakespeare. I bring up this example because the impact of this commercial theater was tremendous on popular music as well as the cinema. Parsi theater influenced Indian cinema's form—a disaggregated combination of comedy, melodrama, action—as well as its adoption of song and dance sequences right from the outset of the talkies era or the era of sound.

Parsi theater informed Phalke's self-perception as well as accounts of his life and career as someone primarily belonging to the world of performing arts and industrial craftsmanship. His biography bears out this model of authorship as praxis at an empirical level. Phalke was born in 1870 in Nasik, a town in Maharashtra, in a Hindu Brahmin family. He was trained in arts and crafts at the JJ. School of Art in Bombay and Kala Bhavan in Baroda, in drawing, painting, engraving, photography, moulding, architecture, magic, amateur stage acting. He worked in Raja Ravi Verma's printing press in Lonavla and subsequently opened a printing press of his own, Laxmi Art Printings Works, which he quit around 1911 after differences with his partners at the press. Around this time, he happened to see the cinematic passion play *Life of Christ*, hand-colored in 1911, at the America-India Cinema in Bombay. That experience, and the nationalist climate of Swadeshi, motivated him to enter the motion picture business. He traveled to England numerous times for training, including at Cecil Hepworth's studio. His early films, meant to convince prospective investors in the worth of this new enterprise, were scientific in nature: the *Birth of a Pea Plant* used time-lapse photography to document the growth of the pea plant. He chose to restrict his feature-length output for the most part to mythologicals for much of his career, perhaps a contributing cause for his career's decline by the 1930s as other genres overtook the mythological in popularity.[5]

Phalke's writings drew on the distinction between competing forms of authorship as genius, as showmanship, and as craft. In one of his articles for the nationalist newspaper *Kesari* he wrote, "There is no point in a writer starting a bookshop" (Phalke 1987, 53). The distinction between author and proprietor seems the point here. As for craft and showmanship, his writings discuss the utility of the film profession, its importance as an industry, and its alignment with craftsmanship and performing arts. Writing for the cinema ought to be an independent discipline, observed Phalke. The writer ought to be trained in the arts that were most aligned with the cinema: drawing, painting, architecture, cinema, photography, and magic (ibid., 62–63).[6] Contemporary advertisements, too, describe his filmmaking as a form of "manufacture" (Rangoonwalla 1983, 31) (see Fig. 4.4).

Even as he distanced the cinema from the filmed play, his writing drew on the structure of indigenous theater for its style, reminding us of the cinema's cultural alignment with theater. Narmada Shahane, the translator of one of his essays, observes that the essay is structured like a play. Phalke adopts the voice of the *sutradhar* or stage manager who performs an important narrative function in appealing for the audience's appreciation at key moments in the performance while also filling in the audience in the interludes on events not shown on stage. In the aforementioned essay,

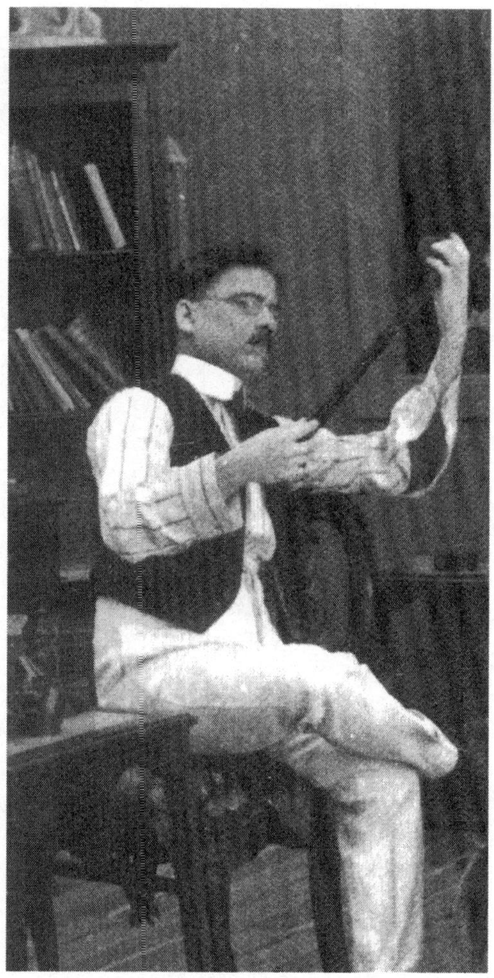

Figure 4.4. Phalke the Craftsman (Source: Wikipedia/Creative Commons License).

originally published in the Marathi language newspaper *Navyug* in 1918, Phalke incorporates an interlude that is structured as a dialogue between himself and an unnamed female voice regarding the various meanings of the word *curtain* and its significance for the cinema. Shahane speculates, correctly I think, that Phalke may have been appealing to the audience of an established cultural form and asserting his affinity with existing performative traditions, given that the essay includes a justification of the cinema as a new medium (Bahadur 1970, 71). Popular biographies and hagiographies of the man, both in regional languages such as Marathi as well as those penned in the postcolonial era, for the most part construct narratives of grit, determination, patriotism, and derring-do, not creative self-expression, even as his technical mastery of the cinema could be noticed. This understanding of himself as a craftsman perhaps strengthens the idealism of nationalist politics that informed Phalke's early film endeavors.[7] I would argue, however, that Phalke was also fully aware that the emerging politics of nationalism did not preclude the commercial traffic in images.

THE CRAFTSMAN IN THE MESHES OF PIRATE NETWORKS

Indrajit Hazra's novel *The Bioscope Man* (2008) shows how nationalism could become a project of selling culture. The novel traces the rise and fall of the "silent-era" star Abani Chatterjee in film-crazed early-twentieth-century Calcutta. Abani's fall from stardom is sudden and swift partly due to the tribulations of unrequited love and partly due to his disastrous and chance entry into a ladies' room. But he also tries to return to grace in the 1920s by shaping the biopic of William Jones (1746–1794), the famous and pioneering British Orientalist, being directed by none other than the visiting German director Fritz Lang (1890–1976). Abani convinces Lang to let him play William Jones's Sanskrit tutor and shift the focus from Jones to the tutor in a production titled *The Pandit and the Englishman*. In this novel, Hazra repeatedly invokes an incendiary nationalist movement taking shape against the backdrop of the popularity of the genres catering to this nationalist imaginary, be they mythologicals, or historical films. The novel's perspective on the relation between nationalism and film culture is witty and fascinating, as is evident in the following extract:

> It was Lalji who brought it to our notice that "nationalism" was becoming the big cultural thing those days. We had reckoned as much when we had staged and screened *Prahlad*, a biscope whose sub-subtext had been "nationalist." . . . At a meeting, Lalji had simply announced that there was much to be gained—in terms of reputation and money—if we took a swerve towards a direction where "nationalism" and "self-rule" and all those fashionable ideas could be hinted at without making them too obvious to the authorities. "Sure it's in your face. Sure, it's banal. And sure, it's not wonderful art. But we are not in the business of social service. For that, there are books and there are sadhus [holy men]. If nationalism is what the crowds want, then nationalism is what we'll give them." (Hazra 2008, 106–107)

There is some historical veracity to Hazra's imaginative reconstruction of nationalism as a lucrative project of branding, as we have already seen. The rhetoric of intellectual property waged in copyright disputes exposed nationalist thought's desire to participate in the commercial logics of empire, albeit on terms quite distinct from those imposed on it by imperial commerce. Nowhere was this more evident than in the Vasudeo Goshi case discussed in the previous chapter, in which a plaintiff who participated in an argument for cultural authenticity could find himself a defendant responsible for the "piracy" of English images.

That said, Hazra's novel is not about the printed image. It is about the cinema. Which is to say, not only did the printed image anticipate the cinema in its mass cultural dimensions, it also set in place certain discursive parameters for discussing the cultural functions of the cinema that in turn informed Indian cinema's identity for decades to come, well after independence.

The cinema, if Indrajit Hazra's novel is to be believed, was no different or even more calculating in its pandering to nationalist thought. To propose that the marketplace became an important measure of success is not to say anything out of the ordinary. Indian filmmakers were operating against tough odds—lack of finance capital from institutions controlled by the British, competition from foreign films that had already recouped their prices in their home markets, stiff tariffs and duties on the importation of technology and materials. Furthermore, the *swadeshi* movement that emerged in 1905 and that avowedly influenced Phalke's enterprise, was also an economic program aimed at self-sufficiency in the production of goods, as a means to self-rule.

But Phalke wanted to go farther. Patriotism was not an atavistic, territorially bounded sentiment for him. His understanding of his success hinged right from the outset on the hope that his work would find a broader international audience. These calculations of cultural production therefore compromise the stark distinction between India and the West, one Phalke was supposed to have ridden to success in laying the groundwork for an Indian cinema. For, not only was Phalke operating in a tough climate for indigenous filmmakers, he was also operating at a moment of significant piracy of prints. Situating acts of cultural creativity within this context is necessary both for a more nuanced cultural history of this moment and to destabilize its fundamental semantic beacons (and lodestars). By the time Phalke entered the motion picture business, piracy and the circulation of junk prints were already rampant, with authentication of prints near impossible precisely because of the global nature of the circulation of film in the early cinema period.

These contexts ultimately became the impetus for the Indian Copyright Law of 1914, an Act that was a replica of the 1911 UK copyright act;

the latter offered protection finally to photographs, sculptures, works of art and film. In that Act, a dualism in the conception of cinema was evident: films were protected both as part of dramatic works and also as a sequence of photographs. Hence, a law firm's advice to the American consul in India in 1928: register the published scenario of the American film headed to India in both the UK and in India for copyright purposes, and make certain that the scenario accompanied the imported print (Indian Cinematograph Committee [ICC] 1928, 4, 404).

By the 1920s, Hollywood reigned supreme on Indian screens and took great interest in controlling piracy. Absent a copyright treaty between the United States and the UK that accounted for India as a destination for vast quantities of American product, the many secondhand, recycled prints of American films coming in via the UK would have to be registered in the UK and in India to cover all bases (ICC 1928, 4, 406). Piracy was a concern not just for the Americans. The Pathé-India representative testified to a government committee that pirated films were being registered under the Cinematograph Act of 1918 (an act that was instituted primarily for censorship purposes) under new titles (Harold Lloyd's 1923 film *Safety Last*, he claimed, was being screened in India as *Sky High*) (ibid., 404).

With the motion pictures, too, it seems that piracy originated precisely at the point and moment in the itinerary of the film print where legitimate rights were conferred. As one Indian film entrepreneur put it:

> Some exhibitor in the foreign countries having made a legitimate arrangement to exhibit a motion picture by contract with the original suppliers or their Agents, thus obtains possession of a film. While this film is in his possession he causes to be made a photographic duplicate of the film in his possession. The copies or reprints from the wrongfully made film are placed on the market and sold. Such unauthorized copies are called pirated films. (ICC 1928, 4, 405)

Official and popular accounts of cinema in South Asia have never discussed Phalke in the context of piracy or even copyright disputes. However, recognizing the world of piracy and copyright disputes around him reminds us that Phalke's desired itineraries for his own films were as expansive as the disputed printed images that preceded him.

In the forces that shaped his career and decision making, Phalke was not that removed from the other printing presses we have already encountered, and was indeed subject to the same pressures as a printer such as Vasudeo Goshi. The more obvious historical grounds that motivate such a comparison of these two figures include the fairly straightforward one of the direct influences on Phalke's cinema of the printed images that preceded him. As with the printing presses, Phalke's motivations were also avowedly nationalist. He aimed to yoke indigenous film production to the politics of the Swadeshi movement of economic self-sufficiency that had emerged in the early twentieth century as the first major response to the extractive economic policies that sustained empire (Barnuow and Krishnaswamy 1980; Watwe 1987: Rajadhyaksha 1993). The combination of nationalism, commerce, and definitions of authenticity informed Phalke's work just as much as they had, the printed images considered earlier. Just as the presses had established a link between national identity and commodity flow, the political beliefs that motivated Phalke's film work and the context in which he worked readily attested to a similar connection.

What Goshi had done was to reverse the dominant direction of the flow of goods, which had involved the steady colonial expropriation of Indian artifacts for imperial museums in Britain, one that could be traced back at least to the calicos of the late eighteenth century, produced in Britain with Indian designs (Kriegel, 2004). Goshi had engaged in the duplication and sale of a "British" image, and it is difficult to not interpret Goshi's piracy as running at least at a tangent to the dominant flows of culture and capital from the empire to its possessions. He had found a lucrative Indian market for an image whose copyright rested in Britain and reproduced it in India for a neat profit. If this was called piracy, it was also a (counter-) theft of empire's possessions.

Let me propose here that for D. G. Phalke as well, imperial geography and India's place in that geography became crucial aspects of his rationale for entering the film business. It would be a stretch, perhaps, to claim that Goshi's appropriation and reproduction of a British image was of the same order as Phalke's seeking inspiration for his first film and finding it in a Passion Play, *The Life of Jesus*. Nevertheless, both instances involved an engagement with geography that must be considered both literally and for its symbolism. For instance, the realization that the cinema figured as territory quite literally underscored his fascination with the medium. As he put it: "Mountains, rivers, oceans, houses, human beings, animals, birds, everything on the screen is real. The miracle of the visual appearance of objects is sometimes caused by the play of light and shadow. This is the magic of the filmmaker" (Rajadhyaksha 1993, 47). Phalke's comments signal the importance of the ontology of the medium and its indexical and affective intensity. British authorities, too, recognized the power of the photographic image to open up a sensuous register and disrupt preexisting discourses. This was in evidence in the ICC testimonies regarding the deleterious effects of the cinema on impressionable subjects of empire (Mazzarella 2009, 75–76). For Phalke, then, it is precisely this sensuous immediacy that captures landscape and *figures* "India" as territory that marks the cinema as an appealing medium to engage as a new profession, particularly out of nationalist sentiment.

Phalke bound this affective intensity to the iconicity of mythological figures as he chose a story from a Hindu mythological as his first movie, *Raha Harishchandra* (1913).[8] Phalke was also, of course, aware of both of these possibilities entwined in the photographic image, one predicated on sight and the other on belief. Therefore, he could speak of the miracle of the photographic image's capacity to envision nature while also situating the referent of his subject matter in a preexisting iconographic and textual system. If the icon and the index were bound together, so was the symbolism of the image that was that of nationalism, produced allegorically by considering a movie of *Indian* gods and goddesses as a nationalist gesture.

Phalke was also reversing the duality of original and imitation that had characterized Britain's relation to India since the popularity of Indian calicos in Britain. The proximate precondition for copyright disputes is mechanical reproduction, of which the cinema was perhaps the most emblematic medium, one that imitated and reproduced life itself. Phalke, however, was not immune to the mimetic seductions of the cinema. The *Life of Christ* inspired him to make similar moving images of Hindu gods. Rather than concocting a story out of his own imagination, Phalke found inspiration for the subject matter of his earliest films from a passion play. He mobilized, in cinematic form, existing mythic iconography from Indian printed images as the equivalent of the passion play he had witnessed. What he did with the *Life of Christ* was what the British claimed they did in the late eighteenth century with Indian calico designs. He "Indianized" the passion play, just as the British were "inspired" by and "Anglicized" Indian calico, infusing it with the British national spirit and identity. In both instances, inspiration is separated from what results from it, the latter (*Raja Harishchandra* the movie) replacing the former (*Life of Christ*) in presence and priority. So geography was important in being figured in the indexical image as well as being represented in that image symbolically.

Geography was also at stake in a material sense; Phalke's filmmaking endeavor interceded in the directions in which cinematic goods typically flowed between India and Britain at the time. His desire was to circulate Indian film westward into Europe, when in most cases American and European films were flowing toward India. He sought to insert his own practice as a comparable frame of reference to films produced in Britain and the United States, which dominated the screens in India until the arrival of sound in India in 1931. Brigitte Schulze (2003) contends that Phalke was acutely aware of the *film d'art* or *kunstfilm* as a prestigious genre and marketed his films for an English-speaking middle class, advertising in English language newspapers such as the *Bombay Chronicle* rather than in national-ist Marathi-language newspapers such as *Kesari*. He was motivated by an outward-directed glance at international film culture and an attempt to align his work on par with the products of that culture.

The significant point to make here is that this international ambition was in no way incompatible with the demands of nationalist self-sufficiency. The Swadeshi (self-sufficiency) movement that emerged in answer to the British partition of Bengal in 1905 was the first major mass mobilization of the century against British rule. Phalke's descriptions of the origins of his film practice make it clear that he thought Indians ought to produce Indian images for Indians, an attempt to mark a level of difference at the level of an idealized national imaginary. The stakes, Phalke claimed, were high: the failure of his indigenous film production would "have been a permanent disgrace to the Swadeshi movement in the eyes of the people in London" (Rajadhyaksha 1993, 49).

However, even for Gandhi, whose opposition to industrialization in all forms was well known and who saw the production of handspun cloth (Khadi) as a revival of the self-sustaining village republic, the Swadeshi movement never foreclosed commodity consumption. Rather, it sought to encourage a politics of consumption as a way to engender political identity formation, as a mode of imagining the nation materially through the consumption of goods produced within the nation (see Trivedi 2007).

Phalke needs to be situated therefore within the discursive ambit of "piracy" in which inspiration and plagiarism, borrowing and theft, the licit and the illicit, possessed highly fungible meanings. As a precursor to Phalke, Goshi's piracy stands as a dramatic action that arrests and then reverses a combination of material practices, physical spaces, and politics that had mapped out the space of imperial finance and the flow of goods in favor of Britain. India's place within that system was as a source of raw materials and a reliable destination for finished goods, compensating with its export surplus for Britain's dismal trade deficits in a period of increasing inter-impe-rial rivalry (see Sarkar 1989). Goshi's piracy in India of a British-produced image whose copyright rested in London stands as a "struggle over geogra-phy" (Legg 2007, 275). Phalke's own faith in the cinematic figuration of territory, his desire to produce an *Indian* version of a passion play and his desire to circulate Indian films westward, are similar steps in the struggle over imperial geography, a struggle that copyright law had not even begun to fathom, let alone regulate.

In his time, however, other Indian filmmakers did not always share Phalke's aim of putting Indian images into wider circulation. By the late 1920s, Indian filmmakers were thoroughly suspicious of the optimism under-lining Phalke's desire to make an "Indian" passion play that could also cater to audiences in the West. For this reason, interviewed by the Indian Cinematograph Committee set up expressly to consider the possibility of a quota of screens reserved for British films in India in return for a like quota for Indian films in Britain, Indian filmmakers made it clear that they did not think Indian films would find a ready audience in Britain. They may have been right. Sean Cubitt argues that "it was only when Swadeshi products like Phalke's films began to circulate in the West that it was possible to see them commodified (in this, similar to the European market for village homespun cloths), a process sped up by the overseas audience's ignorance of the source stories" of Phalke's mythologicals (Cubitt 2004, 62). I do not disagree that the movies' circulation divorced them from an audience more familiar with the source narratives of the mythologicals, making them more vulnerable to being consumed as Orientalist spectacle. But viewed from Phalke's perspective, we witness in addition to a Western audience desirous of oriental spectacle, the desire to circulate Indian gods and goddesses far beyond Indian shores, troubling the territorially bounded nature of nationalist thought.

The filmmakers who shot down the idea of a quota for British films in India and, conversely, Indian films in Britain, may have understood cultural difference in a manner unlike Phalke (for whom an Indian film seemed worthy of circulating far and wide). Their conception of cultural difference was also unlike that of the printing presses of the nineteenth century (for whom prohibiting circulation of Indian images abroad was a matter of protecting profits). Their skepticism with the idea of a quota was expressed on the eve of the advent of sound, which also saw the emergence of a viable indigenous film industry in India. They were perhaps confident that Indian cinema could stand on its own over time. Nevertheless, for those eager to assert a national culture as a marker of difference, as well as for those eager to brand that national culture as a way of participating in global flows, such as the printing presses and D. G. Phalke, one thing stood in common: cultural difference, identity, authenticity were forged on rather cosmopolitan grounds.

Phalke's international ambitions testify to the geographical conundrums that have intensified in recent years since economic liberalization and enormously complicated questions of originality and cultural authenticity. India's mammoth commercial film industries have long been accused of plagiarizing Hollywood plotlines. Within the film industry, "Indianization" serves as a defense against this accusation. Ideas and storylines are presumed to be nonproprietary and the process of "Indianization" (exemplified, among other things, by reformulating the source narrative within the dramaturgical mode of melodrama) significantly alters the Hollywood movie into a form specific and sensible to audiences of Indian popular cinema (see Ganti 2007). This process is a localization of the geopolitics that shape Indian media's relation to globalization. Western nations are willing to aggressively prosecute Indian movie piracy on their own shores because they stand to ultimately benefit from uniform proprietary regimes as their media companies enter Indian markets. Even as combating piracy becomes part of a discourse of legitimacy for Bollywood, a "formal limitation of inspiration" is now being imposed on Bollywood's routine borrowings of Hollywood storylines (Athique 2011, 87).

The formal limitation of inspiration is only a recent development in a much more complicated history of Hollywood's presence in India, from its post–World War I dominance of screens in India (when it edged out British, Italian, and French productions), to its attempts at cultural diplomacy during the Cold War era (Govil 2011). Conversely, Indian cinema was, of course, never entirely free of Hollywood. Its adoption of the fundamental rules of classical continuity editing while interlacing those rules with indigenous regimes of vision, is one form of this tethering (see Vasudevan 1996; 2000). The idea of the commercial film as one (often speculative and commercially impelled) replication and variation among many other films of culturally familiar and longstanding traditions of narrative and dramaturgical form, asserts the importance of genre as a set of conventions and expectations (Thomas 1981) and reinforces the mass-cultural, reproducible form of the cinema. Phalke is a distant precursor of both of these attributes: he "Indianized" a text from a different cultural framework and inaugurated what became the genre of the mythological.

Between and before Phalke and the cinema of the postcolonial and (our) millennial moments stands a complex genealogy of the cinematic auteur, one whose work is necessarily trapped in the constellation comprising imitation, inspiration, and authenticity.

CINEMA AS MASS CULTURE
IN POSTCOLONIAL INDIA

The matrix within which the cinema emerged was one characterized by commerce, profit, piracy, industrial craftsmanship, and an encounter with Hollywood. Phalke was not immune to this matrix. And the colonial state saw Hollywood's presence in India as cause of suspicion, an influence upon the masses that could not have happy consequences. The newly independent Indian state inherited these suspicions. It marginalized a range of popular and highly commercial forms of audio-visual culture: popular cinema, the ubiquitous printed calendar image, film music and songs. In contrast, it engaged in the conscious patronage of the classical performing arts and the "art film" through various cultural institutions (Krishen 1991; Sundar 1995).

The basic milestones of this cultural history are now well documented (Barnuow and Krishnaswamy 1980). The central contradiction as far as the cinema was concerned was that even as it was the dominant form of mass entertainment in India, the postcolonial nation-state refused to recognize it as an industry, let alone patronize it. In the eyes of its detractors the cinema was a toxic combination of commercial appeal and cultural relevance, one that nevertheless needed the state-granted legitimacy of an "industry" status to move into respectability or, as has been the case more recently, to rationalize its workings toward a corporate ethos. The refusal by the Indian government in the 1950s to allow the broadcasting of film music on the state-run All India Radio is one of the more notorious moments in this history (Punthambekar 2010). The cultural institutions established by the new nation-state privileged classical Indian culture (classical music, dance, and theater) over its modern folk, street, and mass cultural counterparts.

The infrastructure and institution of the cinema was also at stake. Theater construction hardly kept pace with the popularity of the cinema, because the scarcity of construction materials meant that nation building had to attend to other priorities. By the mid to late 1940s as well, the star system had transformed the film industry. The family-run closely knit studio system of the 1930s was replaced by the influx of speculative financing by profiteers who had made their fortunes during the war years in armaments and other heavy industries.

Not till the 1990s did an epochal shift in economic policy motivate the state to transform its own function with regard to the culture industry. This eventually happened in 1998, when following economic liberalization, the government granted industry status to cinema. The film industry itself adopted the mantra of corporatization as it discovered lucrative export markets in the West in its "Bollywood" mode, and, combined with India's place in new knowledge economies and network society hubs, the state has now become an active facilitator of media flows including that of the cinema (see Rajadhyaksha 2004; Govil 2005, 2006). But till the 1990s, the culture wars in India pitted patronage and delegitimization, culture and commerce against each other. Indian commercial cinema was caught in the crossfire. The "golden age" of Indian cinema, the movies of the 1940s and 1950s, embraced the Nehruvian dream of modernization. But they also embraced the cultural politics of that dream and participated repeatedly in the project of their own delegitimization. *Pyaasa's* suspicion of mass culture ought to be seen in this light as the film industry justifying itself in the eyes of the state by abjuring a central component of its imaginary—mechanical reproduction.

POSTSCRIPTS: REMINISCING THE AGE OF PRINTS

In an extraordinary essay published in 1954 (but perhaps written earlier in the twentieth century), Bengali historian Jadunath Sarkar (1870–1958) looked back wistfully at the days when printed pictures were an essential part of the experience of living in the city. I reproduce an extended section from the essay:

> These old prints required for hanging them a setting, which is now no more to be found. Take *A scene on the Ganges* [1790s] by [Thomas and William] Daniell, with its flight of steps leading down to the water and the temples on the ghat [banks], or an ancient Banyan Tree dwarfing the greenery in the background. The ideal place for hanging it is the hall of the old type of mansions, which once adorned Russell Street and Theatre Road [in Calcutta], but have now all disappeared. There is a lofty bungalow with deep cool verandahs shaded with bamboo screens, thick brick walls, and trees all around. In the spacious hall free from glaze, the master is seated at ease. There is no sound except the monotonous creaking of the punkha [cloth hand-waved fans] or the snoring of the punkha-cooli [fan-waver] when he follows his master's example by dozing off into an afternoon nap. Today all that background is gone. Gardens and lawns have been eaten up by ferro-concrete; verandahs have been cut out as uneconomical waste of living room; and there is the maddening whizz of the electric fan ahead, while from outside comes the jingle of the tram car, the hooting of motor horns, and the eloquence of the Magnolia ice-cream man trying to shout down his rival the Happy Boy vendor. Therefore, it is in the fitness of things that the modern Burra Sahib's [important official] drawing room in Calcutta is decorated with the picture of some American film star with a liberal supply of paint and a minimum of clothing. (Sarkar 1954)

Sarkar's reminiscence is being voiced with a sense of a wide-ranging transformation that had already taken its toll. However, the bygone era Sarkar is invoking was no less the product of modernity than Sarkar's own historical moment. The "old type of mansions" popular in the nineteenth century were themselves products of the Bengali encounter with British styles. Where precolonial architecture had emphasized the interiority of the courtyard as the center of domestic life, Bengali houses in the nineteenth century had adopted the neoclassical façade, hitherto popular with the British, as an essential component for the architectural and public performance of status and wealth. The focus on interiority was replaced by the need to be connected with the busy streetscape, rather than removing residents from it (Chattopadhyay 2005). Verandahs were central to this flow between interior and exterior space. Venetian blinds shielded the interiors of these verandahs from public gaze but offered a public view for the resident. Domestic and commercial space spilled, via these verandahs and facades, to the sidewalk and streets.

Given that colonial modernity had already reshaped Calcutta's urban architecture, we could go one step farther and assert that the "old type of mansion" in Sarkar's essay is no simple object of nostalgia. Even as the represented space of a utopian past in Sarkar's essay, it was a product of a worldview that superimposed as in a "dissolving views" optical entertainment, multiple temporalities. The picturesque landscapes and views in the prints made from watercolors and oil paintings painted in the late eighteenth century by visiting European artists, such as Thomas and William Daniell, cast a long shadow over Sarkar's memory of the nineteenth-century city of Calcutta from his location in the twentieth century.

My point in making these observations is that such erasures and temporal modifications of the history of modernity as are evident in the essay, are themselves quintessentially modern outcomes and statements. The machines of Sarkar's memory adopted the tactics of the very contraptions— the magic lanterns, dioramas, phantasmagoria shows—that were the screen practices preceding the cinema derided by him.

It is part of the paradox of a modernist articulation such as Sarkar's that it should distinguish so starkly between its own historical moment and a prior one. The film poster's capacity to condense its historical moment in the mid-twentieth century is normatively subordinated to the essentially similar work performed by an earlier print in an earlier century. Both the eighteenth-century print and the twentieth-century film poster invoke their respective environments, evocatively described by Sarkar, but only the former is seen as being in harmony with its environment. The film poster, nestled within the ferro-concrete blocks of twentieth-century Calcutta, captures the hyperstimulus and noise of technological modernity and is viewed as simply a symptom of degradation. Was Sarkar's distinction between past and present, rural and urban, peculiar to colonial modernity? One of the ways in which Bengalis coped with the effects of modernization was to craft a series of distinctions between the inner spiritual domain and the outer material domain; between the modern present and the traditional past (Chatterjee 1997). Calcutta in the nineteenth century was often juxtaposed to the values and traditions of a rural, idyllic Bengal. In Sarkar's case, that idyllic setting is the British country life transposed to Bengal in the paintings of visiting European artists, providing us, even in displacement and fantasy, a historical glimpse into the lifestyles of elite Bengalis in the nineteenth century, the objects they consumed, and the cosmopolitanism of their fantasy spaces.

Sarkar's essay is decidedly not an unambiguous lamentation for the loss of the aura, and for multiple reasons. To paraphrase Walter Benjamin here, "resting on a summer afternoon," Sarkar follows with his eyes the long shadow cast by the branches of a Banyan tree in an old *print*.[9] To the extent that Benjamin's now iconic definition of the aura directs us to pay attention to the chiasmic relation between past and present and proximity and distance that makes an image (and can make any image, even a natural one, even in the immediate present) a resonant auratic object,[10] Sarkar's essay, in the very act of narrating social history, works to produce the aura of the images he describes. He condenses and conflates multiple temporal registers—the early modern (1700s), the modern (1800s) and the present of his own moment (1900s)—to make a case that the image in the mansion exists at a distance and a remove not only from *his* historical moment but presumably within its own historical moment as well, whether that is the moment of its production in the 1790s or the "whenever" depicted in the painting. This is the basis of its auratic potential. By the same token, we could say that the film poster too is auratic, even if Sarkar may have disagreed with this claim, "a supra-mundane visionary form of art" (Haggard 1987–88, 62) nestled in the "ferro-concrete" blocks of twentieth-century Calcutta.

There is a second, simpler reason why Sarkar's essay, even as it bemoans the modernity of the cinema, is not a lament over the loss of the aura. It is the printed image, the duplicate, that the essay valorizes, not the original watercolor or oil painting. As Sarkar writes in the same essay:

> Most of the drawings done in India were reproduced in England as prints because there was a large and enlightened demand for them by men who could pay well. It was the fashion to decorate the houses of our British rulers and merchant-princes and of the Indian nobles who imbibed a new taste from them, with such prints, and it was therefore worth one's while to print them and satisfy two markets, Home and Indian.
>
> But Daniell's elephant folio size plates (144 in number) were very costly, and so, for poorer art lovers a small size edition in mezzotint was issued, three parts bound in one volume. Similarly, Grindlay's *Scenery Etc on the Western Side of India* (1826) contained 26 fine steel engravings in one volume at a reasonable price.

Mezzotints, acquatints, and steel engravings were intaglio methods of print-making that were overtaken—in Europe and in India—by the successes of lithography, photo-lithography, chromolithography, and oleography. Nevertheless, the fact remains that these were prints, not original paintings.

It is in contrast to this awareness of the power and appeal of print culture that *Pyaasa* stakes its position against mechanical reproduction. It seeks to abjure the social basis of the experience of art's aura. It denies the possibility of the politicization of this aura that was central to the visual culture of nationalism. Instead, it seeks an experience immersed in Romanticism and untouched by the technologies of mechanical reproduction. That this perspective is to be found *in a movie,* Benjamin's quintessential example of the medium that obliterates the distinction between science and art, and enables a new form of political participation, may seem the ultimately ironic refutation of Benjamin's prognostications. Ironic or not, this abjuration of technical reproducibility was the cinema's attempt to participate in the politics of its own marginalization as a way of earning cultural legitimacy with the state and with cultural elites. If one line of inquiry into the cinema's relation to print culture takes us from the calicos through to Phalke's enthusiastic and inspired embrace of the inauthentic, another line takes us from Phalke to postcolonial Indian cinema's defensive search for cultural authenticity in which technical reproducibility, and the mass formations it engenders, emerges as the source of a profoundly unsettling mob mentality. *Pyaasa's* concluding scenes depict a mass audience that is as fickle in its allegiances as it is violent, as it celebrates Vijay's poetry one minute and nearly kills him the next for his refusal to participate in a celebration of his work by this mass audience.

Finally, it would be worthwhile to note one other aspect of Sarkar's essay. The essay, written by a Bengali man and ranging in its references from late-eighteenth-century watercolors to early-twentieth-century film posters, is an expression of a very specific kind of modernity, one filtered through the tastes of the educated Bengali male. Given that the vast majority of movies screened till the arrival of sound were foreign films (the French firm Pathé's imports that included mostly American fare, which overtook in number French *and* British films after World War I), we may even have to argue that the subject that consumed the American films was not the same elite Bengali subject that hung a Daniells print on the wall of his mansion in a quiet street in Calcutta. That is to say, the exclusionary tastes of an educated Bengali male can reveal niche audiences and rifts in the consumption of a cosmopolitan, mechanically reproduced mass culture.

PART III

INTERMEDIALITY

5

THE EMERGENCE OF TOPICALITY

• ◆ •————• ◆ •

Snapshot Cultures and Newspaper Photojournalism

This chapter delves into a configuration of film, print, and photography that emerged in the same years as the rapid popularization of the religious and nationalist chromolithograph discussed in the preceding section. At its core is a consideration of the emergence of amateur, newspaper, and snapshot photography and the manner in which these practices produced a discourse of topicality that became quite central to early cinema's engagement with politics (a matter I take up in detail in the following chapter).

Histories of photography have attended more to the grand official photographic projects by the colonial government than the more prosaic forms of amateur and topical photography that emerged in the 1880s.[1] At the same time, the centrality of the chromolithograph has produced an influential account of the emergence of a national cinema. Both these circumstances (the emphasis on official colonial photography and the emphasis on the chromolithograph) have obfuscated the ongoing history of photography, which did not cease with the arrival of the cinema. This history has much to tell us of the emergence of the cinema as a "real-time" medium of truth telling, as a referential medium bound to the constraints and opportunities of topicality.

In addressing this lacuna I attend primarily to amateur photography, because it operates on the cusp of a shift in paradigms of representation: on the one hand, reformulating preceding conventions of photographic representation, and on the other, anticipating and engaging with the new possibilities of the moving image. Amateur photography of the sort I discuss here was largely a European affair. That does not, however, diminish its importance for a history of the cinema. In fact, precisely because those involved in amateur photography constituted a subculture of sorts, one gets a remarkable picture of urban modernity through European eyes in an imperial context. The conceptions of relevance and topicality that emerge, however, are not restricted to European life in South Asia. For these conceptions shaped understandings of the medium for Indians but in ways not easily obvious from the vantage point of a national cinema–oriented historiography.

This chapter follows Chris Pinney's (2008) recent exploration of the history of photography in India as it overlapped with the arrival of the cinema. Pinney is interested, as I am here, in linking the history of photography with that of the emergence of the cinema, and in highlighting the potentially incendiary and uncontrollable possibilities of a new kinetic medium that could magnetize its relationship to its consumers, the audiences on a vast scale. My concerns are similar but I present somewhat more mixed results with respect to the cinema's relation to photography, for the cinema could as easily be used to buttress state authority as it could to undermine it. Furthermore, even prior to the emergence of the cinema, a vibrant subculture of amateur photography set aside the imperatives of official colonial photography in favor of an embodied engagement with new kinds of cameras, new technologies of mobility, and hitherto uncovered subject matter. At the same time, this subculture also reformulated traditional colonial genres of photography such as archaeological, ethnographic, and landscape photography, governed respectively by the paradigms of salvage, surveillance, and the found object.[2] Finally, as we will see in the next chapter, as amateur photographers encountered an increasingly politicized public sphere, they sometimes unwittingly captured the contentious grounds of urban modernity in India. As a political nationalism gained steam, the cinema amplified the possibilities of how one might engage with politics. As an institution, the cinema spilled over into public spaces and in turn allowed public life to spill over into its spaces.

For now, in the current chapter, I want to describe the transformations wrought by amateur photographers to the conventions of representation that had governed the use of photography throughout much of the nineteenth century.

BICYCLE PHOTOGRAPHY

In the United States, the hand camera became increasingly popular by the late 1870s and an important moment in its history was the announcement of the Kodak camera in 1888. The same year also saw the announcement of the halftone process. With it, photographs could now be typeset on the same block as text and this vastly amplified the reproduction of photographs in print. It also combined the market for images with the market for newsprint and standardized photojournalism as an ingredient of the daily newspaper.

In India, the instantaneous image did not win universal approval from photographers. To paraphrase one argument, the instantaneous picture had its strengths in being scientifically accurate, but that did not necessarily make it the most appropriate pictorial representation of movement. The instant image resulted in unnatural poses (a man's leg raised in the process of walking and frozen into an image, went one example). Or it simply failed to convey movement itself since the snapshot of a train traveling at sixty miles an hour would no more convey movement than a snapshot of the same train standing still.[3]

The hand camera's rapidity of exposure and its ability to capture the unplanned moment also threatened to undermine the European photographer's role in what had hitherto been a deliberative act. In an immensely evocative characterization that recalls Walter Benjamin's famous description of photography as the "optical unconscious" of the early twentieth century, writer George Ewing noted: "The chief purpose then of the hand camera is the recording of scenes from life, the catching of the spirit of humanity, and the perpetuation of unconscious revelations of character."[4] If the unconscious was to govern actions, what then was to become of the photographer? Ewing opined, "I am decidedly opposed to the aimless exposure of plates one after another in the hope that a picture may result. Train your hand and eye to secure pictures whenever they appear; regard purposeless exposure as the root of all evil."[5]

The conscious refusal to exercise deliberation risked its loss altogether. But to exercise it, one needed some form of training and, we might add, habituation. In this way, deliberation is preserved as a necessity to offset the excesses of the technology, albeit as an effect of training and habituation. The entire paradoxical formulation—agency and volition acquired through training and habituation—acknowledges what is novel about the hand camera (its propensity to minimize deliberation and encourage mindless exposure) while constricting that novelty into the comforting frame of entrained deliberation. That said, the "aimless exposure of plates one after another" captures the virtual promise of this new instrument of photography for those first encountering it; its potential implications as they saw it, measured against the practices of wet-plate photography that were still all too familiar at the time Ewing was writing this guide. It describes what the hand camera could enable: the aimless exposure afforded by pressing the button.

Ewing's careful balancing of deliberation and reflex was soon overcome by a new entity: the bicycle. Hand cameras did not achieve a mass market in India, but they ushered in leisure- and tourist-driven subcultures of "bicycle photographers"[6] and snapshot photography that offer a striking glimpse of a shared urban infrastructure in which Europeans and Indians experienced the same events but from radically different perspectives. The 1890s was the decade of the bicycle craze in Europe and America and photography and bicycling became twinned passions for many, including the amateur photographers in Calcutta.[7] The bicycle became part of a constellation of changing perceptual experiences, celebrated as new and therefore modern.

Cycling offered new sensory thrills for the European in India. *The Journal of the Photographic Society of India* (henceforth *JPSI*) made mention of the thrill of "coasting"—as the hobby was called in Europe (a word with unknown provenance, the editor confessed)—on a bicycle downhill, letting the bicycle gain increasing velocity as it went "whizzing" down the slope. "The feeling is akin to that one used to experience on a swing when as a boy, one swooped with a yell of delight along the arc it described. . . . The element of danger there undoubtedly is in 'coasting' only increases the pleasure."[8] The hand camera as a device of enhanced portability encountered the bicycle, a new mode of transportation characterized by the promise of rapid movement.

The earliest references in the *JPSI* celebrate the bicycle's compatibility with photography. But they also underscore the need to imagine the bicycle, the camera, and the photographer as a total entity in which each of those elements was inseparable from the others. If anything, the discussion along these lines demonstrated the material problems of fulfilling the promise of self-propelled mechanical motion, whether bodily or visual. One article offered advice on the ideal photographic equipment, on bicycle clothing, medicines to take on bicycling expeditions, the ideal amount of weight a bicycle could carry without posing a problem of balance for the photographer, and the maintenance of the "machine" (the bicycle). The article's author James Waterhouse's discussion ties the hand camera to the bicycle as a matter of necessity, but in doing so it also sutures basic elements of the cinema (celluloid) into the assemblage of the still image and the mobile gaze. A hand camera, celluloid in the form of roll film, and the absence of printing and developing materials that might weigh the bicycle down, were all requisite for mobility and success, Waterhouse contended.[9]

THE ETHNOGRAPHIC AND THE PICTURESQUE IMAGE

Seen in light of Ewing's observations on the unconscious and the thrill of coasting, the bicycle and the hand camera were both part of a constellation of perceptual experiences that destroyed old habits of vision, a destruction that nevertheless resulted in representations that were understood through familiar preexisting paradigms.

Such was the case with archaeological and ethnographic images. One writer in the *JPSI* proposed that "labored ideas of picture making" ought to be replaced with daring attempts to "portray things as they are," an aim particularly suited for the native quarters of Indian cities with their "crowded tenements peopled by an extraordinary diversity of widely diverging nationalities . . . [b]azaars infinitely more curious than anything New York can show."[10] The writer described the allure of "peepul and banyan trees, ox-drawn traffic and sunlit camping grounds—an old world story of slow quaint Oriental life enveloped in a dust haze" (83).

This "Old World" story, however, entailed a very new form of seeing. It was new because it was a highly self-reflexive nostalgia for slow-moving societies. The nostalgia produced an image of these societies saturated with duration. The newness of this particular formulation of nostalgia is also clear when compared with official British photography of India's ancient architectural ruins and monuments undertaken since the 1850s. Christopher Pinney (1997) has termed this kind of photography of architectural ruins as operating under the "salvage" paradigm. Photography would document and preserve for posterity those aspects of South Asia already past and under threat of obliteration from the modernizing influence of the British presence. In contrast to the salvage paradigm, the "slow quaint Oriental life enveloped in a dust haze" being celebrated by this writer in the 1890s was not so much an ancient past at risk of being forgotten, as it was an ongoing present that the photographer could now capture.

On the one hand, the rhythms of time of this coterminous present were being ethnographically constructed as radically other and putatively unlike the accelerations of time and space enabled by the halftone, the bicycle, and the hand camera. On the other hand, the "infinite peace of spreading fields with their patient cultivators, and the mud-walled village and the meandering village" could be recognized as such only when the thrill and speed of perception, of mobility and multiplication of instantaneous images, of their rapid dispersal in print in vast scales, had all become the new normal (83). This paradox of the new and the old as co-constituted entities coexisting in a compacted simultaneity, was clear to the writer. The article goes on to exhort its readers: "Aim at capturing Life as you see it from the windows of the train. Think how new and yet how old are these silhouettes of the East—new because few artists have attempted them, old because they have appealed for countless years to all that is sympathetic and appreciative in man" (83). The premium placed in the article on "proportion," and on an idea "perfectly worked out" in advance in the interest of depicting a woman at the well, or a ploughman turning at the end of a furrow, or a bowed crowd in a mosque, can be misleading if interpreted as an eschewal of spontaneity in the interests of a stable Orientalist vision. Far more significant is the way in which the enhanced mobility, portability, instantaneity, speed, spontaneity, and profusion of detail became the conditions for the possibility of images depicting the obverse of these traits. "The rule to follow is never to let the interest be destroyed by multiplicity of detail which cannot fail to overwhelm the leading idea of a picture . . . the crowd in Chitpore Road, Calcutta can be trusted to flow as it usually does" (84). It was up to the photographer to select the enduring image from the flux of life and the multiplicity of detail offered to the eye equipped with new technologies for seeing and encasing sight.

Moreover, the increased frequently of street scenes in the *JPSI* can be seen as a sign of the recession of an older understanding of the picturesque as something to do with rurality. Sights and scenes "we pass every day" became part of the journal's published halftone images. The result was the visual construction of an alternate, pre-Kodak temporality, but one enabled by the Kodak (see Fig. 5.1).

"No. 1. This represents the common or garden bazaar tum-tum (cart) waiting to complete its load of passengers. The entire absence of hurry and indifference to the passage of time so characteristic of the native, is clearly

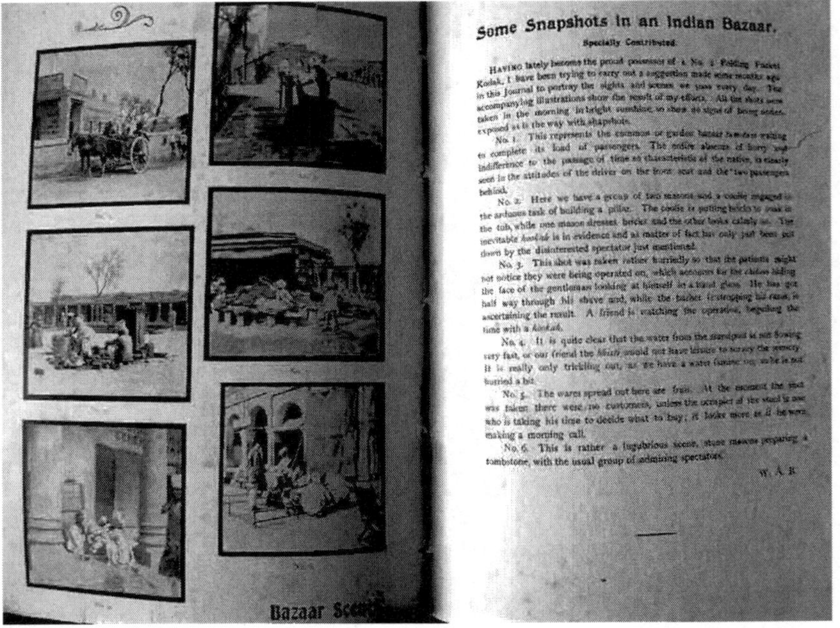

Figure 5.1. "Some snapshots in an Indian bazaar," *Journal of the Photographic Society of India*, vol. 17, 1903, np (Source: Asiatic Society of Bengal, Kolkata, India).

seen in the attitudes of the driver on the front seat and the two passengers behind." Mapping the snapshot in the atlas of lived time specified its significance. The hookah visible in one snapshot "has only just been put down," we are told of another picture. The water from a pipe "is not flowing very fast . . . only trickling out" in another image. "At the moment the shot was taken there were no customers" at a fruit stand depicted in a third image. "The hand of the barber has obscured the face of a gentleman who is getting a shave, observes the photographer regarding a fourth image."[11] Over and over again, the precision of the moment emerges as deliberately singled out in the natural flux and evanescence of time.[12]

Where nineteenth-century glass plate photography or the landscape photographer might have turned the picturesque into a premeditated and serious aesthetic project and achievement, the snapshot camera turned it into a democratized and casual search for found objects. Landscape, ethnography, news, and serialized depictions of movement were all conflated as part of a twentieth-century picturesque. An Englishman opening a bottle of beer, a passenger boat on a canal in Travancore, and even a reader of the *Illustrated Weekly* (a man in a chaise lounge reading the newspaper) became examples of a reading public that relied on print capitalism to produce an imagined European community in India (see Fig. 5.2).

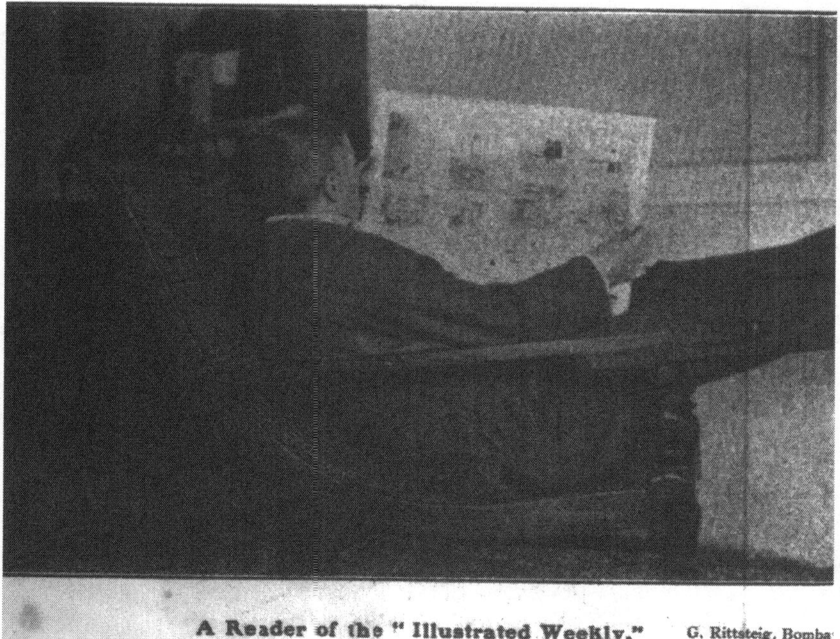

Figure 5.2. A reader of the *Illustrated Weekly*, Nov. 15, 1905, Supplement First Page.

The "mass image" is Gerry Beegan's (2008) apt phrase for the photojournalistic mass-produced image. With respect to the illustrated press in the UK in the early twentieth century, Beegan contends that the mass image enabled a reading public to envision itself. The English-speaking and -reading public in India also saw itself in the halftone images of newspaper photojournalism. In India, the reading public saw itself ensconced within the rituals of everyday life in an empire. Those rituals included sporting events, official ceremonies, and inaugurations.

There was also the copious amount of travel and tourist photography that presented readers with something of a happenstance picturesque, or the picturesque of found views, curiosities, and objects. The found and ephemeral object had always been an organizing trope for colonial appropriation. Indeed, as WJT Mitchell notes, the found object is central to the aesthetic of the picturesque: a "picturesque" view/object that is discovered, as if accidentally in the course of exploration. Object-hood itself, Mitchell notes, is endemic to discourses of imperialism and colonialism. The division between art objects and mere, unredeemed object-hood, between art and non-art, is tested and forged when the culture is involved in a colonial encounter (Mitchell 2005, 116–21).[13]

It is in the context of the casually discovered picturesque that amateur photography redefined ethnographic photography as well. Take, for instance, photographs staging the encounter of the native with modern technology that would begin to appear in English-language newspapers such as *The Illustrated Weekly of India*. One is titled "A Study in Expression" and depicts a group of Indians from Kurseong, a hill station in Eastern India, congregated around a gramophone player and looking at the camera (see Fig 5.3). The other one, titled "Feminine Curiosity," depicts a photographer and an Indian sari-clad woman on either side of a field camera resting on a tripod. The photographer, his head stuck under the black cloth of the lens/viewfinder, is in the act of taking a picture. The woman is not posing for the picture as one might expect. Instead, she is peering into the lens on her side of the camera. The photographer looks through his viewfinder at the woman, but the woman, instead of posing for the camera, has decided to look back through the lens (see Fig 5.4).

Humor at the expense of the subject was, as Fatimah Tobing Rony has observed, frequent in travelogues of colonial territories (Rony 1996, 84). What gives the image its "curiosity value" is that the woman is shot in profile, her body bent in curiosity almost at a right angle as she peers through the wrong side of the camera lens. What we have here is photography's ability to create "a newly technologized body on a mass scale" (Chaudhary 2012, 2). The woman becomes part of the assemblage of the camera and we are offered a radically new view of the most unexpected (for the European

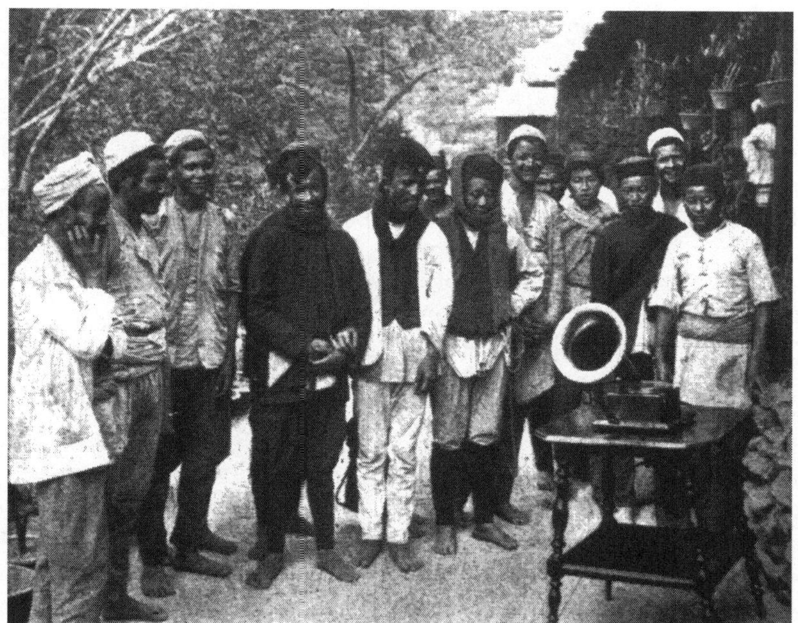

Figure 5.3. "A Study in Expression," *Illustrated Weekly of India*, Aug. 22, 1906.

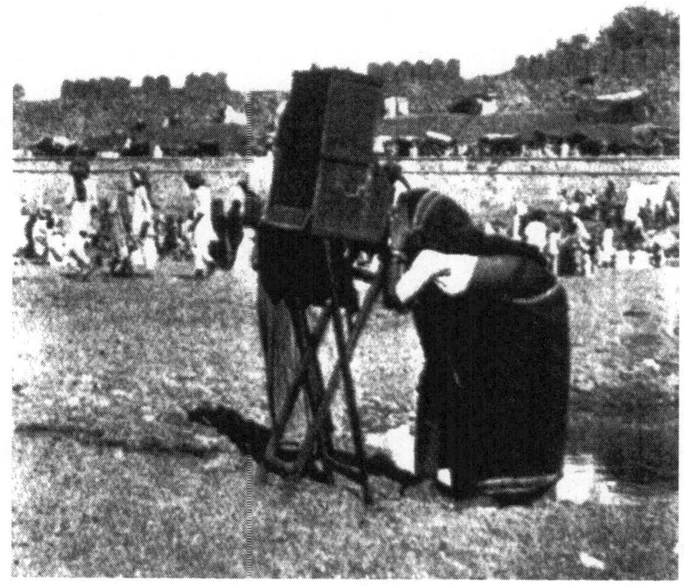

Figure 5.4. "Feminine Curiosity," *Illustrated Weekly of India*, Oct. 10, 1906.

readers of *The Illustrated Weekly*) sort of body modernized by technology: a sari-clad Indian woman.

The body that is "technologized" however, is not the same in the two photographs. The gramophone in the center of a group of men in "A Study of Expression" captures the communitarian possibilities of amplifying sound in space. But more important is the conceit of staging a moment of encounter captured through facial expression that is now up for study by way of the photograph. The photographic camera in "Feminine Curiosity," on the other hand, reveals the power of the camera to become a prosthetic extension of the senses. The image trades on the humor that even a sari-clad Indian woman of a different lifeworld could incorporate the camera into her embodied vision if she so wished. So clear is this phenomenology of mechanical vision that it produces a noncoincidence between the gaze of the photographer that took this snapshot, and the gaze of the subject. The photographer looks at two subjects, his snapshot counterpart on one side of the camera and the woman on the other side, but both subjects are looking not at the photographer's camera but at each other from either side of the camera that is between them, locked in an assemblage that is oblivious to the camera directed at it. The camera has revealed the habitus of the European snapshot in India.

The "snapshooting" of the ethnographic image indicates as well that in British India, the hand camera and the halftone blurred the boundaries between news and observation, between editorializing and reportage, between amateur and professional journalism. The newsworthy event and other forms of topical representation (building fires, urban construction projects, sporting, political and social events, tramcar accidents) constituted relevant public information rendered in the halftone and now accessible to a reading public. By the same token, however, what was formerly an ethnographic project of the colonial state was now topical and relevant for a much wider reading public. Of course, the colonial state's ethnographic projects had always been driven by commercial considerations of dispersal and sale for a consuming public that might purchase the images by subscription. But that public had been largely located in the European metropolis, and the limitations on reproduction and dispersal of the photographic image had restricted the size of that public. Now the vaster scales of reproduction and dispersal had transformed the subscription image into a mass image. Contextualized by the prosaic aspects of everyday life, the halftone diluted the racial and paranoid epistemology of ethnography. Thanks to the amateur hand camera enthusiast for whom taking a picture anywhere and anytime was now easy, and thanks to the mass image of the halftone, Indians were now a proximate part of the everyday life of resident Europeans. Their alterity was contiguous with the newsworthy, the topical, or just the downright curious image. The picturesque and the ethnographic turned banal (but not boring) thanks to the halftone image.

PHOTO-ILLUSTRATIONS AND FILM

What political salience do these mundane ethnographic and picturesque modes carry? The dilution of a "colonial sociology of knowledge" (Cohn 1996) by the snapshot and the halftone underscored a complex relation between the public and the private, a relation the cinema would play a crucial role in politicizing, as we shall see in the subsequent chapter. The hand camera's marketing and uses in the United States produced a clear distinction between the public and the private. This distinction is predicated on a further division of representation between the halftone (the public mass image) and the family snapshot (the private moment). Kodak's marketing ultimately defined the snapshot as a selection of significant private moments for the family album, and public life became the domain of the newspaper halftone (Savras and Frohlich 2011, 63–66). This had not always been the case, for in the pre–hand camera days, public figures and events used to be routinely included in family albums. Thus, the eventual separation of public figures and events from private figures and events implied a distinction, to put it somewhat simplistically, between the political and the personal.

These two sets of distinctions cannot, however, be taken for granted in British India. For one could argue that the halftone image of the early-twentieth-century newspaper turned the public sphere into an object of private consumption for the European reader. For the European, the private was not restricted to the family album. It included an entire people, the public property of empire reproduced as image for private leisurely consumption.

This interchangeability of domains mirrored the mode of photojournalistic production. A glance at photo-illustrations in newspapers such as *The Statesman* and the *Illustrated Weekly of India* makes clear that amateur snapshotters supplied a significant portion of the images published in newspapers, and newspapers sought out these images. Hence, the *JPSI* thought it worthwhile to proffer advice on amateurs' contribution to photojournalism with specific reference to India.[14]

The example of the Delhi Durbars (1877, 1902/03, and 1910/11) illuminates the way in which the public and private were metonymic in significance and experience for Europeans. The Durbars were borrowed from Mughal and other South Asian courtly traditions and reinvented by the British. Their original function was to serve as rituals of gift giving and receiving that established hierarchy between the king, his subordinates, and the subjects at large. The giving and receiving of cloth was the most important of the Durbar's rituals. It signified an incorporation of the body of the subject into the king's body. It was this tradition that the British borrowed and enacted three times, in 1877, 1902/03, and 1911/12. All three Durbars were multimedia events involving photographers, filmmakers, and newspaper journalists. The first one of the twentieth century, in 1902/03, attracted British film producer R. W. Paul, who made at least four films of the Durbar; the Gaumont film company, which may have hired the services of Bourne & Shepherd (the famed photography studio of Calcutta and Simla) to do the actual photographing; the American Biograph Company; the Warwick Trading Company; and one Indian filmmaker, Harishchandra Bhatavdekar, aka Save Dada (Bottomore 1995). Stephen Bottomore's essay catalogs the innumerable "Kodak fiends" stomping the grounds, as well as Indian photographic companies such as Bourne & Shepherd, and Underwood and Underwood, the London stereoscope company, and numerous foreign illustrated magazines, which reproduced photographs from the event in profusely illustrated editions.

Two versions of the 1903/03 Durbar are available to us in different media that are worth comparing: R. W. Paul's film on the Durbar, and a photo-illustrated book released by a Madras-based company (Hoe and Company) titled "Delhi Durbar Album 1903." Let us compare the two for what they tell us of the language of early cinema and its continuities with photo-illustration. Paul's film, titled *Coronation Durbar at Delhi 1903*, comprises three distinct views or vantage points from which the Durbar events are presented. In the first view, a long shot of a wide field depicts formations of soldiers moving from left to right and right to left simultaneously along multiple planes.

In the next view, which actually comprises a sequence of many shots, all from the exact same vantage point, a steady and unending stream of Indian soldiers on horseback and on foot, march from right to left past the camera, which is placed a medium distance from the path of the soldiers' procession. Officers overseeing the parade flank the soldiers on both sides. On the far side (that is to say, in the background of the image), the officers face the camera (and us). The parading soldiers occupy the middle ground. An officer observing the soldiers occupies the foreground and his back is turned toward us. The point of view inscribed in these shots is that of the imperial officers who are overseeing the parade. The shots are part of the strategy of filming common to early cinema that could be termed "fragmentation" (Gaudreault 2001). When faced with an event that involved action that is continuous, serial, or repetitive in nature, the filmmaker adopts a stop-and-start method of filming the event, turning on the camera only when the event is underway, so as to avoid including any unnecessary hiatus that might be part of the repetitive action. In this case, we never see the frame empty, as it would have been in the interim as one contingent of soldiers paraded by and another contingent approached the path in view of the camera. Instead, multiple shots show exactly the same action: soldiers marching past our view. The "in vivo" editing, or editing in the camera by simply stopping the recording, instead of editing after the filming has been completed, achieves an impression of intensified "photogrammatic"[15] and temporal continuity, as if the action suffered no gaps, no empty moments in its unfolding.

The effect of this technique is to construct an endless monumental duration to the imperial staged spectacle of the colonial army marching past that suppresses the possibility of being distracted while watching an action repeated over and over again. It does so through a combination of movement, the very possibility of which provoked wonder in contemporary accounts of the cinema in India as elsewhere, and fragmentation, which preserves the continuity of the action but accentuates its impact through repetition. The images of early cinema, Burch argued, "carry inscribed in them the need to be seen and re-seen; it is inconceivable that an audience of the period, any more than one of today, could have reckoned that they had seen them definitively after seeing them once" (Burch 1990, 17). It is this inscription that is harnessed here, even in a film where there is little of the polycentrism and surfeit of information, the inexhaustible details to be observed from an everyday event caught on camera, that characterized the early Lumière films. The need to see an action repeatedly is harnessed here as a valorization of temporal indeterminacy, as if to suggest that the spectacle of empire is not bound to customary temporal coordinates.

The third view is a relatively brief medium shot of a crowded field with Indians, some in the uniform of lower-level sepoys, some civilians, squatting and standing on the grass while two elephants obstruct them from view, passing right to left. The film ends at that point but the contrast of the third view with the first and second, which had emphasized orderly formations, is conspicuous, as if the last shot were filming the casual backstage of a much grander ritual the dimensions of which this short film had barely begun to intimate to us. This is the kind of back scene that would attract the attention of British painters such as Mortimer Menpes and Indian photographer Deen Dayal, who created "a non-exotic, non-heroic dramatic visual register" in their depictions of Durbar activities and spectators. In attempting to look in the margins of these events—at Indian spectators, or views from an unconventional perspective—for subject matter, these figures undermined the imperial spectacle of the Durbar, and (amateur) photography played a key role in affording new perspectives on the event (Rajan 2012, 168; see also essays by Dewan, Mathur, and Pinney in the same volume).

In some ways, the photo-illustrated book of the same event replicates the continuities the Paul film tries to achieve through assembling thirty-one numbered plates. The serial and repetitive nature of many of the consecutive images in the book parallels the fragmentation and repetition of the film. The book comprises a series of bird's-eye views or long shots of fields, processions, and mass congregations of dignitaries under canopies. The film has no intertitles. But in the book's table of contents, plates 4, 5, and 6 are titled, respectively, "Procession of ruling chiefs in the arena," "Procession of ruling chiefs," and "Procession continued." The same procession is shown three times as the reader flips from page to page.[16]

On the other hand, the photographic camera was more amenable to being carried through multiple locations than the cinematographic camera, resulting in a far more expansive view of the proceedings. The three images mentioned above show three distinct locales: the huge arena or maidan (field) that had been specially prepared for the Durbar; outside Delhi's Red Fort constructed by the Mughal emperor Shahjahan in 1639; and a street in Delhi. Where the viewer of the film could only have focused on the figures in a relatively small number of camera setups, the reader of the photo-illustrated book was provided a tourist's tour of the spectacle coursing through different spaces. The desire for expansiveness exceeds the title of the book, which transcends the Durbar to incorporate views of Delhi's famous monuments. The book ends with five plates of views of other iconic monuments of an older Mughal Delhi: the Kutub Minar, the tomb of Safdar Jang, the mausoleum of Mughal emperor Humayun, and two plates of the Jama Masjid mosque, also built by Shahjahan in 1656 (one a daytime view, the other of the mosque illuminated at night).

These additional images exceed therefore, simply a cinematic staging of a timeless imperial spectacle, to incorporate the possibility of a private reverie of visual commodity consumption of architectural grandeur as a form of vicarious tourism. The frontispiece for this book mimics a privately owned royal photo album in its design: oval insets of Edward VII and Queen Alexandra, as if we were looking at bejeweled cartes-de-visites, in the center of an ornate square boundary. This halftone image album introduces a significant aspect of modern life: the commodity-as-image, a tool for consumption that engendered a new form of work, the work of visual consumption (Crary 1999, 116). By the same token, it ushers in a new form of consumption, attentive and distracted at the same time, a perusal that moves from page to page, not purposefully looking for anything in particular (Beegan 2008, 14) (see Fig. 5.5).

In the combination of filmic continuity and "mass image" perusal, of attentiveness and distractedness, we witness multifaceted protocols of spectatorship: some highly formal and hieratic, as in the Paul film, some more flexible and informal, as in the illustrated book. The illustrated book transforms spectacle into tourism for a private European civilian or elite

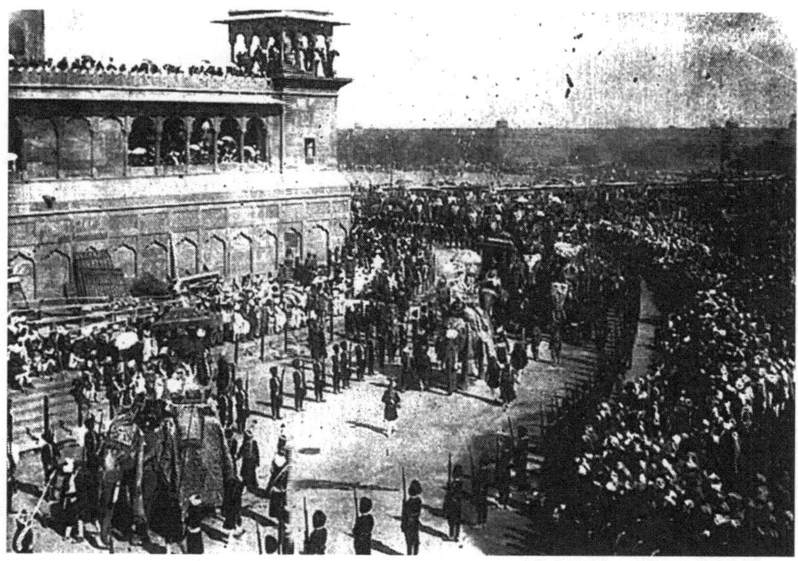

Figure 5.5. "State entry. Their Excellencies Lord and Lady Curzon," *Delhi Durbar Album*, Hoe and Company, Madras, 1903.

Indian as the ideal purchaser and consumer of the book. The continuities between the amateur photographer and the amateur home movie in British India in the preindependence era seem conspicuous. In an essay that sets a lucid research agenda on official and amateur movies produced by Europeans in India, Ravi Vasudevan (2011) points to a certain "movement outwards . . . from home to the official colonial setting" within the span of a single home movie, suggesting that the European amateur home movie and the official educational film exploited "an indiscriminately available visibility" (89). The official and amateur film shared "a similar locus of public authority" as well as the "objectives of displaying colonial development achievements" (89).[17]

The ethnographic images discussed earlier also bespeak a certain desire to reconstitute (in the still image) and reenact (in the moving image) a certain reality for the viewer, "as if the depicted events reassembled for the spectator were to be made sense of as if the action was happening along an immediate temporal and spatial presence and continuity" (Griffiths 2013, 53). Their form of casualized ethnography may be understood as a powerful assertion of the camera's ability to reveal new truths about unsuspecting subjects. As I will describe below, precisely such an understanding of the camera becomes part of the state's presumption about visualizing and apprehending crime through the cinema. The camera produced certain articulations of detection and unseen surveillance. The Kodak is of course, central to this process. The caught-in-the-act moment was impossible and impracticable in the pre–hand camera days. Photography's use in capturing, indexing, identifying, and classifying criminals went back in India to the 1850s. But for a variety of reasons—the uneducated eye, the untrustworthy native informant, the difficulty of picking out an individual from large batches of images—a naive faith in such uses of photography gave way to the anthropometry of Alphonese Bertillon, adopted erratically in India. The body in "bertillonage" becomes a text. It becomes legible; it speaks itself. But bertillonage too, produced its problems—of cost as well as a classification system that was not necessarily time-efficient. The fingerprint, pioneered in India, replaced photography as the authoritative imprint.[18] But with the potential exception of the fingerprint, common to these organized methods of using photography in criminology was the conscious acquiescence/submission of or potential subversion by the photographed subject. That precondition is annulled with the emergence of snapshot photography. The body that could speak itself is transposed now to ethnography, which can now capture unsuspecting subjects and thus, with the aid of photography, also speak itself into authenticity. How these articulations of detection and unseen surveillance inform the vocabulary of commercial Indian cinema ought to become part of a history of film style in Indian cinema, a history that remains to be told. Such a history might reveal a much deeper seepage of topicality and its spatiotemporal coordinates into the fiction film.

For now, I want to pursue this line of thought in two directions. First, public engagements with visual methods of criminological detection shared the fundamental premises of the casual snapshot ethnographer. This was the belief that the camera could capture what may not be seen by the eye. Second, the history of criminology and its use of the technologies of vision found a much more programmatic expression, not surprisingly, in the early documentaries produced by India's government-run documentary unit, *The Films Division*.

MIMESIS OR EXEMPLARITY? CRIME FILMS AND PHOTOGRAPHS AND THE LEGACY OF TOPICALITY

The promise of fortuitous sightings turned the camera itself into a fetish and the Kino-Eye acquired a generalized authority as a metaphor for the possibilities of acquiring facts and insights that would otherwise be elusive. This faith embodied in the expensive hand camera and its application in everyday life is evident in the peculiar spate of petty thefts of the Kodak camera at the turn of the century and the ways in which those thefts were discovered. In Bombay in 1903, a nineteen-year-old man was arrested after he stole cameras from his friend's photographic store (where he was employed) and sold them to the famous photographic studio of Bourne & Shepherd (henceforth B&S). The employer noticed the cameras that had been stolen from him were now at the B&S studio and realized that his own employee had stolen the cameras and sold them to the studio. A plan was hatched. The conditions for the crime were reconstituted, this time as a trap. B&S placed a preplanned order for cameras from the photographic store. The proprietor of the store dispatched his friend, the suspect, to B&S with the cameras they had ordered. When the suspect arrived, B&S was able to confirm the identity of the man who had sold them the stolen cameras in the earlier instance.[19] Was it a sensibility attuned to the camera eye that understood that replicating the actions that were involved in the crime could lead to the apprehension of the thief?

It would seem so, because the cinema and photography became essential to crime solving. Assassination attempts targeted at British officials drew requests by authorities for any cinematographic and photographic records that might have been taken at the time.[20] Consider the image published in Calcutta's *The Statesman* of a Calcutta street as the scene of a crime, taken with the camera in the middle of the street. "Broad Daylight Dacoity in Calcutta," says the title of the photo. The caption describes the crime: the audacious robbery of 95,000 rupees "snatched" by three men in a motorcar. The photo marks a spot (indicated with a cross) in the foreground. The caption says, "The photograph was taken yesterday at exactly the same hour as the robbery was committed the preceding day. The busy atmosphere of the street demonstrates the thieves' daring." The spot, we are told, "indicates the scene" of the crime. Here the emphasis on the time of day is meant to assure readers that the event occurred at an instant that was unlike those that preceded or followed it. An additional aim would be to ensure that the street looked just exactly as busy as it did that unique instant of the robbery. Both aims necessitate a reenactment of the act of seeing the crime, an act that is now in the past, with a machine that would capture the ideal viewpoint. That viewpoint is predicated on a camera that was absent the previous day. The camera now constructs an idealized, mechanical view that is humanly impossible. This, of course, is part of Walter Benjamin's account of the camera as a reflexive shudder, a shock of an instant that produces an image that replicates the scene but in so doing also reveals the machine at the heart of the visible (see Fig. 5.6).

The "spot" seems too precise to be called a "scene" and it certainly does not cover the portion or area of the street that may have been the scene of the crime. It reduces an area into a point that seems like an attempt at precision that overreaches for its aim. And why is the spot even necessary?

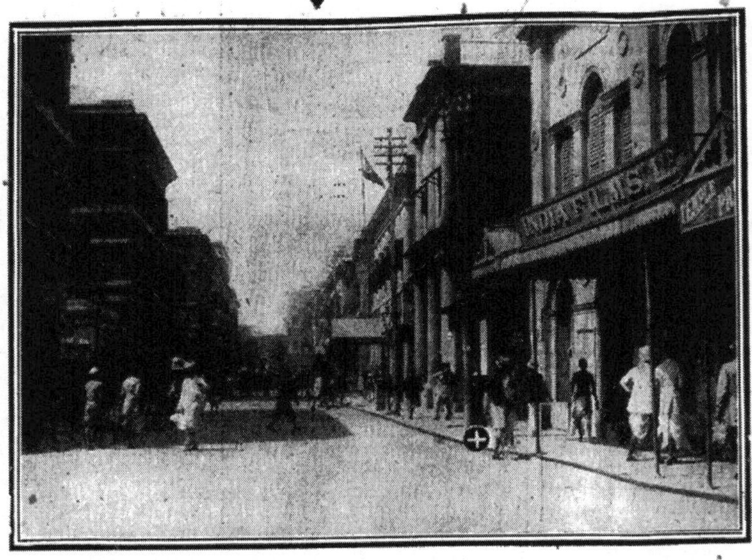

Figure 5.6. "Broad Daylight Dacoity in Calcutta," *The Statesman*, March 3, 1908, 10.

What does it tell us except that something exceptional took place on this perfectly ordinary-looking street a previous day; that all that the photo can do is to indicate where it took place and describe in the caption how it took place. It is one of those delicious historical details that the board of the commercial establishment right by the spot of the robbery says "India Films S. L." Even that is something the human eye might have skipped if not for a retroactive registration by the camera.

If the newspaper banks on its ability to offer visual illustration, the authority of that illustration, indeed its very existence, is necessarily contingent on a reenactment where the human eye is replaced by the camera eye. The authority of the reenactment becomes an important component of the state's utilization of this new technology both for its still and moving image production. Once a record produced at the very moment of the event is no longer permissible because it threatens the stable experience and regulation of time, the state cannot do much other than to reenact its ideal moments.[21] Time exists at a lag for the state. In the case of the still photograph, it arguably bolsters the authority of the camera. The image is consumed in a newspaper, as news.

But when these protocols of collecting and displaying photographic evidence are utilized in the cinema, the duration of a movie and its need to tell a story cancel the forensic power of the camera, replacing it with a melodrama in which the cinema's place is ambiguous and not necessarily authoritative. Such is the case with documentaries produced by the independent Indian state under the aegis of Films Division. I turn to one such documentary.

BLACK SHEEP (1953)

Photography's function as a site for reenactment is ultimately shared by informational movies produced by the colonial as well as postcolonial governments. *Black Sheep* (1953), made not long after independence, captures some of the statist discourses around crime as well as the place of vision in the apprehension of crime. Produced by the Films Division, the movie depicts the indictment of an industrialist who runs a coal factory, the manager of a power works company and their respective male assistants, for corruption. Made shortly after independence, the movie depicts a nation-building period when electricity was rationed as part of a planned economy. The industrialist seeks extra energy for his factory and bribes the manager of the power works company (presumably government-owned, as most major infrastructures were at the time) for more than the allotted supply. A young, idealistic male managerial employee of the corrupt industrialist (one of the few characters to be named as Satish) is witness to the machinations and chooses to collaborate with the police in collecting evidence and eventually jailing the corrupt parties. The bribery of the manager of the power works company by the industrialist (for extra power for his coal plant) takes place on the occasion of the industrialist's daughter's party and is seen by the police surreptitiously (see Fig. 5.7).

The movie's point is made clear in its last scene: if only there were more honest employees who would choose principle over obeisance to corrupt bosses, the police would have a 100 percent success rate with regard to convicting the corrupt. The narrator in that last scene links honesty to the need for law enforcement. He argues that the latter would no longer

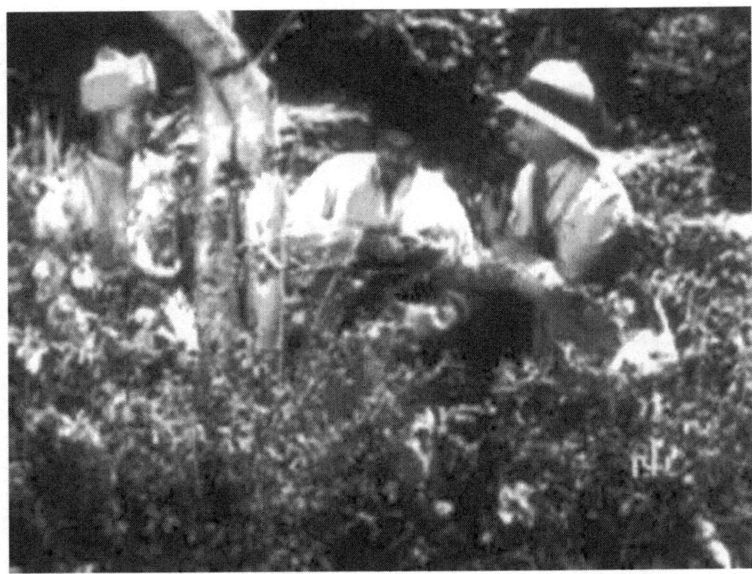

Figure 5.7. The honest employee hides and watches his manager's corruption. Frame from *Black Sheep* (1953, M. Bhavnani, Films Division of India).

be necessary if more people were honest. It concludes with a rhetorical question: "As a taxpayer wouldn't you prefer that?"

Black Sheep is intended to be didactic. As such the movie is narrated in voiceover and the situations described in the narration are enacted almost entirely with no diegetic sound so that the narrator paraphrases exchanges between characters. In the first scene, we see a police officer working at his desk. The narrator tells us that "we want you, all of you" to meet this policeman who works for a special unit of the police and who has a story to tell "us." At this point, the policeman looks up to the camera that presents him frontally to us and hails us as his co-citizenry. "My story is not a pleasant story." But, he says, it is one that happens to all of "us." As he starts to introduce the man whom he calls "the first character in our story," a dissolve takes us to the enactment of the story by characters. The enactment will remain in place through almost all of the film. Only in the last scenes will the policeman return to stand outside of the story as he does in the first scene, and impart a message that explicates the moral system the film wants its viewers to adopt.

The first notable element of this movie, then, is the narration. In this movie, three layers of narration are at work: the biographical author outside the text (in this case, a director working under the aegis of an institution, The Films Division), the voiceover narration within the text that can be considered an author mediating between film and viewer, and the "first person" narration of the policeman who takes over the task of narration. And that's excluding the movie's narration as a process that takes place at the level of form and structure. This is a didactic film produced by the national documentary films unit, the Films Division, an entity inherited from the British and owing its origins in significant measure to Griersonian traditions and indeed to Griersonians such as James Beveridge (Roy 2007; Garga 2007). The trifurcation here reinforces at multiple levels the authority of the narrators, for all of whose roles in this particular film the postcolonial state apparatus is an elementary condition of possibility.

But the story also threatens the ocular powers of these multiply reinforced authorities precisely because of the multilayered narrators. The undermining of the film's sources of authority is evident in the crucial scene in which the police observe the act of bribery, the exchange of cash, from behind the bushes. During trial, the accused argue that there is no "evidence" of an exchange of a box containing a handover of cash. At this point, the narrator says, "our case looked pretty hopeless." It is par for the course for melodrama to enact these sudden reversals. The police's account of events cannot be taken at face value, and the policeman who addressed us at the outset and who is now sitting in court as one of the diegetic characters nearly admits defeat. The dispiriting turn of events is reversed in the next instant when the police produce a witness "whose testimonies would be difficult to refute." The motion picture camera saves the day (Fig. 5.8).

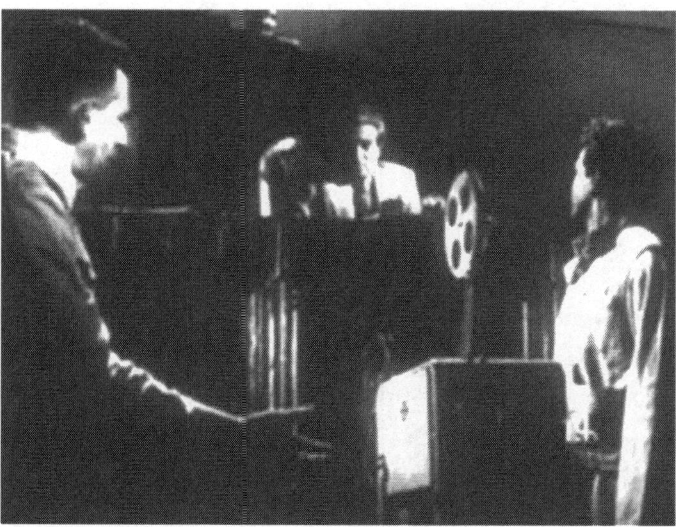

Figure 5.8. The motion picture camera saves the day. Frame from *Black Sheep* (1953, M. Bhavnani, Films Division of India).

The policeman reveals that the exchange was recorded on camera and a projector and screen are wheeled in. A frontal shot of Satish, the whistleblower, wielding a movie camera interrupts the time of the courtroom as a clarifying flashback even though the camera barely registered the act of camera surveillance at the scene of the crime as it actually played out earlier in the movie. The blinds are lowered in the courtroom. The film is projected. This time the narrator observes that "we changed lenses to get a closer view." A medium close-up shows a hand grabbing another person's hand and pulling out a bundle of currency from the pocket (Fig 5.9).

Here, reenactment produces a creative manipulation of an evidentiary record as we see a close-up of the act of apprehension (even though the earlier footage is revealed in long shot). The camera trumps human action: mechanical seeing precedes physical doing. But even the camera is not enough. At the end of the movie, the officer produces a note from the wad of money that exchanged hands as evidence while pointing to the fingerprint of the corrupt manager on the note.

The cinema therefore appears in this movie as an adjunct to more authoritative sources of evidence.[22] Let me also propose that there is something of a quandary that is posed for narration by the enactment of the scenario of corruption. Like the photograph we have encountered earlier, this movie too is a reenactment, a re-staging of what is supposed to occur commonly in everyday life. As such, it is torn between mimesis and exem-

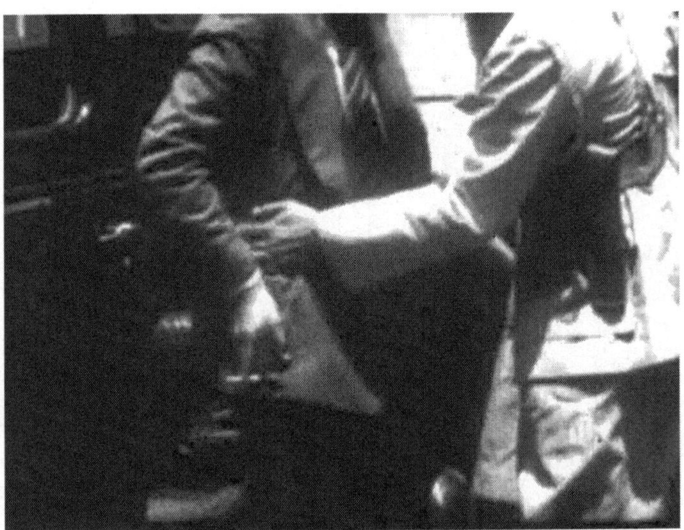

Figure 5.9. The act of human apprehension is edited into what is supposed to be hidden surveillance footage.

plarity. The mimetic part of it is that it aims to confirm a preexisting truth. It is an imitation of a real action. It stands in as evidence for the real. As Ivone Margulies, who proposes this distinction, puts it, such is the case with partial reenactments, say in docudramas, where the reenacted portions are supposed to show what happened as it happened (Margulies 2003). On the other hand, the fully reenacted film aims to exceed the demands of mimetic representation and generate real action. This too is part of the aim of this didactic film: if only there were more of the young honest men who are willing to be whistleblowers, as the narrator rues toward the end. The film's credits make it clear that the characters are imaginary and furthermore, the narrator refers to the people in the drama as characters one, two, and three. This dual compulsion—to let the reenactment stand on its own and on the other hand to ensure that it retains its exemplarity, its exhortative potential—produces a problem for the various levels of voiceover narration when it comes to realism. The narrator often performs his paraphrasing of the conversations that occur, as they are occurring, and with a frequently stilted expressivity to dramatize the scene, acutely calling attention to the enactment.

Another brief moment makes the tension between mimesis and exemplarity evident in the abrupt shift between diegetic and non-diegetic sound. Diegetic sounds are almost entirely absent, except for one odd but telling moment. The exchange of money takes place in the form of a gift-wrapped box, a camouflage for the money given by the industrialist's young daughter to the general manager (and the narrator notes that this is odd because it is the girl's birthday party, not the manager's, and the gift ought to be given by the manager to the girl). But as the industrialist calls for his daughter, we hear the daughter's name shouted out aloud by a voice other than the voice we have heard thus far narrating the story—Pushpa! Pushpa! The timbre of the sound is distinctly different, flat (that is nondimensional), loud, originating in a different ambience, which we now have to accept on faith as the soundscape of the diegetic world. While it is clear this sound too is postsynchronized like the narrator's voice, it is unlike the narrator's in sounding unrehearsed and not sounding as proximate in perspective.

Black Sheep and other public service messages on film (*Fitness First* from 1951 on the need for physical education, *For Your Safety* from 1960 on traffic rules) reveal some discomfort with the principle of self-evidence because it threatens to undermine the authority of the state as narrator. In these films, the utilization of reenactment as a dramatic strategy reinforces the "authenticating aura" of the medium of the cinema (Margulies, 220). But what is it that is being authenticated here? The credulity earned by the movie or fantasized by the state depends for its efficacy not so much on the image's ontology as on the narrative community's amenability to the epistemology produced by the state. Yet, these films are very much the product, albeit ambivalently, of the cinema's emergence as a powerful medium of communication and expression, one that occurred alongside the rise of the mass photographic image in its snapshot and printed form. If the cinema supplied the implicit duration and movement to the still image, it also reenacted the still image's punctuated authority.

In the next chapter, I want to examine a range of discourses and texts that enable us to put together a picture of the cinema's place in urban life. The ethnographic images of the woman in front of the camera and the men collected around the gramophone also produce an implicit narrative around modernity. How did the cinema's presence in public life signal an engagement with this urban modernity? The same images also point to the imagined communities shaped by visual images. *The Times of India's Illustrated Weekly* did not simply present ethnographic curiosities. It also explicitly imagined a normative public sphere in the Habermasian sense in, for instance, the photograph of the reader of the newspaper. Were other imaginations of a public culture possible at the time, and to what extent do these imaginations straddle multiple media?

6

POLITICS ACROSS MEDIA

· ◆ ——— ◆ ·

The Partition of Bengal (1905) and the Cinematic City

How did the cinema participate in the event, affect and significance of urban life? How, in other words, could the cinema produce a variant understanding of the public sphere, one quite distinct from the playground of the European amateur photographer and photojournalist that I have discussed in the preceding chapter?

Against the backdrop of the first major moment of nationalist mass mobilization against British rule starting from 1905, this chapter follows the interface between film, print and photography as it weaves its way in and out of urban politics. Of course, any consideration of urbanism and the cinema in the early twentieth century must also acknowledge the relation between cinema and the experience of modernity (on which more below). Thus, we have a constellation of issues that come together in this chapter: the emergence of the "mass image" in newspaper photojournalism, amateur photography and the topical film; the role of this intermedia constellation in engaging urban life and politics; and the nature of the modernity that is being shaped and experienced in this historical moment. My aim here is to return the discussion of cinema and modernity to a contextually specific framework, in this case that of the political history of nationalism.

My method here is speculative; with no singly defined grouping of images. I stitch a somewhat filigreed network of interactions between media and public spaces. In some cases, I follow events as they move from one medium to another. In others, the more general political and social contexts allow me to trace connections between media. While the shared subject matter between a movie and a halftone is the more literal of the mediated transferences that occur in the process of turning the everyday into the mass image, this chapter also seeks to capture the phenomenology of the experience of modernity within which the cinema became so central.

There is a strong formal component in film studies discussions around cinema's relation to modernity. The cinema did not just share subject matter—that of the experience of modern life—with the media of its time (such as print journalism). As a medium, it emblematized the perceptual-social experience of modernity in its formal mechanisms, and this aspect has been absolutely central to the critical theory and urban sociology that have informed film studies' engagement with this question. Prima facie, British India, and Calcutta as its most important city at the start of the twentieth century, were no exception to the phenomenological dimensions of modernity as already extensively outlined by other scholars. Nor are critical theory and urban sociology paradigms (the Frankfurt School, Walter Benjamin, Georg Simmel) irrelevant in the Indian context.

In making mention of this intellectual framework, I'm following the lead of Zahid Chaudhary (2012) whose discussion of nineteenth-century European photography in India draws centrally on Walter Benjamin and Maurice Merleau-Ponty to describe how photography operated for the European eye. Chaudhary argues that the highly conventionalized images produced by the British in India (the picturesque landscape, the paranoid ethnographic image, the archaeological ruin, the postcard memorabilia of famous battles fought by the British in India) served the function of turning India into a modern phantasmagoria for the British. The conventions such as the picturesque functioned akin to habit, filtering sublime and uncanny experiences of India through the comfort of repetitive convention. Following Chaudhary's lead, the last chapter searched for a cinematic imaginary in the still photographic image by attending as much to the form of the photographic image as to the phenomenology of the photographic experience.

The cinema catalyzed the printed photograph and snapshot, revealing itself as a potent ally that subsists in the still image as virtuality, and the still image in turn supplied the authority of its stasis to the reenactments of the moving image. If the snapshot produced instantaneous time, the cinema endowed that instant with the potential for dynamic movement. Images of actions, of natural and mechanical processes, of matter in motion, abound in the newspapers of early-twentieth-century India. Examples include images of the welding of rail lines producing flying sparks captured by the camera, the serialized depiction of a building being built from foundation to completion, the depiction of disastrous fires in the city, and so on (see Fig. 6.1 and Fig. 6.2).

However, there is also much that prevents any wholesale application of modernity theory as a hermeneutic to non-Western locations. Leo Ou-Fan Lee's observations on Shanghai's encounter with modernity apply in large part to Calcutta as well. Both cities were more culturally hybrid than Paris, given the European presence. This produced a complex situation for

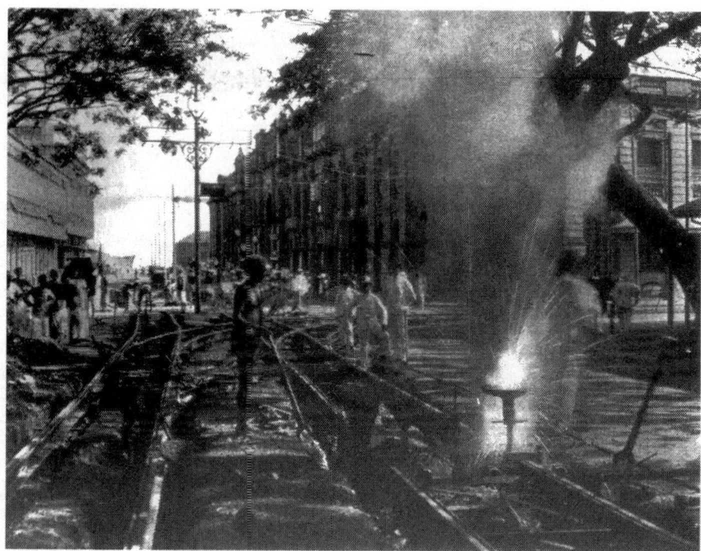

Figure 6.1. "Prize photo: Welding rail joints on the Colombo Electric Tramway. The Photograph was exposed, developed and printed and in no way was worked over by hand," *Illustrated Weekly of India*, May 2, 1906.

Europeans and non-Europeans: "mixed company but separate lives bound together by the infrastructure of urban life" (Ou Fan-Lee, 6) that resulted in the uneven experience of the institutions and emblems of modern life, depending on whose life was at stake. In both cities, although perhaps less so in Calcutta, modernization occurred at a rapid pace in a condensed period of time, quite unlike Europe's long encounter with not one but two revolutions (industrial and communications) over a longer period of time. In Shanghai, intellectuals lacked the detachment and "reflective mentality" of the flâneur because they were enamored of "lights, heat and reflection" (39) and walking for them was an act of traversing the lived space of the city (and not a fine art). In India, Sandra Frietag (2002) has contended that as nationalism saw mass mobilization, it was the politically engaged "processionist," not the solitary flâneur, who embodied movement through urban space. And the absence of the street walker in Benjamin's account is a critical lacuna one must take seriously because it has bearing for locations such as Shanghai, Bombay, or Calcutta as well. Finally, in Shanghai, the movie theaters, dance halls, and cafés became the alternatives to traditional Chinese entertainment since arcades in the Benjaminian mode were out of reach for Chinese intellectuals. In Calcutta, as we shall see, the cinema spilled out into public space and drew selectively from that space to define its functions, which exceeded that of entertainment.

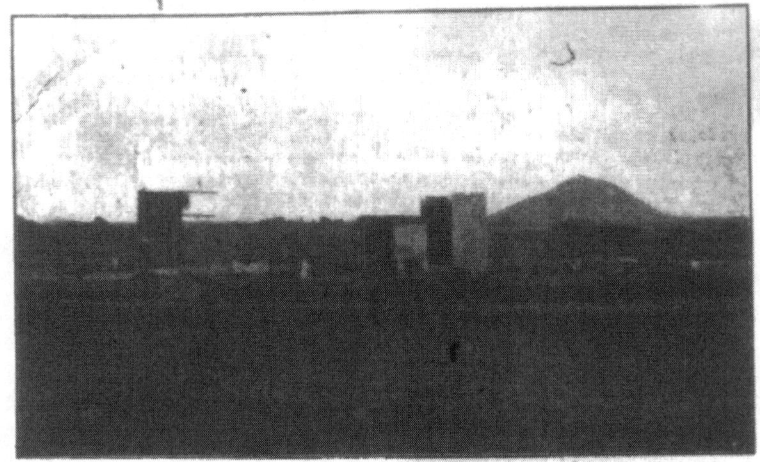

BUILDING OPERATIONS SOON AFTER COMMENCEMENT.

The construction of the bungalow seen in these photographs, was undertaken by Messrs. Marsland, Price and Co., of Mazagon, on the reinforced concrete system throughout including the flat concrete roof, and serves as an excellent instance of the rapidity with which the work by this system can be carried out.

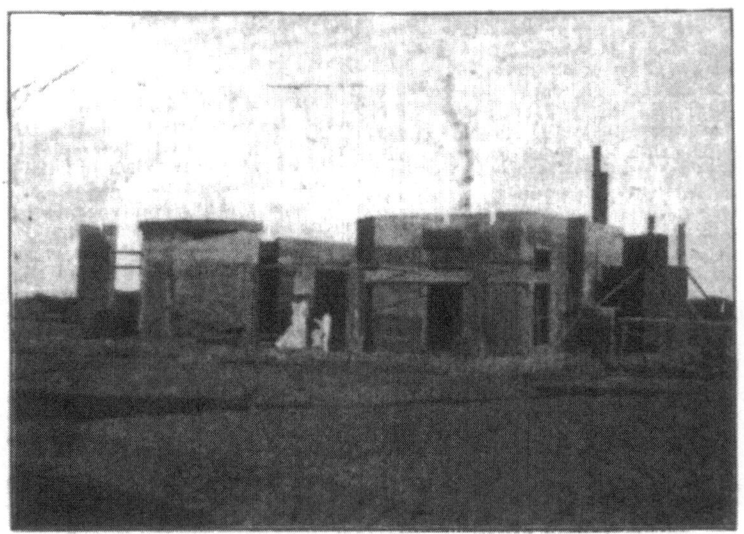

A FORTNIGHT AFTER.

This photo was taken when for the most part the main walls were set up.

Figure 6.2. "Rapid Housebuilding in Nasik," *Illustrated Weekly of India*, September 16, 1906.

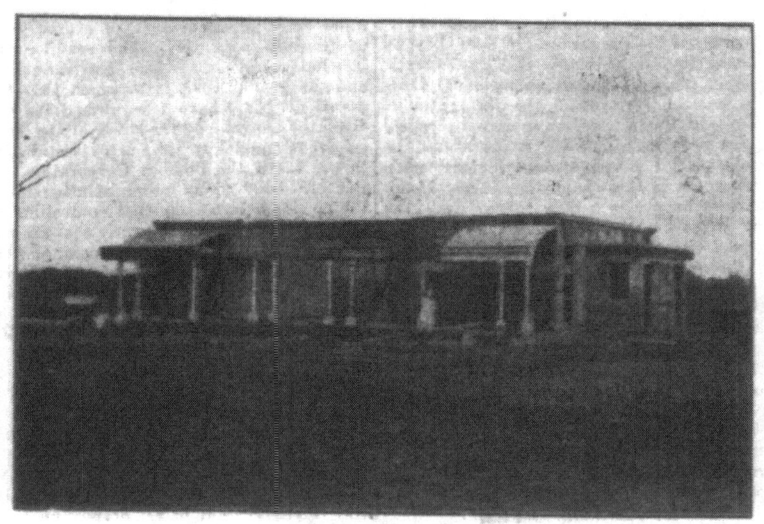

THE THIRD STAGE

Photo taken five weeks from the commencement, when the walls were finished, and the roof was on.

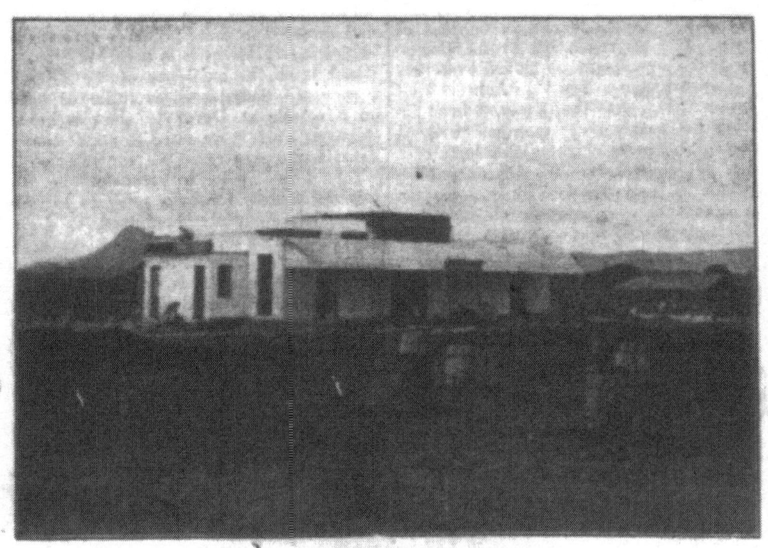

THE COMPLETED BUNGALOW.

This last photo was taken when the bungalow was practically complete with the exception of the finishing touches and the fitting of the window-frames and doors, which were all ready to go in.

This bungalow which had been erected in three months, comprises a centre room 28ft., by 16ft., with two bedrooms on each side 20ft. by 16ft and bathrooms to each.

Figure 6.2. *Continued.*

Lee's emphasis on urban life and the experience of modernization as a shared infrastructure obviates the need to posit two distinct modernities that are culturally separated. The thrill of rapid movement and the delight of a heightened mobility of vision enabled by the bicycle and the hand camera were expressed by European amateur photographers, and the aerial views of the city that appeared in English-language newspapers transformed lived space into the abstract vision of the concept city. At the same time, however, the sensations experienced by the urban laborer welding tramlines against fiery sparks, the explosions of anarchist bombs directed at the British, and the new possibilities of collecting and moving through urban space en masse also constituted the experience of modernity. And as in China, the visual culture that emerges at this moment is a "technologically and culturally mediated" vernacular that blurs distinctions between various media even as it foregrounds the shared urban infrastructure within which political and cultural distinctions were shaped (Zhang 2005, 3).

A preliminary example illuminates the extent to which various screen practices and forms of imaging combined to produce a vision of urban space. A report published in the *Times of India* of Bombay in February 1900 described Lord Northcote's arrival to the city of Bombay on Febuary 17, 1900, as the newly appointed British governor of Bombay province.[1] In the account, the narrator travels through the streets of South Bombay, passing one urban landmark after another and recording his observations of the crowds gathered to welcome the new governor.

The report encapsulates the central concerns of this chapter. How did technologies of vision transform perceptions of urban space? In this transformation, how did the cinema emerge and play a role as a topically relevant medium in India? And how specifically did its affinities to other media, particularly print and photography, ensure the embedding of the medium in everyday life?

The author of the report lists ideal viewpoints for the procession and describes his own changing perspective on the crowds gathered to celebrate the arrival of the new governor as he traverses through those viewpoints. An evolving view of the city emerges through the description, one that combines the anecdotal with the topographical in the manner of the composited panoramas of battle scenes in the nineteenth century that combined close details of the battle with broad views of the setting and scale of action. As Allison Griffiths observes, the composited panorama resonates with the medium of film and the possibilities of editing (Griffiths 2013, 44, 55).

> The verandahs of the Bunder Road were full of spectators. Handkerchiefs were waved and hats raised as the party passed. The Sailor's Home had its flags, and the Wellington Foundation decorations was [sic] still more interesting. It was covered

with natives . . . thrilled with the portentousness of the whole
thing. The bend of the road towards the Oval was a great stand-
point. . . . Turning up by the Corporation buildings, a still greater
display of bunting came into view, and across the road appeared
a cloth bearing the inscription "Welcome to Lord Northcote."

Enter the cinema.

A cinematograph in a shop halfway down the road to the delight
of the bystanders had been made to play "God Save the Queen,"
and the operator beamed with delight to hear the brightness of
his idea praised.

It is unclear if what is being described is a cinematograph or a gramophone.
Regardless, the currency of the cinema was enough to produce a man with
a movie camera in the midst of an urban spectacle. This telling detail is
followed by still further descriptions of the immersive and encompassing
viewpoints in the language of the panorama, invoking scale, co-presence
and virtual travel. As the procession climbed up Bombay's Malabar Hill,

rising gradually, the view became more and more beautiful until
it burst forth at last like a magnificent panorama. Far to the left
the great city unfolded itself like a map, its huge buildings faintly
outlined in the distance through smoke and mist shrouding its
toiling thousands. In front of Back Bay glimmered in the sunlight,
which yet had failed to dissipate the vapors that gauzelike hung
over it. Who would say, looking at these rich gardens and green
trees relieving the solidity of the architecture that this was the
Bombay of famine? Who would say that in a scene so lovely
there could be such loathsomeness and misery, as plague?

The aerial vision gives full expression to a "human geography" in
which human elements of this encompassing vision become surface phenomena, a part of an urban geography. The ecstatic perceptions thrown up
by the writer's technologized perception of space see city and crowd as an
organic whole, emerging in time. We might consider this to be the sublime
counterpart to the rationalist, weaponized view from above that became
part and parcel of aerial photography in the early twentieth century (see
Amad 2012).

The adjectives used here amplify a poetics of real time and change: rising, bursting forth, unfolding, shrouding, and glimmering. Notably, the city
as urban space and spectacle and as cartographic concept emerges through
the combined work of panoramic, cinematic, and cartographic visions. This

intermedial vision that we might be tempted to see as a perfect replay of now familiar historical narratives around modernity and the cinema ends, however, in a dramatic reversal. The city as spectacle runs up against the harsh reality of the city as a documented space of famine and deathly plague. The cinema had a role to play in both kinds of cities. In what follows, I want to trace the emergence of a politicized public sphere, first in the European subcultures of amateur photography and then more generally in newspaper photojournalism and in the cinema, but against the backdrop of a modernizing city.

CINEMA AND URBAN SPACE: FROM IMPERIAL RITUAL TO NATIONALIST POLITICS

Two years after the Delhi Durbar, in 1905, Bengal was partitioned into East and West Bengal. East Bengal comprised a predominantly Muslim peasantry, and the partition was viewed in retrospect in nationalist historiography as a classic example of British divide-and-rule administrative rationalities that ultimately pitted Hindus and Muslims as communities with divergent and competing interests vis-à-vis the state. The partition provoked a vigorous backlash in Calcutta and the agitation against partition launched the Swadeshi movement, a form of economic nationalism meant to promote Indian industry by boycotting goods of British manufacture. This movement was the first major attempt at mass mobilization by the nationalist Indian National Congress and would lead to many others.

If the amateur private European photographer seemed blissfully removed from the emerging political scenarios, his bicycle excursions with his cameras, however, captured the impending drama. New photographic technologies, the modernizing city, and the state's role in this process came together in dramatic ways that would later be picked up by the cinema. Snapshot photography, even through the eyes of "Eurasians" (another contemporary word for Europeans who were born and lived in India), tokenized the fissures in the imperial body politic in India. Consider an example that encapsulates two major preoccupations for the British, both administratively and scientifically: technology and natural disasters. How these preoccupations were visualized says as much about the enabling technologies as the subject matter of the visualizations themselves. One of the first essays illustrated with halftones was published in *The Journal of the Photographic Society of India* (*JPSI*) and described a natural disaster, the earthquake of July 1897 that hit vast regions of Bengal, including Calcutta, then the capital of British India. The earthquake became the occasion for the photographer to reflect on much more than solely the natural disaster, for the article was titled "The recent disturbances seismic and social in Bengal." An illustrated catalogue of devastation and ruin coupled with social unrest, the article began with a description of the destruction of colonial bungalows in Darjeeling, a verdant tea plantation hill station north of Calcutta. The first halftone accompanying the article is simply a view of a devastated bedroom in Annandale House. Subsequent images were more dramatic as the writer described his train journey through the earthquake-stricken zone while drawing on Jules Verne–like imagery:

> The train I travelled by being one of the first to run through [the devastated area], did not attempt to run in this part, but crawled: and as the line in some places was like a switchback railway, with the additional variety of one rail being often higher than the other, the traveler experienced on a smaller scale the sensation of pitching and rolling at sea, while the gaping cracks on either side made one (one at least) feel as if at any moment the train might drop through on a voyage of discovery to the earth's interior.[2]

Armed with a photo-jumelle[3] and a stand camera, the photographer sought to capture the huge cracks in the earth at various railway stations along his train route in Bengal, and the image that accompanies such a description is a wide-angle view of a railway station. A split in the ground runs from the extreme right of the foreground of the image all the way to a vanishing point in the center of the background of the image, with clusters of men standing and squatting all along the right side of the split. A portion of the train juts into the frame on the left, also receding to meet the split in the rear. Technology and natural disaster meet in the image in the receding point of the image[4] (see Fig. 6.3).

After describing one more image (of a fractured bridge), the article moves into a different territory altogether: that of the social and political unrest in Calcutta. The shock of the initial earthquake had been followed by numerous tremors, we are told, and a prediction that more would follow:

> And sure enough their fears were justified in Calcutta . . . only this time the disturbances were not seismic but social, and one of their effects had been, with something analogous to the "Expulsive power of a new affection," to drive thoughts of the earthquake out of the heads of those who are not too painfully kept in mind of it by the dilapidated condition of their houses.[5]

What exactly was the cause of this "expulsive power"? A tiled hut used by Muslims for prayer on Barrackpore Road in Calcutta had been marked for demolition because the land belonged to the government. Opponents had promptly sought to rebuild the mosque even bigger than its original size, had been arrested for doing so, and the demolition had resumed. Clashes ensued. "The rioters derived much help from the recent earthquake which bountifully

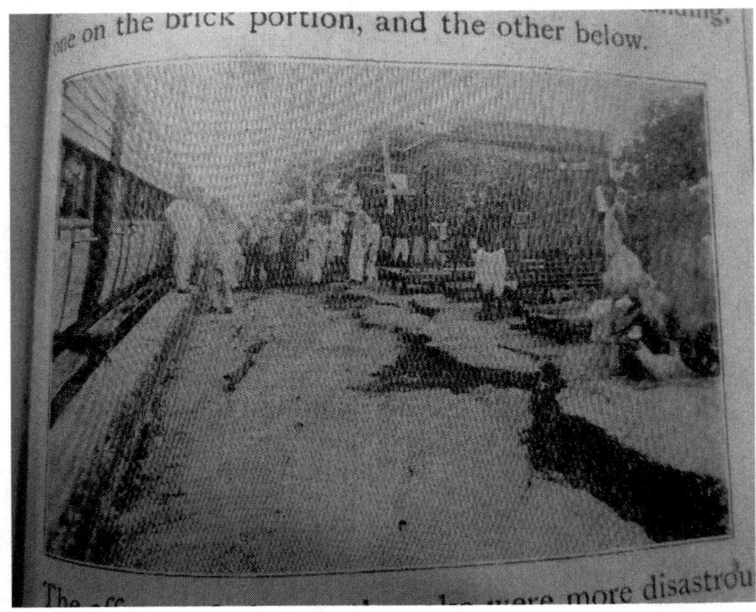

Figure 6.3. The convergence of technology and natural disaster. "The recent disturbances social and seismic in Calcutta," *Journal of the Photographic Society of India*, Calcutta, Aug. 1897, 352–53 Courtesy Asiatic Society of Bengal, Kolkata.

supplied them with brick bats: these they used more valiantly in attacking the carriages of European ladies and gentlemen who had occasion to pass along the streets of the northern part of the town on the evening of the 30th June."[6] Subsequent to the riots, the photographer-author visited the site of the disturbances and took a photograph of the demolished mosque, a view from a considerable distance of a tall pile of rubble of rafters and brick with the small figure of a man in the foreground. He concludes: "I should have liked to get a few representative rioters into the picture, and though there were some Mohamedans looking on sulkily from round corners, I did not care to invite them into the picture for fear that I might be guilty of inciting a riot."[7]

In these four photographs, an amateur European photographer achieves a visual and semantic equivalence between social unrest and natural disaster. From the initial photograph of the destruction of a domestic space to those of railway stations and bridges to finally the riots around a demolished mosque, all become signs of disaster and all were indicative of the capacious and metonymic nature of the gaze that tied these varied events to each other. In the process, both natural disaster and social unrest become subsets of a more general sense of a geography in turmoil. But this abstraction conveyed in an often tongue-in-cheek and occasionally sarcastic tone also obfuscates the dramatic nature and specific political contexts of the essay's linkages, as well as the portents of more trouble to follow in coming years, in particular the partition and the protests that followed.

The agitation against partition inaugurated new modes of protest, involving newly visible and audible forms of political expression. The Indian National Association, the first avowedly nationalist organization, organized meetings in Calcutta, and attendance exceeded expectations and ran into the thousands. The date of the partition, October 16, 1905, served as occasion for the closure of places of commerce such as bazaars, fish markets, public baths. Spontaneous demonstrations and planned processions became increasingly part of the theatrics of the agitation. Authorities were acutely aware of the political resonance of noise and restricted political expression. In response, nationalist organizers produced tactical pairings of political conduct and physical movement designed to circumvent prohibitions. For example, the Swadeshi movement's rallying cry, *Bande Mataram*, was prohibited on the streets in one instance. But organizers interpreted the prohibition as applying only to dry land. As waves of protesters headed to a protest location by boat, they chanted slogans on the ferry en route to that location, while staying silent once on shore.[8]

Property and public space, therefore, including the spaces of entertainment, became sites where the project of modernizing Calcutta into something closer to its European counterparts met with resistance. By the second decade, the process of Calcutta's urbanization was linked to the aspiration to transform Calcutta into the "second city" of empire, following London. Warehouses of businesses were encroaching upon and spoiling promenades such as Strand Road, complained the gentry. Open spaces, rather than being used as gardens, were being converted at a rapid pace into football grounds whose barricades would now display "lurid pictorial advertisements." Or they were being transformed by the erection of shops, private clubs, movie theater tents, and skating rinks.[9]

The cinema was an important element of this process of urbanization. The Calcutta Corporation leased land in a prime location for erecting a Bioscope theater to J. F. Madan, the most influential and powerful of the motion picture companies at the time, a move that was resented both in the corporation proceedings and in the press.[10]

These transformations of older spaces of elite leisure (promenades and gardens) into crowded spaces of commerce and urban entertainment signaled changes in other respects as well. Roads were tarred for the first time. Motorbuses were introduced. Tramlines were installed. The postal service was modernized and individual postboxes were assigned to each business. Real estate speculators were in plenty. Grand commercial buildings and sumptuous flats replaced the older neoclassical-style houses of the sort we have encountered in Jadunath Sarkar's reminiscences. These new constructions provoked concerns of the eventual bursting of the real estate bubble, concerns that at the same time were tinged with pride that the "city of palaces" was finally being drawn into the logic of a healthy capitalist instinct.[11]

As buildings were being torn down and the earth dug up, occluded history could occasionally surface as hierophany, a manifestation of the sacred (Ricoeur 1995, 49–50), and pose a challenge to the transformation of the city. Thus, in the middle of Calcutta's property boom, a slum had been torn down because the land was sold to a man of the Marwari community (a merchant community from the Northwest, currently the state of Rajasthan, that had settled in Calcutta). The new owner, who was a Hindu, wished to set up a school on the site. Two large snakes emerging simultaneously and ominously from the loose earth scared the workers digging the ground of the slum. The crowd that congregated, however, found in place of the snakes a stone tablet with Arabic inscriptions in memory of a descendant of the Prophet who had died on that spot 218 years before. A Muslim mendicant "appeared on the scene and assumed charge of what he regarded as the shrine of a great saint and began to decorate the spot with flowers and perform religious rites." While the mendicant had to be charged with criminal trespass and arrested, an investigation revealed that the land was originally known as Fakir-katakia, a resort for mendicants and beggars, and had been a Muslim burial ground.[12]

The process of modernization and the turmoil of the nationalist movement that had been engendered in the preceding decade justified outlawing various aspects of urban public life, such as public religious acts. At the local level, the concern over the Muslim riots published in the aforementioned article from the *JPSI* was a result of what Sumanta Banerjee terms "the structural criminalization of the public sphere" in India by the turn of the century (Banerjee 2006, 112). That in turn meant criminalizing public gatherings of people as potentially unruly mobs threatening peace. The newspapers of the 1890s are rife with references to riots by Muslims, and sporadic bursts of violence directed at the state apparatus by crowds of people that often included non-Muslims as well. The "snapshotting" of a riot by the Eurasian photographer ought to be seen therefore as an interlacing of technologies of vision, urban planning, and state control and not just as a marginally amateur hobby with fortuitous and dramatic results.

In retrospect, it seems difficult to untangle visual culture and entertainment from political violence, natural disasters, or public health crises. These seem linked, even if in some instances only circumstantially. The circumstantial links are worth noting, with one brief example, that of reports of news from Calcutta for readers of the Bombay newspaper *The Times of India*. By the end of the first decade of the twentieth century, news from Calcutta seemed a bizarre combination of complaints about dull entertainment pickings and dramatic political violence. Calcutta had become a hotbed of political radicalism, or a "seditionist center," as one report put it (see Fig. 6.4).

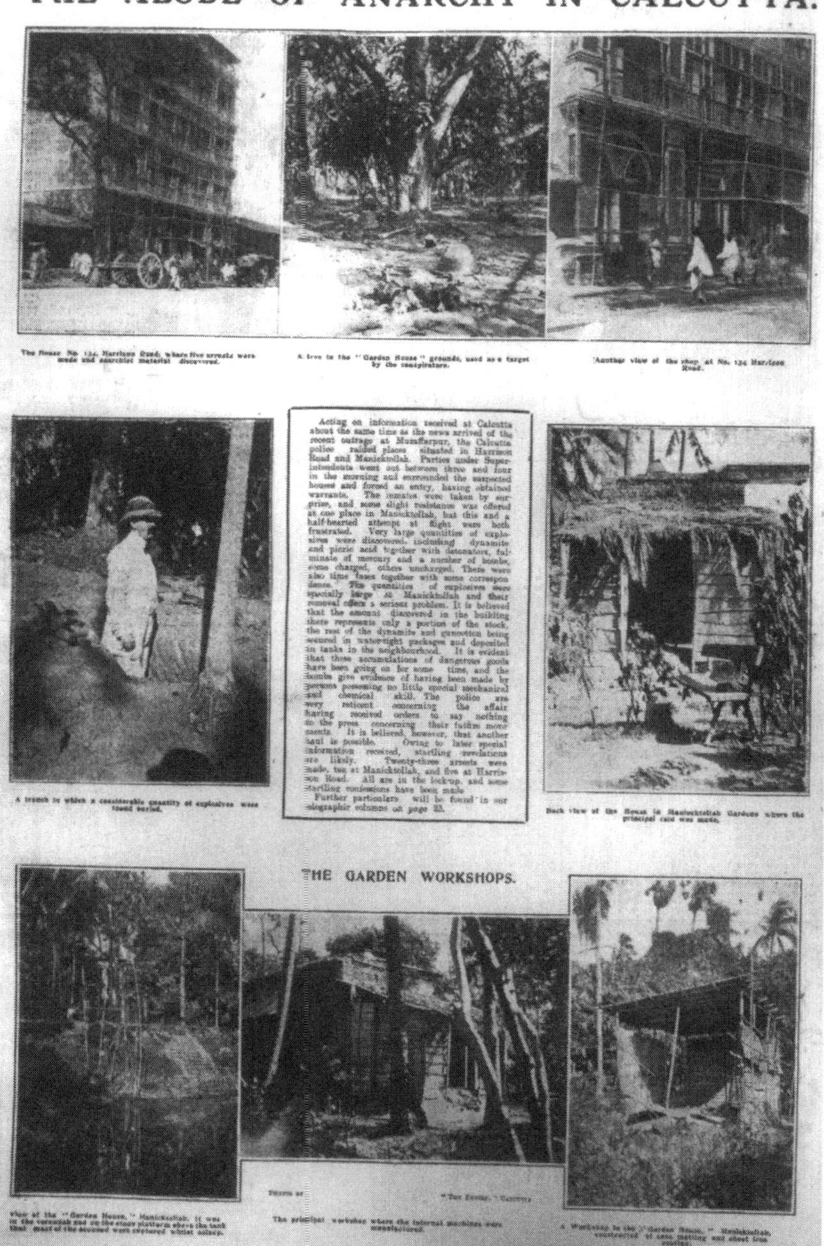

Figure 6.4. "The abode of anarchy in Calcutta," *Illustrated Weekly*, May 13, 1908.

Frequent assaults on Europeans were being reported and "the native press [was] bound the sure and certain road to confiscation with their war songs, reviling, and incitements to violence."[13] Such observations shared column space with reports of "practice riot scares" designed to test the Calcutta police's ability to suppress political activity. And the same column also included laments about the paucity of dramatic societies in Calcutta (ascribed to Calcutta's social caste system). The column concluded with the following observation: "In the meantime our after dinner amusements are practically limited to Cinematographs and Gramophones."[14] Theatrical and cinematic entertainment drew on the increased scales of photographic production enabled by the halftone, promising halftone pictures of scenes from their productions as souvenirs for members of the audience.[15] Newspapers carried illustrated supplements separately for sale. Some were prepared by U. Ray, the art filmmaker Satyajit Ray's grandfather and a pioneer in halftone. One notice advertised the notable figures that would appear in such a supplement, mentioning by name representatives of two domains of public life: a famous actress and nationalist figures.[16]

CINEMA AND THE STANDARDIZATION OF TIME

The imbrication of entertainment and politics continued apace and intensified as the partition protests gained steam. The year 1905 was significant for another reason. Ritika Prasad (2013) notes that it was the year when a standard railway time in relation to the Greenwich Meridian Time became operational in India. The first train had run in India in 1853 and by 1905, approximately 250 million people used the railroad. Indians grappled with railroad time in various ways, as it was integral to the experiential dimensions of colonial modernity. Prasad shows that the standardization of time evoked varied responses among Indians—from a celebration of temporal acceleration to a lament about the loss of the experiential dimensions of travel at a nonmechanized pace, to the emphasis on punctuality by leaders such as Gandhi himself (even as Gandhi shunned industrialization and saw the railways as part of the problem).

The adoption of railway time in civic life, combined with the arrival of cinema, produced a significant shared priority between entertainment and other aspects of political and social life predicated on mass mobilization: an appreciation of the instrumentalization of public time. Preorganized events rallied people into political crowds or paying audiences, into tactical communities or transient consumers. The temporal attribute of meeting at a preassigned time binds the cinema as a timed program to the political protests of the period. Thus, the date of the partition, October 16, became an event to be commemorated, with protests on its anniversaries organized in advance by virtue of being announced in advance.

Entertainment cultures likewise participated in this form of timekeeping. For example, theatrical entertainment served a palliative function in light of the plague of 1902, or so claimed the Classic Theater in 1902 in newspaper notices for its productions. Those notices invited audiences to measure the day in terms of time spent inside the theater away from the contagion of the plague.[17] "To be forewarned is to be fore armed. Plague is in our midst, the season is bad and the only preventive is hilarity and play. Midday performance serves the purpose of amusement thoroughly and as the whole affair finishes before midnight, it will as well serve well the purpose keeping fresh both the mind and the body."[18]

There were, of course, more literal transferences between entertainment and politics, transferences that were technological and as with our previous examples, having to do with the eventfulness of public life. Dramatic political events migrated between film, photography, and print media, sometimes completing each other's functions. English reporters took back with them cinematograph pictures to illustrate their remarks on the "insurrectionary districts" of Bengal but were asked by authorities to suppress them.[19] Bengal partition cartoons were being advertised in newspapers for sale as illustrated booklets: Swadeshi and Boycott depicted "in most humorous, witty and telling cartoons," announced one notice.[20] Swadeshi politics marked many moving picture shows. Perhaps the sullen Mohamedan in the photo-illustrated essay discussed above may have taken part in political activity himself, and if so, the cinema as well as newspaper photojournalism would have covered it. The Classic Theater's shows were advertised as being "under the patronage of the Swadeshi leaders" and in aid of the Swadeshi movement. Hiralal Sen (1866–1917), one of the first Indian filmmakers, filmed the massive demonstrations and protests that followed in the wake of viceroy Lord Curzon's decision to partition Bengal in 1905 into East and West Bengal (Rajadhyaksha and Willemen 1994, 210). In addition, another contemporary film exhibitor in Calcutta, The Elphinstone Bioscope Company, also organized screenings of the demonstrations, which were advertised in *The Statesman* in September 1905. The notice went:

> On account of uncommon rush the Company have decided to send the original negative Film of Bengal Partition procession to Messrs. Gaumont & Company, London and have kept the positive for the next candle light performance on Sunday, 21st September 1905. . . . For one night only The Great Partition Movement Monster Meeting at the Town Hall. . . . The Grand

Demonstrative Procession on Bioscope Worked by Electricity . . . 12 Selected Pieces from Different Plays. (Ray Chaudhury,
1992)

These films of major political protest and turmoil have unfortunately
not survived, but their import is clear: they conflated movement in multiple
senses of the term. The films were registrations of incipient nationalism in
the form of moving images. Movement was involved at another level as well,
in the political mobilization of the gaze of the protesters who were taking
part in processions coursing through public space. To recall Sandra Frietag's
observation, these processions offer a model of the urban and mobile gaze
quite unlike that of the flâneur whose key attribute is detachment. Street
processions became effective modes of mass mobilization, both for explicitly
political purposes and for seemingly religious festivals that were occasions for
nationalist political activity. If the Delhi Durbar film and illustrated souvenir
showed how recorded time could mutate in form into graphic matter on the
pages of a book, to be read in leisure time, the Hiralal Sen and Bioscope
company's films showed how events in real time were transformed into moving image spectacles of recorded time. The snapshot photographer empties
the gaze of his Muslim counterparts of substantive political content by simply
noting their sullen stares, as we saw in the preceding chapter. Hiralal Sen's
and the Elphinstone Bioscope Company's films of the processions, on the
other hand, record the mobilization of those stares in the form of a procession
through urban space. The motion pictures conferred movement and captured
events the state would not have approved, such as riots or mass mobilizations.

Can we see images of masses and crowds as metonymic of those that
gathered inside the movie theater? Masses, gatherings, and crowds are important and recurrent elements of still and moving images of the time. Masses
both represent and constitute a problem, sometimes at the logistical level,
for representation. Are they emblematic of colonial power? Are they indexes
of anticolonial resistance? Are they measures of the vitality of a normative
public sphere posited by authorities? In the snapshot of the lone Muslim in
the "social and seismic disasters" essay discussed earlier, the mass of bricks
behind him enables us to measure scale: his diminution relative to the
destroyed structure. But the mass of bricks also echoes a different kind of
mass, that of the riotous and frightful mob of which the aggrieved Muslim
is implicitly posited as emblematic. The mass of bricks is what Gustave Le
Bon would call a crowd symbol (Brill 2006). Other figurations of masses
emerge in the images: the political procession in the Hiralal Sen film, the
organized masses of soldiers in the Delhi Durbar films, the casual onlookers
in the bicycle photography article. For the film historian, images of masses
concretize the possibility of envisioning a cinematic public.

A distinctive aspect of film exhibition in South Asia was its form of enterprise that sought to reach dispersed, niche audiences as part of the culture of traveling picture showmen. In this case, the exceptionality of South Asian film history hinges on the frequent and longstanding ability of the cinema to escape the customary patterning of its enterprise around the regularized congregation of its audience, and to instead travel to those audiences in their dispersed and temporary locations. The movie audience becomes not an indifferent mass but a multitude of "multiple singularities" (Hardt 2006, 35).

But in urban areas, audiences were imagined differently. Where the traveling showman sought a dispersed viewership, an urban exhibitor enumerated the cinema crowd in relation to the cost of infrastructure. The link between movies and industrial labor, both involving masses, is indicated in an article on air-cooling systems that makes incidental reference to movie theaters. The article notes that the cost of operating an air-cooling system in cinema theaters would be 1.5 annas per person in a half-filled movie theater. The article only makes this single reference to the cinematograph in its discussion of new air-cooling systems and their impact on worker efficiency.[21]

The cinema's palliative function in gathering crowds indoors as opposed to the fraught plague- and pandemic-ridden urban spaces outdoors has also been noted earlier. This palliative function implicates the cinema as an institution that disciplines access to public space. This discourse was evident even in the traveling exhibitions, as with the exhibitor we encountered in chapter 2 who testified before the Cinematograph Committee that masses could be easily made to view films under any circumstances outside of permanent exhibition structures. A discourse of control thus permeates the rhetoric of flexible spectatorship even when voiced by Indian entrepreneurs.

Authorities saw things differently. They saw movie audiences as impressionable masses whose exposure to the movies—especially American ones—risked undermining British authority and the image of European culture in India. The movie hall, far from being an instrument of hegemony, was a space of regulatory concern (Dass 2004, 2009; Mazzarella 2009). Yet its relation to what was outside of it in the street was neither continuous nor disjunctive. It was the function of specific circumstances in specific contexts. If the purchase of time, privacy inside the theater, and reprieve from the elements were features of early film culture in the West, the purchase of space outside of the theater was also an essential element of film culture. In that sense, it is not the text that allows us to extrapolate the mass audience; it is the latter that constructs the cinema (Thiessen 2012). Precisely for this reason, I find the extensive images of crowds in photographs of the period particularly beguiling as metonymic and interlocked pieces of a historical picture puzzle that, put together, enable us to visualize the audiences discussed extensively in the Cinematograph Committee report.

The cinematic audience emerges in various ways and sometimes in passing. For instance, a postindependence Films Division documentary from 1970 titled *Jalianwala Bagh* uses temporally indeterminate or even anachronistic stock footage of crowds at political events from the preindependence era.[22] In the documentary, a reference to the Delhi Durbar of 1911 includes a brief shot of dignitaries walking up to the Durbar and offering their salutations to the Viceroy that might very plausibly have been shot at the Durbar in 1911. But at other moments in the same film we cannot tell that the aerial views of massive congregations of people happened at that particular event being depicted by the documentary film. A bird's eye view of huge crowds pans for a half-second across a billboard for a movie: the movie is *Alibi*, a 1929 Hollywood crime film. But the event being described by the voice over narration is the 1920 Calcutta meeting of the Indian National Congress in the aftermath of the massacre of civilians by the British that occurred at Jalianwala Bagh.[23] The split-second shot of *Alibi* is suggestive. It offers a visualization of the extent to which cinematic sensationalism and political sensation inhabited common spaces (see Fig. 6.5).

Likewise, enthusiastic and cheering crowds in cities such as Calcutta and Rangoon received the end of World War I in 1918, reported the *Times*

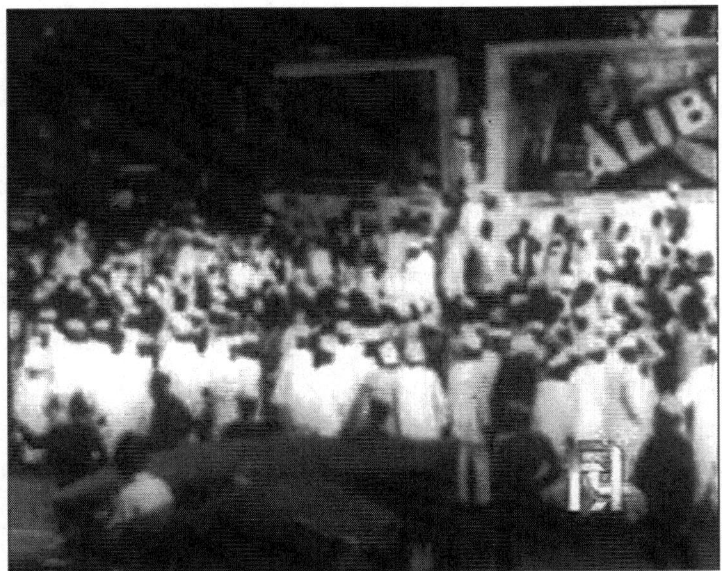

Figure 6.5. A frame from *Jallianwalla Bagh* (1970, Films Division of India).

of India. "There was much animation when it was announced in hotels, picture houses and theaters. . . . News was displayed at intervals on a screen as the telegrams were received at the newspaper offices" and in Rangoon, "the titles announcing the armistice were met by enthusiastic crowds who broke out into patriotic songs."[24]

Audiences were indeed hailed by movies as participants in a critique as well as consumption of modernity. However, the late emergence of the institution of stardom, its fan discourses on the surfaces of fame and public life (which refused to pry into the private domain of female stars) and its imagination of public space as a field of gossip and rumor (Majumdar 2009) suggest more complex ways in which cinematic publics become part of an imaginary of the cinema. The Indian Cinematograph Committee testimonies' extensive references to masses, crowds, and audiences are worth consideration here. Each of these words carried with it connotations of scale, class, education, and box office value. The word *mass* was almost always used as a generalized characterization of the population, attached to an attribute such as lack of education or propensity to be improperly influenced by the medium. Hence, the "illiterate masses" or the "impressionable masses." As such, it carried with it an adjectival function. *Crowd*, on the other hand, was not as much of an abstraction as mass. Unlike the word *mass*, a crowd was potentially enumerable and finite. And unlike masses, crowds were not always invoked negatively. They could mark the difference between box office success and failure (a movie could draw "good crowds" or not). The word *crowd* could also mark the boundary between art and commerce, between taste and the absence of taste, and could specify the ethnicity of an audience. First-class theaters drew "cosmopolitan crowds." Religious pictures drew mostly Indian crowds. The crowds were attracted to amatory scenes in movies. If masses connote a despatialized population, crowds are narrower and are located around the vicinity of the cinema. They are what one found outside the theater. Their legibility was most evident when they were visible outside. The word *audiences* further localized masses and crowds into finite, located collections of people, often in the context of some imagination of the space of the movie theater in front of the screen.

The cinema's institutional and commercial appeals to potential customers encompassed all three modes of constructing moviegoers and in so doing shared the task of the discursive construction of audiences. Promotional material can imagine audiences as preexisting constituencies compatible with the movie's textual address. Such was the case with Phalke's mythologicals in South India. Exhibitors characterized and advertised the appeal of going to watch Phalke's religious narratives in the idiom of religious devotion, so that the cinema "remediated religious performance" through the imperatives of a capital-intensive business (Hughes 2005, 219). Meanwhile, political leaders were appropriating the idioms of religious festivals to mobilize the masses toward the cause of nationalism. Both cinema and politics recoded the mass as a devotional one—the former for drawing audiences; the latter for political mobilization. The two domains—cinema and politics—intersected on the ground of nationalist mobilization and an emerging politics of electoral representation for Indians, coding the crowds attracted to the cinema as expressions of nationalist pride. While print capitalism could have unified an elite reading public, it fell to the cinema, however, to become in Hughes's words "a new frontier of mass participation" (232) in representational politics while also being lucrative.

Ranita Chatterjee's groundbreaking work on urban film culture in Calcutta underscores the heterogeneity and fragmented nature of Calcutta audiences that cannot be simply divided into elite and subaltern. Even as the geography of film exhibition seemed divided between the European and Indian-dominated portions of the city, exhibition practices imagined "a complexly layered audience and not just a simple division between the elites and the masses" (Chatterjee 2011, 155). Traveling cinemas were closely tied to lower income levels outside of urban limits. Intertitles in multiple languages catered to Calcutta's various linguistic communities. Film release dates and their scheduling were drawn from the practices of Bengali theater, including the customization of program during the festival season. Theaters could be divided into not two but at least four categories: those catering to European, Anglo-Indian, elite Indian, and exclusively Indian audiences. Reading the ICC reports, Chatterjee discovers a much more nuanced understanding of audiences by the Calcutta film industry than by those conducting the ICC hearings. More than in Madras or Bombay, the Calcutta film industry seemed closest to a situation where masses and crowds gave way to complexly imagined audiences.

In Bombay, the imagination of the masses as impressionable fueled the drive of both the nationalist elite bourgeoisie and the colonial state to control the cinema. But the modernity that was emerging was one that neither the colonizers nor the nationalist elite could entirely control. It was emerging in the bazaars among the working populations and the youth as a fascination with thrilling action adventure-romance serial films with plenty of stunts, both the Hollywood and Indian variety. This is a fascination with a global mass culture, with advertising, fashion, romance, new modes of sexual relationships, and new foundations of the modern self as an autonomous individual. Bhaumik calls this emergence a "globalization from below" (Bhaumik 2010, 57). His argument here closely parallels Miriam Hansen's argument regarding classical Hollywood as a form of vernacular modernism (1999). This fascination with globalization could be nationalist, too. If I understand Bhaumik correctly, the sheer numbers of people amassed by nationalists as a show of collective strength and consensus against British rule were not the same impressionable masses imagined by the colonial or nationalist elites. Instead, these were masses born of the belligerence of a "modern individual autonomy" (58) because of which being modern could serve the needs of being nationalist while exceeding those needs as well.

That said, there's much to qualify Bhaumik's formulation of vernacular modernism as a form of "globalization from below." The criminalization of urban space and of nationalist activities, and the use of cinema as a crime-solving mechanism in state-produced documentaries, paints a more complex picture of the vernacular modernism of film. Indeed, for the masses gathered outside that could also look up and see a billboard of a Hollywood crime film such as *Alibi*, the sensational crime films could well have reminded those masses that crime was a mode of social exclusion and differentiation. In India, as we have seen in the preceding and current chapters, the cinema could easily serve as co-conspirator of the British and then the postindependence Indian state in utilizing sensationalism to produce models of upright citizenship. In these respects, South Asia shared much with Latin America, where too, as Rielle Navitski's (2013) spectacular research demonstrates, popular sensationalism in the movies was hardly a confirmation of the cinema's status as a formal expression of the sensory intensity of modern life. New York's or Paris's sensory intensity was not to be found in Mexico City or Sao Paolo or even Calcutta. In Mexico and Brazil, the cinema was an import and consequence of contact with European modernity, not the expression of it when local conditions were so radically different than in Europe or the United States. And as in India (perhaps even more so), in Latin America the cinema was endorsed by elites and the twinning of sensationalism and crime became the expression of elite anxieties about social change.

With these qualifications in mind, the still images of crowds I consider here can be considered the raw data that are translated into a discourse about masses, crowds, and audiences by the institution of the cinema. There is, of course, a vast chasm between the printed page and the moving image, between the grain of the halftone image and the indexicality and iconicity of the moving image. Yet, in the absence of documentary images of movie audiences, the following photographs capture the same gatherings that would be mobilized on and off the screen by movies, cinematic institutions, and the nationalist movement alike.

THE EMBLEMATIC AND THE TIDAL CROWD

Crowds could be made to take on a wide variety of meanings in relation to political authority as well as agency. Perhaps the most obvious function of the crowd is to stand in for the event at which it is depicted. The eventfulness of the function, its scale and importance, and its relation to political order or disorder are indexed in the way crowds are framed.

Hiralal Sen's partition movies of processions have not survived but the photo-supplement of the Bombay-based *Illustrated Weekly of India* published two halftones of partition-related gatherings that took place in Dacca in East Bengal. The full-page spread of October 3, 1906, bore two large half-page photographs arranged vertically and separated by captions, occupying the full length and width of the page. The page bore the conspiratorially inclined headline, "The Truth in Photographs." The first one was captioned "The mass meeting of Mohamedans held in Dacca on October 6th to protest against Sir Bampfylde Fuller's resignation," and the one below it was captioned "Another view of the mass meeting at Dacca." Both pictures showed a large gathering of people in a vast open ground, as symbolically laden in their meaning. The camera's distance from the crowd and slight elevation of view conveyed the size and scale of the gathering. In both, the framing depicted a crowd that is supposed to be emblematic of the absence of a gap between rulers and ruled, an "orderly model of the formation of the body politic" (Schnapp 2006, 5).

The accompanying paragraph below the second one reinforces the emblematic nature of these gatherings. The crowds were proof of the absence of a gap between policy and public. The crowds were one with authority. In this case, the policy in question was the partition of Bengal. The resigning official Sir Bampfylde Fuller had been the first Lieutenant-Governor of East Bengal after partition, and criticized for his heavy-handed clamping down on partition-related agitation. Nationalists in Bengal saw his resignation over differences in policy with the British government as a victory. But the *Weekly* sought to demonstrate otherwise with these photographs, to prove that the partition expressed the desires of the Muslims in East Bengal. Depicted in an act of prayer, Muslims were described as protesting the resignation of Fuller as a loss to their community in Dacca, ranged as they were in this narrative against Hindu nationalist agitators.[25] Aside from such partition images, the emblematic crowd emerges frequently in images of gatherings commemorating events presided over by British dignitaries.

At the same time, *The Illustrated Weekly of India* also carried pictures of emblematic crowds protesting colonial policies. Such was the case when later that month the *Weekly* carried two images of "Partition Day," identical to the layout of the two halftones just discussed and likewise occupying the full page of the weekly. The first picture was captioned "Partition Day in Calcutta: a morning mass meeting in Beadon Square. The speaker seen on the platform is Moulvi Leadat Hossain." The second picture is captioned "A big mass meeting on Partition Day at the Federation Hall Grounds, Calcutta. The speaker at the time this picture was taken Mohammed Moulvi Yousef Ali, Khan Bahadur"[26] (see Fig. 6.6).

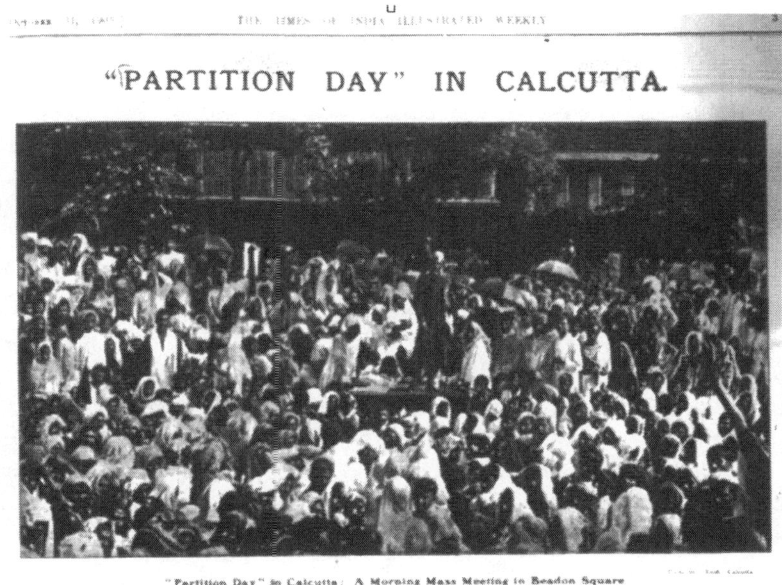

Figure 6.6. Partition Day in Calcutta, *Illustrated Weekly of India*, Oct. 31, 1906.

If the crowd becomes emblematic of empire's loyal subjects in one pair of photographs related to partition, in the other pair the photographs show crowds emblematic of the gatherings that would appear with increasing frequency as the nationalist movement against the British grew in scale. The picture captioned "big mass meeting" shows the crowd receding into the depths of the image, as far as the eye can see, stopped only by the houses and trees at the very end that run widthwise and mark the boundary of the grounds in which the meeting is occurring. The speaker's podium, raised above the crowd, also stands tiny and distant from the camera's position. Even within this obviously limited space, it seems as if the space on the other side of the podium is much larger than what we can see: the space of the crowd farthest from the camera seems compressed and telescoped into a much narrower body of people.

By contrast, the numerous "orphaned snapshots"—without attribution and date—at the Nehru Memorial Museum and Library in New Delhi capture the chaos and movement of nationalist mass mobilizations. These snapshots are from a later period, the 1930s, unlike the partition agitations in the first decade of the twentieth century. The most obvious difference is the implication that the camera's framing of the image is inadequate in conveying the scale of the crowds or the chaos or dramatic nature of the events. In some photographs, empty space in the foreground dramatizes the human action in the rest of the image. Other aerial bird's eye views capture massive gatherings that could be interpreted as ambiguous, depicting a congregated crowd that nevertheless veers on dispersal as the people on the edges of the gathering, walking in various directions and off the frame, become the loose threads of a piece of woven fabric of bodies. Both the fabric and the thread, however, are clearly larger and longer than what the snapshot can contain (see Fig. 6.7). In other images, marching battalions of riot police, or processions, supply direction and guide the eye in a movement across the image. Buildings with billboards and motorcars attempting to weave through the crowds remind us of the presence of other elements of everyday life.

Images such as these depict crowds in their "oceanic" mode as tidal surges, frequently dangerous ones. If, with emblematic crowds, the leader—or a voice—emerges as one out of many, in contrast, in the human "ocean-oscapes" the leader taps into the tidal surges of the multitudes (Schnapp 2006, 5). The emblematic then could also contain the seeds of the "political sublime" (Schnapp 2006, 7), an experience of "shock, immersion and somatic risk" (Schnapp 2006, 5) delivered through attempted depictions of

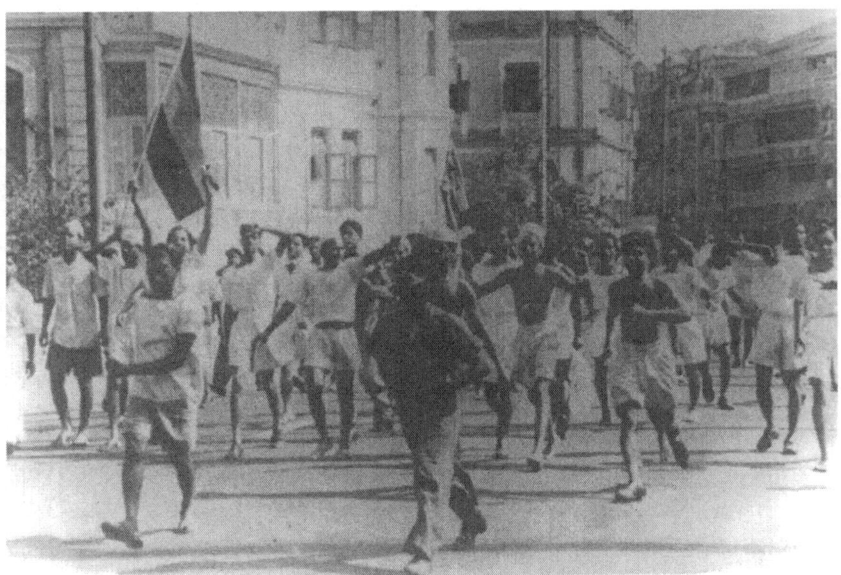

Figure 6.7. A tidal crowd. Date and photographer unknown. "India's Independence Movement, 1857 to 1947." Photo: Press Bureau of India. New Delhi, India.

"tidal" masses.[27] We do not know where filmmaker Hiralal Sen stood or what his vantage point was in relation to the procession of protesters he filmed. But we can assume that Hiralal Sen's filmed records of partition protests were meant to convey, at best, emblematic crowds that were mobile and mobilized against state policy.

FACING THE CROWD

Were other ways of envisioning crowds possible? A snapshot from the Nehru Memorial Museum and Library's archives—again, its provenance and date uncertain—depicts a vast seated crowd from an elevated position nearly on the same level as the roofs of the buildings across the street. Much of the seated crowd is shown in profile as it is facing a speaker outside the visible space of the image. But in the background, swaths of seated onlookers are clearly looking at the camera. What is this image trying to convey?[28] For one, right across the street, is the curved awning of a photographer's studio with the words M. L. Vishwakarma and Company. Only the awning is visible, as the vast crowd blocks the entrance. It could be that the photographer saw this as a prime opportunity to capture an event but perhaps also produce a marketable and dramatic image of his skills.

What does it mean that the crowds look back at the photographer? The aforementioned photograph is not an example of the exhibitionism of lynch mobs that look back at us, as in photographs from U.S. history. Nor can we think of the masses in photographs such as these as emblematic masses that are formally posed intentionally to look at the camera. These are not those who look back at the camera because they have no choice but to do so, as with the subjects of nineteenth-century ethnographic photography. Finally, there are the masses that don't intend to look back but catch the cameraman looking at them. It is the last kind that we have before us here in this image. Political theorist Ariela Azoulay proposes that we restore time and movement to the still image in the manner of watching a movie. Rather than looking at a photograph or seeing it, we watch a complex encounter between photographer, subject, camera, and viewer. The photograph emerges therefore, as one element in a civil contract, a covenant, whether intentional or not and maybe imposed, maybe not, in which the subjects, the viewer, and the subject matter interact with each other. From this perspective, the political is not a trait of and in the image but "a space of human relations exposed to each other in public" (Azoulay 2010, 251). The photographic act does not usher those already considered citizens into a certain space in front of the camera. The act itself, Azoulay argues, can be seen as claiming citizenship. Thinking along the same lines, we could say the image records the moment when the compact between photographer and subject is rendered visible and as a result ushers photographer, subject, and viewer into the space of politics. We may not know the provenance of the numerous snapshots of rallies, processions, strikes, and lathi charges (blows by baton-wielding police, on protesting subjects). But Azoulay's framework allows us to restore time and movement to the snapshots and to consider their political efficacy for Indians.[29]

Moving images depict this dynamic as well. They depicted crowds for a collective audience that had to see itself as one and could see a version of itself on screen. Nowhere is this clearer than in the famous opening nationalist-patriotic song in *Kismet* (1942) in which a group of singers demand that aggressors of the world leave Hindustan because "Hindustan is ours"—*Door Hato! Door Hato! Door Hato O Duniya Walon Hindustan Hamara Hai.* In the context of World War II, the song was prima facie a voice of support for the allied war effort and directed at the fascist aggressors. But as with so much of the semantic subterfuge of nationalist mobilization, its lyrics were also clearly targeted at the British. The shot reverse shot structure presents the singers addressing the camera frontally and demanding that aggressors leave Hindustan. Roused by the song, the reverse shot shows the audience no longer seated but standing, fists pumping and repeating the refrain being sung on stage. The audience too is depicted in a frontal address to the camera. The conventions of editing tell us this is a reciprocation of glances between the diegetic audience and performers and that it demonstrates the power of mass entertainment to produce a community in the event of its performance. But the scene also powerfully doubles the strength of its direct address, ensuring that we remain the audience to whom the on-stage performance and its off-stage mimesis are directed. The crowd that looks back at a camera in a movie was not new, of course. But it wasn't solely the result of indigenous, devotional modes of seeing, such as the *darsanic* gaze. It also possessed a more prosaic lineage in the visualization of topical crowds in photojournalism. Would it be too much of a stretch to claim that the direct address of the patriotic song in *Kismet* is also the scripted residue of the encounters forged in the still snapshot? Don't both forms posit a civil contract of political expression otherwise denied by the state?[30]

CONCLUSION

The forms that emerged in print media at this moment from the halftone process—newspaper photography, the photo-illustrated book, and the snapshot—pose a problem for the historian in that they are not amenable to being archived. The newspaper photograph and the snapshot are ephemeral objects even as they are ubiquitous. The printed image in a daily newspaper has a short shelf life of one day, till the next morning's newspaper makes the previous day's news irrelevant. Furthermore, the image is surrounded by text, by captions, and by other news items. It may serve to illustrate the printed text that surrounds it. If so, to archive the printed photograph in and of itself becomes an act of decontextualization. On the other hand, it may exist independently of the news items surrounding it. If so, rather than acquiring a stable presence for itself, the photograph acquires a transience bound to the transience of the reader's gaze that will soon turn to the next page.

The snapshot likewise lacks an independent existence. It is too often wedded to the instantaneous and the accidental. It is both a record of and a form of the "marginalia of history" (Chakrabarty 1996, 2143). Quite apart from its presence in domestic/home/private photography, the snapshot also serves as the source for the photograph in the newspaper or the photo-illustrated book. In both of these capacities, it becomes the embedded visual infrastructure for the forms it generates and is often not available any longer as a singular object. This same trait, however, is also proof of the promiscuity of both significance and dispersal of the snapshot. The snapshot's tenacious survival fossilized in other media guarantees it a longevity and discourse that it may be unable to marshal on its own. It is this intermediality that makes the snapshot worthy of consideration in a genealogy of the cinema.

Neither the halftone nor the snapshot can be tamed by a positivist archival impulse. Therefore, rather than search for one single preconstituted archive, this chapter and the preceding one have searched for the cinema's presence and portents in a widely dispersed (in function, format, location) set of images, moving between and across them and across media in the interest of a speculative historical exploration. What if this fundamental archival instability is an implicit and taken-for-granted part of the popular cinematic imaginary in India today? What if historiographical self-consciousness is fundamental to the cinema's presence in everyday life? In the next chapter, I take up this possibility in examining the forms of film historiography that have narrated Indian cinema's origins.

PART IV

ARCHIVES

7

THE ABUNDANT EPHEMERAL

· ◆ ———— ◆ ·

The Protocols of Popular Film Historiography in India

There is an unresolved contradiction when Indian cinema's prolific output encounters laments of its poor archival preservation. This contradiction needs to be thought through if the conditions of the possibility of film history in India are to be recognized as such. Considerations of the archival future of Indian cinema must acknowledge the sheer number of films that are produced in India each year. The practical size of India's cinematic output poses an epistemological challenge for imagining an archive in the traditional sense of a site of storage and preservation—but that volume is essential to its cinematic imaginary. With anywhere between six and eight hundred films a year, and seen from the vantage point of the films that do become "visible" by finding exhibition, there is too much "ephemera." One can find a vague echo of this conundrum in the world of film museums entrusted with preservation of film-related materials that ponder over how to collect, catalogue, and cross-reference movie ephemera (Campagnoni 2006). But it is only a vague echo because the word *ephemera* must mean something quite distinct in India. The challenge isn't to track down and locate ephemera; the challenge is to notice it and figure out what to do with all of it. The ephemeral is what exists in abundance. Or rather, it is ephemeral precisely because it is abundant. Who cares for it when there is so much of it?

The problem seems analogous to that of the countless straight-to-video films in the North American context (Lobato 2012). Franco Moretti has invoked the "slaughter-house of literature"—that vast world of literary production that will never be canonized and that needs to be excavated and situated alongside existing canons for a more complex view of literary production (Lobato 2012, 32). With India's cinema, the problem seems doubled. All of it, all of India's cinema (with perhaps the exception of its art cinema) has been clubbed together as the "slaughter-house" of cinema from the vantage point of the Western film critic, at least till the 1980s. Moreover, the Indian film industry's mammoth scale produces its own slaughterhouse of movies that disappear into oblivion.

How film history is remembered, memorized, memorialized, preserved in India is a function of the seemingly perpetually emergent temporalities that have shaped its viability. Historians haven't quite acknowledged the implications of a situation in which old and new media seem to coexist to produce an archive that is not yet one, an archive that can never be a stabilized, closed space of storage and predetermined recall. And I find the protocols of popular historiography addressing precisely this aspect: the open-ended archive. Popular film histories seem to do something quite other than what more sober narrative accounts that count as history proper seem to do. They suggest that not only is the archive of the cinema still in the making, it is also for the taking.

Laments about the abysmal culture of film archiving and preservation in India,[1] and, indeed, about the state of archives in India in general, have been frequent.[2] The recent release of an elegiac, beautifully shot meditation on India's film history, *The Celluloid Man* (Shivendra Singh Dungarpur 2012) points to this sensibility. The movie melds the biography of P. K. Nair, instrumental in the story of the National Film Archive of India (NFAI), with that of the NFAI and in turn the story of Indian cinema. Indeed, as the title demonstrates, the end result is the archiving of Nair himself as a scarce and precious object, like the celluloid that is now a metaphor of a scarce sensibility that recognizes the value of film and need for its preservation.

In contrast to *The Celluloid Man*, the filmmaker Kamal Swaroop's ambitious "collage" of Phalke's life, titled *Tracing Phalke* (2013), turns Phalke's life into a counterarchive of film and cultural history. *Tracing Phalke* is a dense collage (literally) that in a cut-and-paste mode destroys the boundaries between Phalke and his times. As Swaroop puts it in the book's introduction and in interviews elsewhere, the linearity of Phalke's life unravels into an infinite proliferation of inexhaustible threads that turned Swaroop's fascination with Phalke into a decades-long project.[3] Accordingly, *Tracing Phalke* comprises Swaroop's hand-typed "chronofile" of the developments of Phalke's life, accompanied on the chronofile's margins by "simultaneous developments in technology and larger historical events" (Swaroop 2013, not paginated). Swaroop's description of the process is evocative and conveys the impact of media history on film history.

A pair of scissors and a bottle of glue always with me, I went looking for images to put on my typed pages. These were the pre-internet times; I collected fragments by making Xeroxes from libraries or by mining art catalogues. Soon chimneys sprouted out of the heads of industrialists, underwater turtles nudged a pregnant Dwarkabai[4] and an image of Toulouse Lautrec mirroring himself shadowed Phalke's movement into becoming a young man.

When my images began to come together, I no longer knew whether I was putting together or breaking down . . . putting Usha Mantri's[5] face on Ravi Varma's "Sarasvati,"[6] was only making visible the grafting process that had historically taken place in our cinema. But the new collaged "she" became one of my favorite creatures, a griffin. I began to let griffins live in my book. I let myself cut and shift and paste, I let myself associate and dream and keep in images because I liked them. (2013, not paginated)

Elsewhere, Swaroop has observed that the arrival of VHS was crucial to his ability to conceive of a "new philosophy of time."[7] The result is a visually complex experience of Phalke's life that is deeply embedded, in page after page of the coffee table–sized volume, in a variety of narrative modes, primary sources, and images. Swaroop's typewritten "chronofile" jostles for space, visibility, and legibility with extracts from Phalke's writings, Swaroop's objective narration of biographical events, sections of Swaroop's screenplay of Phalke's life for his biopic, and an "indirect free style" of narration[8] in which a third person objective narration of Phalke's life slips into a third person subjective narrational mode incorporating Phalke's thoughts and responses. It would be difficult to offer an abbreviated discussion of Swaroop's work given the density of visual information but two points are worth noting. First, in transforming a biography into a series of visual images (including images *of* text) presented to us in the mode of a bound book whose pages we browse, Swaroop offers an intermediated staging of biography. The cinema is far from absent in this vertiginous intersection of the printed photograph with photographed type, typeset reproductions of paintings, woodcuts, engravings, newsprint, and frame grabs from movies. Swaroop's "indiscriminate" collage recalls (in Henri Bergson's phrase) the "visual dust" of history captured by the medium of film (Amad 2010, 110). As we shall see shortly, the emergence of VHS and its attendant piracies inform the context for the movies I will be examining shortly in greater detail, just as they seem to have shaped Swaroop's own thoughts around Phalke.

Second, we should also note the connections *Tracing Phalke* reiterates between intermediality and topicality that I discussed in detail in chapters

5 and 6. To the extent that the chronofile of time mutates into the space of topical relevance given formal expression and delimited by the pages of *Tracing Phalke*, Swaroop is reflecting as much on the origins of a multimedia infrastructure as he is on Phalke's life. In this, what we have is (akin to Douglas Gordon and Phillipe Parreno's "film" on Zidane made for the televisual and hyperlinked age), a "twenty-first-century portrait."[9]

Furthermore, much like the *Illustrated Weekly of India* and the *Delhi Durbar* album, Swaroop's intermedial endeavor encourages a leisurely perusal of pages, enacting the durations and rhythms of everyday life that are so central to the medium of film and its status as a counterarchival site. As noted in the introduction, the interest in current scholarship on Indian media, in media imaginaries, is an interest ultimately in the everyday as a site for the life and times of a medium. Perhaps in this sense, while *Celluloid Man* turns India's preeminent film archivist into a precious and receding object, *Tracing Phalke* turns India's pioneering filmmaker into an expression of an everyday imaginary.

More generally, it might be useful to briefly survey the range of film histories that appear in popular media. The Films Division—India's state-run documentary division—as well as individual filmmakers such as Shyam Benegal, have produced documentaries on the history of Indian cinema as well as its major auteurs (including Raj Kapoor and Satyajit Ray). Since the economic liberalization and privatization of media in India, there have been diverse new modes of popular historiography. These have included Bombay cinema's own nostalgic invocations of earlier eras of its history in movies such as *Om Shanti Om* (2007). The retroactive colorization of black and white classics such as *Mughal-e-Azam* constitutes a more reflexive industrial stance on the part of a globalizing film industry eager to showcase new resources and competencies, the present technological capacities of recent film and media in India (Walia 2013). Current concerns inflect invocations of the film as a historical artifact grounded in a particular past. Rajadhyaksha (2009) terms these impulses the "golden ageing" of Bollywood (77–83). In contrast to the Films Division documentaries such as the one I will discuss shortly, which align film history with the history of nationalism,[10] the "golden age" of Bollywood emerges as such in the postliberalization era to characterize the films of the 1940s and 1950s. Rajadhyaksha traces this celebration of the 1950s to BBC's Channel 4 programming in the 1980s that showcased the history of Indian cinema in a manner that established the golden age narrative.

Crucial to this narrative are Nasreen Munni Kabir's prolific publications as well as documentaries for Channel 4 on the history of Indian cinema. There is no small irony in Kabir's celebration of Indian cinema in the first decade after independence (1950s) as the golden age, according to

Rajadhyaksha. The 1950s was, after all, the period when the studio system of the 1920s and 1930s broke down because of the influx of independent financiers who lured stars and directors away from studios and inaugurated what would remain the dominant mode of production till the 1990s Bollywood era: a highly disaggregated mode of production reliant on speculative financing (sometimes with very high interest rates) from often less than legitimate sources that turned the film business into a form of money laundering. It also ushers in a highly problematic relationship between cinema and the postcolonial state. Chapters 3 and 4 offered a wider and deeper historical backdrop to that relationship and argued that the distrust of cinema by the postcolonial state as a form of mechanical reproduction can be located in the crosshairs of the uneasy relation between (mass-) cultural politics and the imperatives of commerce and cultural authenticity in the period before independence.[11] *Pyaasa* (1955), I proposed, can be seen as a consideration of the possibilities and perils of mass cultural productions. Here, in the context of a discussion on how film history is narrated, we can add that by the 1990s, *Pyaasa*, along with other films by the same director (Guru Dutt), as well as now iconic films by Raj Kapoor, Mehboob Khan, and Bimal Roy, became part of a golden age of Hindi cinema.

A third genre comprises historical surveys of specific topics pertaining to the cinema that have become increasingly frequent on television. The Indian television network *Headlines Today* has a series called *An Affair to Remember*. Each episode chronicles a particular notable figure (a playback singer, a star, a director), elements of film form and genre (cinematography, the evolution of the action sequence, horror, double roles), notable films (*Umrao Jaan*, *Salaam Bombay*), and themes ("100 years of Indian Cinema," "Stars of South in Bollywood," "Pakistani Artists in Indian Cinema"). This series does not venture beyond a chronology of significant moments, profusely illustrated with clips, voiceover narration, and talking head interviews with relevant film industry figures that alternate between reminiscence and opinion.

All of these genres of film history reveal varying degrees of indifference to the project of a formalized film archive. The absence of an archival imaginary in this conventional sense of respect for the cinema as heritage is not, of course, unique to Indian cinema. Corporate decisions to support archives are often a function of marketing and branding considerations, and television's desire to turn to film history can be seen as a function of cost-cutting practices in relation to producing original content. And if, as *Celluloid Man* reveals, Homi Wadia's son admitted to burning the surviving prints of his father's film pioneering 1931 film for silver (*Alam Ara*, the first Indian talkie, of which no surviving print exists), compare that to the fact that Universal Pictures burned all of its nitrate holdings, also for silver! (Horak 2001, 33–35).[12]

In response to a sharp question about whether contingency—of survival and of preservation—is intrinsic to the film archive, given the sheer volume of images produced, Mary Ann Doane reflects on the historicity of the medium of film. Film is a historical medium not only in that it records something, but also through its own historicity as an object, vulnerable to the ravages of time and to new media. In the face of the seemingly immaterial digital media, movies like *Decasia* (2002) exhibit a kind of nostalgia for a medium in its historicity (Doane 2007, 18). Obsolescence then haunts considerations of the archive. It informs the aesthetics of celluloid as archival material in films such as *Decasia*. And it is a concern not shared by Hollywood or Bollywood. Why mourn, and what is there to mourn, when film history is so easily configured as immersive and interactive experience with the technological resources of the digital age?

What I am trying to get at here is the possibility that there might be other modes of remembering and preserving the history of the cinema, other protocols whose procedures ought to be considered seriously. Given, on the one hand, the poverty of the archive in its conventional sense, and on the other, the "heritage" business of the cinema often run by the film industry itself, what other kinds of film historiography might we consider as germane to the possibility of a cinematic archive (which may not be the same as an archive of the cinema-as-celluloid)? In what follows, I consider two oddities of film history on film that reflect on the history of Indian cinema and produce an unconventional vocabulary of recall.[13]

CINEMA CINEMA (1979)

Cinema Cinema (1979) narrates the history of Indian cinema in the form of a documentary being screened for an audience in a movie theater. The screening of the diegetic documentary is interspersed with a scripted and enacted picture of an audience. The movie alternates between the history being narrated on screen and the audience in the theater and their varied responses to what they see on screen. In doing so, the movie experiments with the project of documentary film historiography while retaining its most conventional features: the voiceover narration, the talking heads, the montage of clips of noteworthy films, and a largely linear progression from Indian cinema's origins to the present. It, however, undermines the narrative in the diegetic documentary and its claims to authority by muddling the divide between documentary and fiction. This, after all, is an enactment of a movie screening, a screening that nevertheless presents us with a documentary of Indian cinema. And if that were not enough, the documentary being screened is narrated by the on-screen presence of the biggest Bombay film stars of the time: Amitabh Bachchan, Dharmendra, Hema Malini, and Zeenat Aman.

Cinema Cinema came in the wake of its director Krishna Shah's earlier big budget 1978 flop *Shalimar*, the story of a gang of crooks seeking to outwit each other in acquiring the priceless diamond Shalimar.[14] Although a flop, *Shalimar* earns the distinction of being one of those rare films in Bombay cinema—perhaps even the first—to be cross-franchised as a novel coinciding with the movie's release.[15] Who was Krishna Shah? A 2003 article, well into the "Bollywood" phase of Bombay cinema, described Shah as the "pioneer of crossover cinema," based in the United States, a Yale and UCLA Film School graduate whose student film had won second place after George Lucas's *THX1138* (1971), and who now had ambitious plans to tap into the Bollywood phenomenon.[16]

Shah was not only a crossover pioneer. In the 1980s, he appeared twice in published newspaper reports as a filmmaker warning against video-cassette-related piracy of Indian films. One of those appearances included a taped confrontation with an Asian shopkeeper in London over the piracy of his own movie, *Cinema Cinema*. The confrontation was later broadcast on a BBC program on the subject of piracy.[17] Another detailed 1980 report and analysis on the impact of videocassettes on piracy quotes Shah saying: "The signs are clear. This is the last decade of the movies, as we know them. All over the world the motion picture industry is dying as a result of this unbelievable phenomenon—the video" (Kagal 1980, 5).

Such portentous pronouncements on the death of cinema in the age of the videocassette contextualize Shah's failed endeavor. *Shalimar*, as well as its follow-up *Cinema Cinema*, are symptomatic of the exceptional position of the Indian director who might seek to straddle the worlds of Hollywood and Bombay Cinema in the 1980s. Each of Shah's two movies, *Shalimar* and *Cinema Cinema*, is an oddity in its own right. His optimism in the potentials of cross-franchising a movie such as *Shalimar* in India, and his assumption that the form of the Indian film was modular and cross-culturally adaptable (remove the songs and you have its Hollywood version) imagines a cinema reconfigured for a global age, but well before that globalization had become the mantra and zeitgeist in India. Shah's globalism is clearly not in the same epistemic space as Merchant-Ivory's Raj nostalgia. That nostalgia depicts an Indian world filtered through the (fantasy) sensibility of a simpler Anglo-Indian past. If Merchant-Ivory looked to British society of an earlier century, Shah had looked to the United States of the current century and the current moment in the late 1960s, well before India's economic liberalization of the 1990s reconfigured its geopolitical and cultural relationship to the United States.

Shah's desire to actualize a future that was yet to happen—a future characterized by (fantasies of) a complementary synergy between Bollywood and Hollywood—makes his films all the more interesting. *Shalimar* becomes an attempted cinematic rendering of that future with something of a utopian cast to it. *Cinema Cinema*, on the other hand, illuminates Bombay cinema's history by localizing its impact at the site of reception, the movie theater. While one globalizes, the other localizes.

Shah's film also exists at a remove from corporate- and industry-led cinematic records of the history of Indian cinema. In contrast to the TV series *An Affair to Remember* that I discussed in the preceding section of this chapter, *Cinema Cinema*, as well as the other movie I will discuss here, *Film Hi Film*, are not incorporated as programming into mass media, and have not to my knowledge been broadcast or transmitted on television. I discovered the two films while browsing an online store selling DVDs of Indian films. One of the consequences of the emergence of online retailers specializing in Indian cinema is the sudden "appearance" or unprecedented availability of movies that may have barely made it to the theaters on their original release or that have been forgotten over the years. Flops such as *Shalimar*, pre-1950s period films and romances, less well-known films of major stars, and even rarely seen iconic films such as *Neecha Nagar* (Chetan Anand 1946) now seem to be available in one format or the other. Who owns the rights to these movies? Who is behind the production of the DVDs and VCDs of these movies? Who uploads these films to sites like YouTube?[18] While answers to these questions can be elusive and in many cases impossible to obtain, online retail seems to have made the obscure examples of India's cinematic output available. As such, then, the two movies constitute a despatialized form of social memory. That is to say, this social memory is no longer rooted in a territorially sited past framed within the parameters of national cinema.[19] Unlike postmodern art that creates and fabricates a new past, here we have an actual past, ready-made and prefab, freed from its temporal origins and its locations of significance, to become the object of nostalgia, including for those who may not have even lived it. This is a past that now belongs to no one institution or country and everyone.[20]

As I noted at the outset, *Cinema Cinema* enacts the event of a movie screening. The enactment's functions are worth outlining. The particular rhetorical and analytical procedures adopted by the movie bind Indian cinema to the site of its consumption. The chronology is dependent for its meaning and affect not on the intrinsic value of the past but on its present reception in the movie theater, emphasized through editing and action and given equal if not more time than the documentary itself. The movie is driven by the desire to watch or discover audiences watching. The black box of the theater is shown darkened only at the outset and at the end to indicate the norm, while it is illuminated through much of the movie as a space of visible social interaction.

In its structure, *Cinema Cinema* replicates the act of moviegoing. The film opens with an exterior shot of Bombay's Edward Theatre (opened in

1918 and still functioning). A line forms. Tickets are purchased, including from touts that sell tickets in "black." Back in the projection room, the projectionist spools the reels of film and a bell rings. The audience takes its seats. A documentary about the history of Indian—but mostly Hindi—cinema commences. The documentary comprises back-to-back clips of notable movies, intercalated with expository narration by four major film stars. The documentary's version of history proceeds chronologically, segmenting the history of Indian cinema into four broad periods and utilizing four stars to introduce each period. In the middle of the screening, there is an intermission. The audience files out. Men line up at the open-air urinal. Others buy snacks while a lady changes diapers. Soon, the documentary resumes. When it concludes, the lights come on and the audience exits the theater, and the movie too comes to an abrupt end, as if it were running on time borrowed from the documentary nested within it.

Cinema Cinema's nested documentary's archival footage is not restricted to Indian cinema, or for that sake, even to fiction. We see clips drawn from Hollywood and Europe, especially in the pre-sound period, and equally copious use of documentary footage of events in India's freedom movement. Nor is the movie's use of footage restricted to live action. A lengthy discussion of the 1928 Cinematograph Committee report is presented as animation. In this, the movie astutely recognizes the excess of detail demanded by a photographic medium such as the cinema, the challenge it poses to conventional historiography, and compensates for the lack of visual records of a governmental and investigative commission by imagining that event and its complex politics in animated form.

The relation between plot and story in this movie is noteworthy. By definition, the plot refers only to the events we see on screen in the order in which we see them. The story, on the other hand, includes what we see on screen as well as events not seen but inferred by us that allow us to construct a fuller story out of what we are watching on screen. The periodic conflation of the screen *we* are looking at with the screen inside the movie theater where the documentary is being viewed by our fictional audience, complicates the story duration. Like a Chinese box, the movie's ninety-seven-minute running time encapsulates its roughly two-hour plotline of events—I am guessing the duration from buying the tickets to exiting the theater. This two-hour plotline in turn encapsulates the screened documentary's seventy-five-year-long story of Indian cinema. *Cinema Cinema*'s running time is less than the duration of its plotline, which in turn is less than the story duration that encompasses the entire history of Indian cinema. The miniaturized world-in-a-grain-of-sand logic would seem to create a larger than life cinema. But it would be more accurate to say that this is reverse miniaturization that accords more priority to the viewing of this documentary by those inside the movie theater, and also to our viewing of this entire exercise in imaginative historiography. It is not so much that a macrocosm opens up inside a grain of sand. More to the point, the seventy-five years of Indian cinema are contained and "tamed" by the event of their narration in a movie theater, which in turn is contained by our viewing of this imaginative act of historiography. Miniaturization at any rate does not imply reduced significance. On the contrary, the miniature can emblematize a much larger order outside of the container that holds it, and the container itself can serve as a material replication of an orderly universe.[21] Perhaps we ought to think of this movie as producing a microhistory of Indian cinema, one that we are being invited to consume.[22]

The documentary is a collection of elements of the history of Indian cinema—of scenes and fragments of canonical films, dates, and personages—whose circumstances are being narrated by major film stars, who may be seen as custodians responsible for the collection or as *sutradhars* (narrators in traditional theatrical forms). In choosing the biggest film stars of the time to narrate the history of Indian cinema, *Cinema* confirms the star-driven nature of Indian cinema. It also situates Indian cinema's history literally and figuratively in the interface—the screen—between spectator and star. Perhaps in the encouragement of star-struck reverie, *Cinema Cinema* desires to transform history into an immersive experience (see Fig. 7.1).

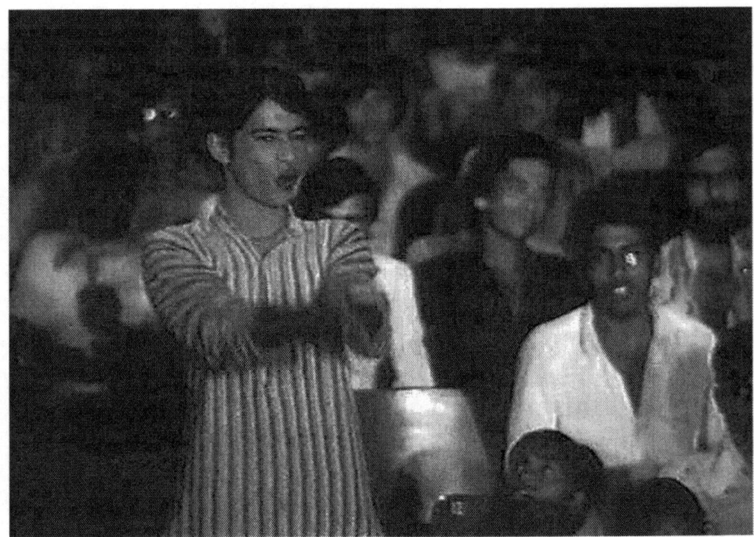

Figure 7.1. An Engaged Audience. Source: *Cinema Cinema*.

The public dimensions of Indian cinema emerge in the mode of viewership at work in the theater, a viewership that is interactive, haptic, profoundly engaged, and resolutely social. These dimensions are revealed in the movie theater. The theater contains a selective cross-section of Indian society. Among them are young couples in love, married couples with and without children, elderly and youthful single men, specifically marked by sexuality or religion as minorities, the passed-out drunk, and the distracted sports buff balancing the latest sports score on the radio with the movie he is watching. And behavioral types: a man picks his ears, another is fast asleep, a third stares at the camera, and a couple holding hands and cuddled together seem distracted more by their mutual love than by the screen. One young man is dressed in a floral-patterned red *kurta*, his face made up with eyeliner and lipstick. We witness his determined flirtation with the exasperated married man sitting next to him.

The architecture of the theater typifies the single-screen theater in India, with the "stalls"—where much of the audience interaction occurs—and the "balcony," where the tickets tend to be more expensive. Shah chooses to situate the entire audience, middle and working class, elite and plebeian, in the stalls, a democratizing impulse, perhaps born out of a U.S.-based director's experience of the cinema and quite unlike the social stratifications of Indian moviegoing.

Cinema Cinema, in its subject as well as the enactment of that subject, compels us to consider various models of the past, of narrating that past. Is its collection of clips a scrapbook or souvenir that might ask us to remember the origins of Indian cinema? Probably not, since the movie is strikingly free of any aching desire or longing or nostalgia for the past that characterizes the souvenir's raison d'être (Stewart 1993). This is brought home both by the star power that presents this history (a commercial calculation) and by the busy happenings in the hall as the movie plays out.

The activity in the hall, with its frequent insouciance to the project of concentrated spectatorship, tilts the documentary to become a collection of materials from the past, which exist to be utilized as the audience may see fit. As Susan Stewart puts it, unlike the souvenir, which is a form of antiquarianism, the collection raids the past and arranges selected elements of the past into a new whole. It is a mercantilist disposition, interested in extracting value, in creating something potentially replicable without the charged desire to delve into the origins of the objects in the collection (153). Even if we judge the documentary to be a presentation of the illustrious patina of film history, its reception in the theater deflates such an assessment.

Accordingly, the audience responds to old clips in *Cinema* with more complex motivations that exceed nostalgia. An elderly man in the audience laments that the quality of movies in the present seem to have declined compared to these older films, diluting nostalgic affection with qualitative assessment. The young couple argues over Amitabh Bachchan's appeal, the woman in adulation, the man with jealousy. The devout woman treats the image as an iconic one, praying when scenes from devotionals appear on screen. Her husband, meanwhile, sulks and complains, making explicit his preference for "serious" New Wave cinema, which the wife dismisses off-hand. And where there is nostalgic bliss, it is for the tunes being played onscreen, an indication not just of the power and longevity of film songs in India, and therefore the porosity of the filmic text, but also the cinema's ability to cater to auditory pleasures at the expense of the visual. There are other, more tactile pleasures. One of the final clips is of a risqué song by Helen, Hindi cinema's foremost cabaret dancer, performed in the manner of the Lavani, a regional genre of popular music in the state of Maharashtra that is often sung to teasing lyrics. The camera's lascivious focus on Helen's swaying hips is intercut with the excited, wide-eyed projectionist in the booth frantically unspooling an entire reel with his hands, as if what is seen on screen could be found and held more concretely in the celluloid in his hands. The past turns into immediately relevant and applicable present.

Yet, to play devil's advocate for a moment, the cinematic image is by default in the mode of a memory quilt, or scrapbook or a souvenir (or a fossil, as Bazin would say). By that ontological standard, this is a movie that offers an indexical trace of the movies. This is, after all, a movie about movies. And as such, the title, with its duplication, perhaps alludes to that fact.

It is one of the pleasures of this movie that it not only converts the indexed past into a series of iconic gestures (the extracted scenes) and faces, but also in the process engages in the task of iconoclasm, subordinating film history to the conditions of its possibility—the screen, the projector, the audience, the reels of celluloid, the building, the box office. The movie's wide-ranging dissection of the cinematic apparatus inventively braids the medium's material tangibility (the film reels, the tickets, the building, the technology, the lights) with its affective intensity (the responses elicited by the movie screen) (see Fig. 7.2).

FILM HI FILM (1983)

While *Cinema Cinema* adopts the conventions of the documentary only to subvert them, *Film Hi Film* (1983) adopts, at least at first glance, the conventions of the found footage or compilation film, in order to tell the story of the film industry.[23] Running almost two hours long, *Film Hi Film* makes extensive use of scenes from unfinished films. This is not so much stock footage as it is "found" footage, or more precisely, "lost" footage being brought to light again.

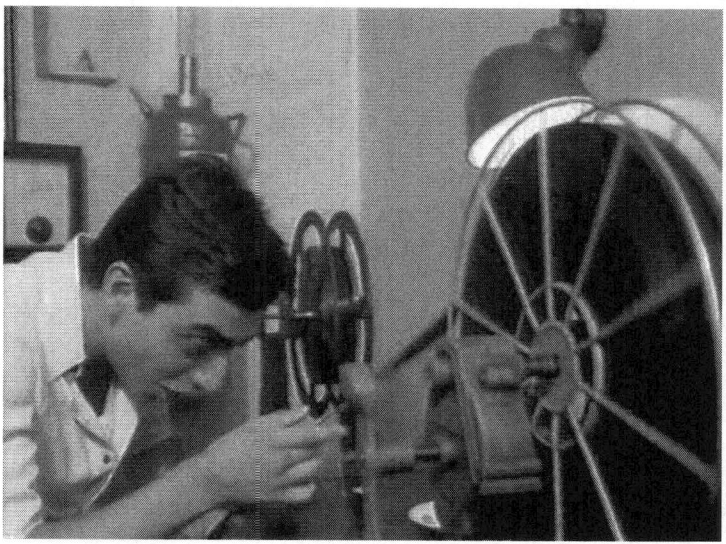

Figure 7.2. Sight turns into touch. The projectionist is seduced by celluloid. Frame: *Cinema Cinema*.

The footage is alternated with a framing narrative about the troubles of a principled but unfortunate film producer. Gyanchand aka Sethji (played by character actor Pran) is a producer who loses his wealth and his money in a bad investment and is reduced to penury. A French journalist researching the history of cinema comes to interview Gyanchand and makes him a handsome payment for his time. Elated, Gyanchand returns to film production with the money. His former crew of technicians work for him at no cost. Rehearsals and production begin. After numerous other trials, the movie is completed, but distributors show no interest. Frustrated, Gyanchand is about to destroy the reels when, miraculously, a former employee, now a successful distributor, has a sudden change of heart. The movie, titled *Film Hi Film*, is released at a glittering premiere, includes a peppy disco number, new actors who are heralded as exciting new stars, and the presence of established film stars from Bombay cinema at the premiere.

This narrative of a producer, whose career, in melodramatic terms, threatens to be an unfinished movie, is interspersed with extended scenes from incomplete movies recovered from film studios.

The relationship of the found footage with the framing narrative is not always explicit, but that seems a function of the fact that the framing narrative is presented as a melodrama of insurmountable hurdles, coincidental occurrences, and sudden reversals of fortunes. The interloping scenes from unfinished films comment on the main narrative. Their distinct nature is also visibly clear in that many of the interloping scenes are from black and white films, whereas Gyanchand's story is entirely filmed in color.

The first found footage segment appears abruptly, without warning, after Gyanchand has lost all his money and been sentenced to five years in prison. The scenes are from a movie made in 1960, *Reporter*, about a reporter (played by iconic film star Raj Kapoor) with a talking dog for company, one that can predict crimes in advance and gets the reporter in trouble. Following closely on the heels of Gyanchand's reversal of fortune, the scenes perhaps point to good men caught up in unfair circumstances. On other occasions, the footage is supposed to be exemplary or illustrative in a self-evident manner. Gyanchand, asserting to his crew that stars are born, not made, invokes Amitabh Bachchan as an example of an actor who was transformed into a star overnight by the movie *Zanjeer* (1973). Mention of Bachchan's name motivates the turn to footage of scenes from two incomplete films.

At times it seems as if the framing narrative wants to satirize the found scenes. In scenes from an unfinished war melodrama, *Shikhwa* (*Complaint*, 1954), a pacifist hero (Dilip Kumar) is imprisoned as a traitor to the cause of war. To save him from the death penalty, his lover Nutan must abandon him and marry the warmongering general. In the version Gyanchand is directing, this war melodrama is translated by his newbie actors but with Buñuelesque transformations. Shot-reverse-shots of the two characters include the presence of a teddy bear in the heroine's arms and two goats that bear the brunt of the hero's wrath.

Perhaps an explanation is not needed. *Film Hi Film* bears the markings of its relative anonymity in the history of Bombay cinema in the fact that neither the scenes of its framing narratives nor the found footage appear in the order they ought to. Also obvious is the less than skillful editing in which some scenes close on shots that linger a tad too long on the actors, as if we were watching a poorly timed amateur stage play. The abrupt transitions to the orphaned scenes seem at times to be a function of possibly missing footage or frames of the Gyanchand segments. Finally, the screen duration of the orphaned scenes is often much longer than the scenes comprising the framing narrative itself, suggesting an economical approach to storytelling where available footage minimizes the need and costs of freshly shot ones. Do these misplacements—and the goats—signal the unknown history of the transfer of this movie from film to cheap VCDs now available online? *Film Hi Film* may have undergone the randomization of use that underscores the idea of footage lost and then recuperated in entirely new contexts.

Regardless of whether intentional or not, the difficulty of following the plotline does not hamper our understanding of the story. This too may be a function of melodrama, and especially the loose dramatic arc of Indian commercial melodramas that makes a scene-by-scene economy of narration unnecessary and fundamentally foreign to a dilatory unfolding. What then does this movie set out to do?

First, I would contend that *Film Hi Film* serves to conventionalize an already highly conventionalized cinema. The reclamation of "orphan" scenes is not motivated by the desire to situate them in a linear and realistic storyline. Writing in the 1980s about the commercial Hindi cinema's own standards or frames of reference, Rosie Thomas observed that in Hindi commercial cinema, the originality of a story line is less important than the screenplay's emphasis on spectacle and emotion. What happens next is less important than how it happens. Moral perturbations to be eventually resolved are more important than unsolved enigmas. The audience's familiarity with the depicted cultural universe, and its expectations about the commercial film form, combined with repeat viewings, take precedence over originality. Finally, a succession of ingredients—action, melodrama, song-dance, and comedy—is more important than a linear development (Thomas 1984).

There is therefore a certain degree of reflexivity built into the commercial film form of Indian cinema. Considering *Film Hi Film* as a form of metatheorization of the medium would therefore be misplaced given that reflexivity is a happy confirmation of the established conventions of this cinema. It is not a symptom of—or for that sake, in this instance, a cure for—an epistemological crisis regarding the photographic image, induced by new media.[24]

Second, scholars of found-footage films have often used the metaphor of waste, junk, and recycling to describe such footage. Found footage has been termed a form of disposable culture reclaimed from a landfill (Danks 2006). However, the impetus that drives this movie's use of found footage is quite unlike in experimental and avant-garde cinema, where the decontextualizing and then repurposing of found footage, can be seen as oppositional forms in relation to the capital-intensive Hollywood. Far from stripping away the context, *Film Hi Film* with its melodrama about a filmmaker seeking to make a commercial film melodrama, restores this found footage to its rightful context.[25] The scenes are from movies that were never completed and therefore could be seen as already decontextualized by circumstance, even before the director reuses the material. *Film Hi Film* performs the function of a salvage operation, rescuing what would otherwise be termed as waste. In this function, it serves as an archive in the most literal sense. It is in this sense that we may consider this a movie less about "found footage" in the sense of fortuitous discovery, and more about "lost footage" searching for a new cinematic home. After all, the titles at the opening of the movie acknowledge many of the major studios in Bombay at the time as suppliers of these scenes.

Third, the framing device undertakes, however ineffectually, a critique of the film industry as it was in the 1980s. The lack of institutional legitimacy for the cinema is conveyed when Gyanchand takes a principled stand to go to jail on his unpaid debts rather than declare insanity, because he sees himself as the better exemplar of an already reviled industry. The highly disorganized mode of production of Bombay cinema is conveyed in his need to take loans from private moneylenders at usurious interest rates. His inability to afford stars, or find distributors who might want to purchase rights for the film after it is finally done, conveys the picture of a star-driven institution. *Film Hi Film* writes history in the best possible way: by filtering an orphaned past, self-reflexively, through its own present. Michael Zryd (2003) explicitly contrasts archival footage—housed in institutions—from found footage, which survives by chance and is discovered by chance. *Film Hi Film* manages to turn found footage into archival footage, where the archive is of the present, as well, and not just of the past.

The movie's metahistoricity, if it is such at all, derives from the most transparent representational function of the lost scenes as they are incorporated into a larger melodramatic narrative and dramaturgical framework. We are watching a movie about movies. What we are watching is a transparent record, a record of movies as the referents of that record.

Nevertheless, a lingering trace of *detournement* as a secondary strategy is also in evidence in the satirizing of the source material that I described earlier.[26] Steve Anderson proposes that found footage films perform "a deployment and subversion of ontological certainty" with regard to the photographic image (Anderson 2011, 70). The footage is frequently employed rhetorically by being decontextualized, repurposed, and recombined. As it is also evident in the sly inclusion of news footage of major film stars arriving at *a* premiere of some other movie, within a montage of shots of Gyanchand being feted at *his* movie's premiere with his cast of unknown nonstars. Inside the theater of the premiere, we are in for another late surprise. The shots of the theater are sourced from producer Shabab Ahmed's earlier production, *Cinema Cinema*. Where now does this footage—that of the theater—stand in relation to the movie *Film Hi Film*? (see Fig. 7.3).

To unpack that question, we may need to return to an aspect of *Cinema Cinema* that I have not touched upon: its status as a "fictional biography" of a real entity, Indian cinema. In that movie, at intermission, the diegetic audience is treated to an advertisement (with jingle) about Air India. So the audiences are paying to watch a documentary on the history of Indian cinema as entertainment, where they would otherwise watch a feature-length fiction. During intermission, they watch an advertisement for a state-owned

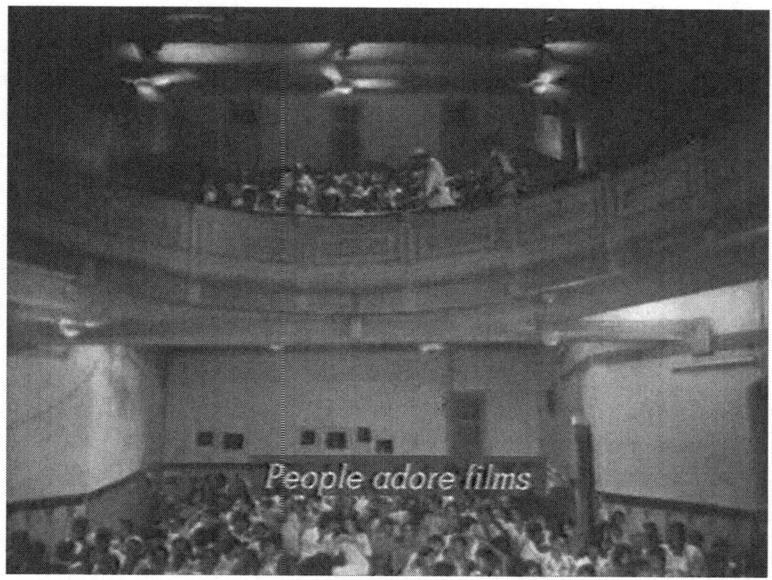

Figure 7.3. This image of the theater appears in *Cinema Cinema* as well as *Film Hi Film*.

airline, Air India hawking the pleasures of travel and tourism, where they would otherwise watch the state hawking something edificatory and didactic. The intermission was when audiences in postindependence India would have been invariably treated to the state's pedagogical documentaries on health and civic issues. In a strange reversal, then, commercial cinema adopts the pedagogical documentary mode, while the state adopts the exhortative mode of travel and tourism. The state peddles the consumerist fantasies routinely peddled by commercial cinema. Commercial cinema on its part, presents its own history as edifying in the documentary mode.

Of course, for the diegetic audience and considered within the terms set by *Cinema Cinema*, the documentary is entertaining. And promises of entertainment by the state (-run airlines) are, at best, worthless intermissions. And again, within the terms set by the diegesis, the space of the theater is the space of real life. However, we also know that the goings-on in the theater are enacted. *Cinema Cinema* confounds, therefore, at least two forms: the mockumentary and the docudrama. It is neither all fiction pretending to be a documentary (the mockumentary), nor is it all fact presented in the manner of a fiction (the docudrama). It might be more useful to say that the realism at work in *Cinema Cinema* is iconic and idealist. As with the commercial Hindi film, it is recognizable and familiar to a narrative community as a cinematic imaginary: the familiar public experience of the cinema (as opposed to an individual spectator and her experience that might be predicated on credulity, or the willing suspension of disbelief). The reuse, then, of the shots of the theater from *Cinema Cinema* in *Film Hi Film* is possible because those images of the theatre are iconic images of a cinematic imaginary, representative. In other words, those images are not being used—or certainly not solely being used—as indexical records of a movie theater. They are not being used for the evidentiary power that permits the narrative context to be rewritten while the medium ensures that the evidence remains unassailable. Instead, what we have is a movie with a relation to history where *kuch bhi chalega,* anything will suffice, if it can convey the cinema's iconicity, its practical existence.[27]

Neither *Cinema Cinema* nor *Film Hi Film* is terribly committed to the historicist project. But the two films also attest to a broader principle of popular film historiography. The miscellany, the collection, and the compilation have served as the dominant modes of writing and narrating film history in popular culture, not anamnesis or recall in the mode of a fidelity to a certain narrative of the past. Nostalgia turns into recollection and classification, not preservation in its archival or historicist sense. The cinema, removed from elite valorization, state-conferred legitimacy, and self-congratulatory industrial nostalgia, becomes a rich repertoire of popular uses in the present.

In contrast, and in conclusion, we may consider a Films Division documentary on the history of Indian cinema *Through a Different Lens* (S. Krishnaswamay 1986) that reclaims film as national history, by redeeming it and emphasizing the cinema's nation-building service in the anticolonial past. The voiceover narration makes it clear that the cinema is "not just entertainment," and that Indian cinema has had a venerable history of patriotic representations countering British imperialism. What follows is a series of clips of movies of the preindependence period. The clips are considered patriotic for thematic and topical reasons (the genre of "the social" that depicted contemporary life and invoked contemporary political issues and themes such as caste, agricultural servitude, widow remarriage, women's emancipation), as well as for allegorical reasons (the historical, the devotional, the mythological). Phalke finds mention roughly at the midpoint of the film for starting a film industry out of patriotic reasons. This motivation, the narrator claims, makes the Indian film industry unique, for its self-consciously nationalist origins.[28]

The desire to redeem the cinema in this documentary is also significant because the movie was made in the 1980s, the same decade as *Cinema Cinema* and *Film Hi Film*. This was the decade when it seemed that the form of the Indian commercial film had truly degenerated into a highly ossified formula. This is the "masala" film (*masala* meaning spice mixture), with the outsized influence of Bachchan on this formula (the ritualization of violence, the marginalization of female characters, the amplification of the star text through multi-starrers, were all features of the Bachchan film). This was also the decade of the deep reach of the underworld inside the film industry (alluded to or thematized in many Bachchan films).

It is therefore significant that *Through a Different Lens* was made in this decade and takes as its premise the idea that the cinema "is not just" entertainment. The documentary therefore serves as a form of "state historiography" functioning as "redemptive texts, structured to offer predictions based on causal accounts of exoneration and blame" (Stoler 2002, 105). In preceding chapters, I have already discussed the emergence of the cinema as mass culture, one in which the blame game was quite central to the state's conceptions of culture with the cinema bearing the brunt of the blame. Here, Films Division produces a documentary that seeks to exonerate Indian cinema, to redeem it. The exoneration is executed by none other S. Krishnaswamy, the co-author of the first major history of Indian cinema to have academic chops, *Indian Film*, first published in 1963 and in its second edition in 1980 (Barnuow and Krishnaswamy 1980). The desire to redeem the cinema in this documentary is also significant because the movie was made in the 1980s, the same decade as *Cinema Cinema* and *Film Hi Film*, the same decade critiqued in *Film Hi Film* for its uncaring cruelty toward a hapless filmmaker, and celebrated via a star system run amok.

While the debates around the archiving of Indian cinema's past continue, I have presented here a parallel world of initiatives whose historiographical gestures imply starkly variant perspectives on what would constitute an archive, on the possibility of an archive, and on the necessity of an archive.

Archives are vulnerable to the "conditions under which they are utilized" (Simon 2006, 194). If we think of history as a practice and mode of production, popular visual culture in South Asia is constantly in the practice of producing its history as a vernacular imaginary. The practices of exhibition and image production discussed in this book therefore also serve as acts of historiography, of generating a history. At the same time, these practices also constitute open-ended archives, reusing the past and putting past fragments to new or reiterated uses. The question of the cinematic archive may carry its prescriptive, nostalgic, and diagnostic elements, especially given the woeful state of India's film archive. But in this chapter, I have taken the archive as a heuristic to describe the cinema's propensity to make its past through relentless reuse rather than preservation per se. To reverse my earlier formulation, the archive is not just for the taking in India, it is for the making.

8

POSTSCRIPT

Two radically different imaginations of the cinema can be found in India today. The first is contained in an article published in 2012 in the magazine *Indian Architect and Builder*. The article describes the plan for a proposed Bollywood museum in Mumbai, designed by the Yazdani Studio of Cannon Design, an architecture firm in LA run by LA-based architect Mehrdad Yasdani. The "museologists" for the project are Lord Cultural Resources, a Canadian firm that describes itself as "a global professional practice dedicated to creating cultural capital worldwide," including in its list of services, "cultural and heritage tourism planning."[1]

Written in a promotional tone, the premise of the piece is that Mumbai is missing a Bollywood museum in which "film enthusiasts can enjoy the Bollywood experience" (!). Yazdani therefore proposes just such a place, a museum whose entire structure

> is like a wave, undulating as you move from the entrance to the various spatial experiences waiting to unfold inside. When the building emerges from its surroundings, it is somewhat reminiscent of a silk ribbon swaying dynamically, complementing the dancer's moves. The building resembles a wave; a central feature in all things typically "Bollywood"—the flow of thought, emotion, storyline, drama, the climax, the lyrical movement of the song-and-dance routine—every facet has a definite rise and fall. (82–83)

The experience of moving through this museum will replicate the "grandeur and stardom" of Bollywood: a red carpet entrance, a movie theater where visitors can get an orientation to the museum, and galleries themed, we are explicitly told, not chronologically but "as per emotions; five emotions in particular: joy, sorrow, angst, fear and love." The museum will also include "working sets" for a behind-the-scenes feel, while other galleries will include "new age" interactive technology to create a film world inside. Exhibition rooms will house iconic memorabilia but the aim will be to create a "living space" and not a "museum-esque artefact box with little emotional connect." The article also mentions a film library and concludes that the wavelike design of the structure will represent "the global reach of Bollywood" that is "like a rising wave, slowly but steadily taking over the world." The museum will be located, the article informs the reader, in Film City in Goregaon (a suburb of Mumbai), and the excitement of possibly running into film stars or into shooting in progress will add to the excitement for visitors.

Renderings of the museum depict aerial views of a "silk ribbon"–like design with three folds, also described at one point in the article as akin to a Mobius strip. Other images, of the lobby and of two halls of interactive media, and one of the front façade of the structure, show interiors bathed in a near-monochromatic pink/purple hue, an odd choice for a piece that uses the world *colorful* at least once. Perhaps this is a matter of being tasteful and toning down the saturated colors associated with the visual landscape of the cinema in India. As Ackbar Abbas puts it in his summary of Walter Benjamin's critique of taste, "The importance of taste increases in direct proportion to the consumer's declining awareness of the commodity's social and technical conditions of production—that is, the less you know about a product, the more important taste becomes. Taste is a highly ambiguous response to the commodity. On the one hand, it bathes the commodity in a 'profane glow'; on the other hand, taste is a 'more or less elaborate masking' of the consumer's 'lack of expertness'" (Abbas 1988). That formulation of taste applies to Yazdani Studio which believes that the "experience" of Bollywood is lacking in everyday life, and only the phantasmagoric aesthetics of a museum would supply that experience. This is the Arcades project come to fruition a century too late (see Figs. 8.1 and 8.2).

One of the interior renderings depicts a spacious hall, with silhouetted visitors. Prominent in the picture are transparent glass tubes descending from the ceiling (imagine sci-fi pods), which contain haloed depictions of contemporary Bollywood stars, the moments drawn from movies. The stars may be holograms; the wall on the right bears a stretch of classic Hindi cinema posters on the lower half while the upper half is covered in undulating violet drapery. A second room depicts a hallway called the "Tunnel of Love," one that includes a screen for the wall, depicting romantic moments, while the rendering, interestingly enough, depicts two young men holding hands and

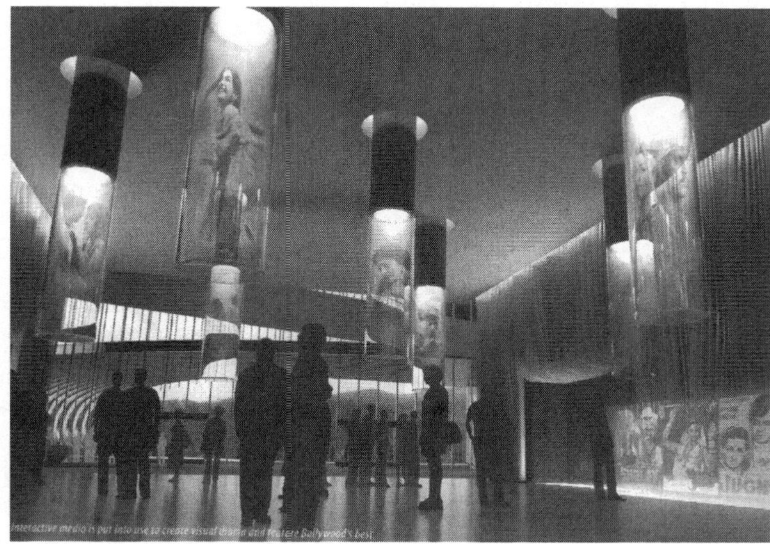

Figure 8.1. Interior of the proposed film museum by Yazdani Studio. Source: *Indian Architect and Builder* magazine, Jan. 2012 issue, courtesy of Yazdani Studio of Cannon Design.

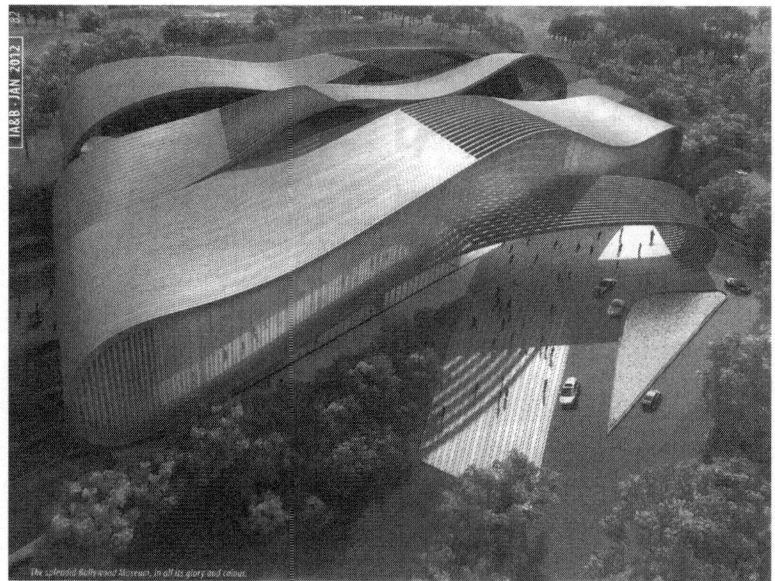

Figure 8.2. Exterior of the proposed film museum by Yazdani Studio. Source: *Indian Architect and Builder* magazine, Jan. 2012 issue, courtesy of Yazdani Studio of Cannon Design.

walking through the space, an observation of Indian homosociality but one that is open to reinterpretation in the context of that space.

This museum follows the trend in film museums elsewhere of renouncing sweeping narratives of film history. A singular emphasis on the material cultures of the cinema, on artifacts denarrativized, encased, and denuded of context, takes their place. Film museums born of personal collections, such as Henri Langlois's early versions of the Cinémathèque Française, comprised objects fetishized by the collector, not objects organized and narrativized by the historian.

While the absence of a grand narrative of Bombay cinema is clear in this proposed museum, its departure from the trend of decontextualized artifacts is more complex. On the one hand, it explicitly eschews the "museum-esque artifact box with little emotional connect." On the other hand, it follows closely the hybrid models of film museums that have emerged at institutions such as the American Museum of the Moving Image or the now defunct Museum of the Moving Image at the BFI. In this latter approach, the artifacts are married to a historical narrative. But the narrative makes no claims to a broad sweep. Instead, thematic organization, sometimes motivated by the location of the museum, attempts a more modest experience of the cinema. This experience makes no claims to comprehensiveness (Trope 2001).

It is striking how closely the proposed Mumbai museum follows this more recent model. A red carpet leads to the lobby of the theater. That lobby is a prelude to a series of thematic galleries organized around the emotions that comprise the classical Sanskrit aesthetic system, which are elaborated around the five *rasas*, or flavors, or emotions. The pedagogical mission of the museum is emblematized in a library and in a simulation of a working set, while the cinephile of the Langlois mode is enticed with movie memorabilia, and the younger generation with an interactive, multimedia experience of Bombay cinema. Thus, the initial lobby is not followed by the equivalent of the movie hall and its theatrical experience. Instead, it leads to an unpacking and reorganization of the aesthetics, production, and technology of the cinema. The emphasis on stardom, which continues to dominate Bombay cinema as its presiding economic logic, is worth noting, since every rendering of the interiors is dominated by the presence of stars rendered in various formats: as holograms in glass tubes descending from the ceiling, as more traditional movie posters encompassing entire walls, and presumably as moving images on walls/screens that run the entire length of the "Tunnel of Love." Stardom is the main pull for the location of the museum, one that might enhance the possibility of running into stars, we are told. Location confers the value of being situated inside the very episteme the museum seeks to reproduce within its walls.

The Bollywood museum's description and renderings share much with the rapidly developing suburbs of postliberalization India, gated enclaves of residence and business whose "state-of-the-art" luxuries speak a strongly temporal imagination of an anticipated and proximate future, a virtual experience that informs real spaces imbued with futurity (Kalyan 2011). The renderings of this particular Bollywood museum don't specify all the materials of construction, but they can be inferred nonetheless. Granite or concrete, glass, and light seem dominant. The light is both artificial and natural, the latter ushered in through the latticework on portions of the ribbon-roofs (which also throw patterns on the driveway in front of the entrance). Natural light is also to be found inside, through glass openings on the far end of the hall mediated by thin vertical lines that might be—and I'm guessing here—pencil-thin steel beams. The museum's materials and form, as an undulating wave, convert the "black" box of the theater into a fluid experience of space. The key element of the cinematic apparatus, the screen, has become, in this museum, part of an immersive environment. But the screen has also become a three-dimensional glass tube, descending from the ceiling from luminous pools of light that radiate seemingly three-dimensional and transparent images of stars.

In this case, the cinema is given a certain architectural form in keeping with the neoliberal ethos of urbanization in India. But the flip side is that the architecture adopts the cinema as a metaphor to produce an ephemeral image of memorabilia, emotions, experience, and immersion, as does Rem Koolhaas's architecture. Nothing in this museum indicates an imagination of the cinema as a record of durability (Tweedie 2010). Both architecture and the cinema become modes of "erasure and eradication" (ibid., 390). Tweedie reminds us that for Koolhaas, the history of the city is a fall from Manhattanism, a desire to build enduring soaring structures testifying to progress, to a new model of the virtual city, characterized by the acceleration of new media and its concomitant generic architectural styles. This is indeed how we ought to read this initiative of a new cinema museum, one that peddles the cinema as a neoliberal exception (Ong 2006). This film museum is symptomatic of the current political economy of Bollywood. But it stands in stark contrast to a different imaginary of the cinema I encountered in person.

In the summer of 2010, I was in Delhi walking through the dense, congested streets of Chandni Chowk, or Old Delhi. I was in search of a lane of repairers and sellers of film projectors. While initial enquiries with shopkeepers yielded directions to the lane, all I saw were shops filled with digital projectors, old and new. I wanted to see a lane full of old film projectors. Eventually, I was directed to a building where I was told a man named Ashokji might be of help. Ashokji took me to a decrepit building long out of any maintenance. As he disappeared into the darkness of the building's entrance, I followed him in total disorienting darkness, finding my way up through the curving and seemingly endless staircase, without light, feeling the walls. Finally we reached a dead end, a door that Ashokji unlocked.

Delhi-ites would call this room the *barsati,* or a small rooftop or attic room. Inside, I found a cot and a bench facing each other along the length of the tiny room. The walls were plastered with an unlikely combination of religious calendars and printed images, of which some were religious "pictures" of Hindu gods and goddesses, and others were depictions of Mecca, Islam's holiest shrine. Then there were still other posters, of sultry semi-clad actresses and heroes with guns, from Bombay's mammoth film industry, in some cases plastered over the religious calendars. On the floor were cans and cans of film reels whose title cards were barely legible.

Still more cans of film and other printed matter jutted out of a shelf on the wall. Ashokji was eager to sell me things. The bench was actually a cabinet whose seat/lid opened to reveal thousands of printed film posters. His younger assistant, who arrived shortly after us, was being instructed to pull the posters out for my perusal. This was not terribly exciting. If I wanted posters and wanted to glorify myself as a serious collector of movie memorabilia, I would be more interested in vintage ones, not reprints. But there was more: hall cards of low-budget horror movies with titles that would not suffer translation, movies that from the look of it were at once softcore porn and grisly violence.

But the *pièce de resistance* of this room was the door that opened out to the tiny verandah and the sunlit view of the congested street below, a door covered in film posters that could compete with any takeout joint decorated in Bollywood kitsch that one might find on Capitol Hill in Seattle, or in the Alberta Arts neighborhood in Portland (see Figs. 8.3 and 8.4).

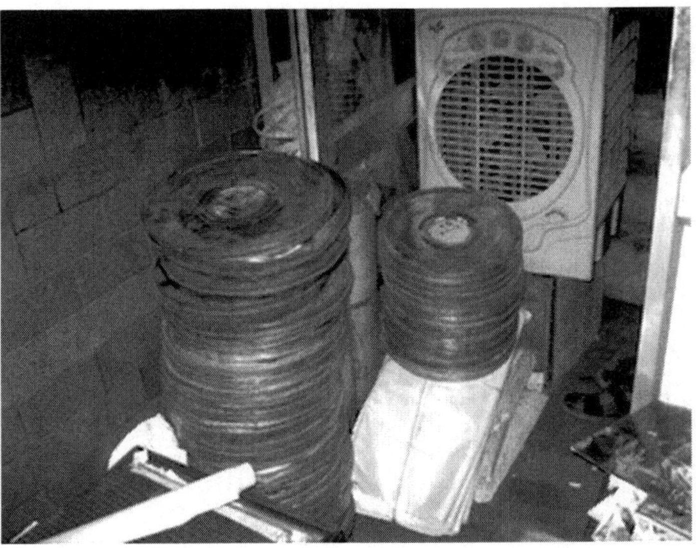

Figure 8.3. Old Delhi, 2010 (Photo: Sudhir Mahadevan).

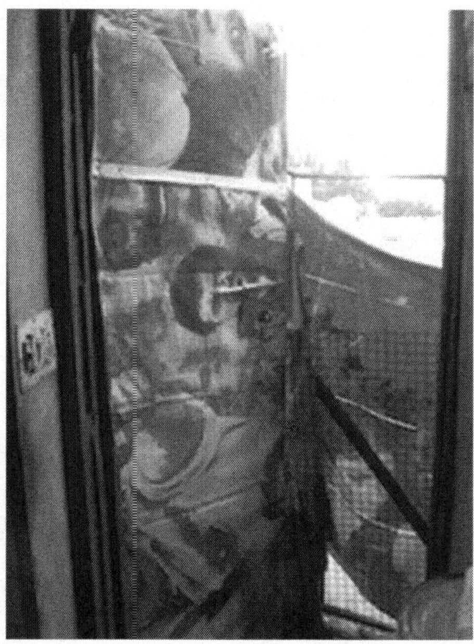

Figure 8.4. Old Delhi, 2010 (Photo: Sudhir Mahadevan).

My trajectory up the stairs of this building in total darkness to a space filled with movie memorabilia, in retrospect, vaguely replicated the experience of walking into a movie theater a little late, feeling one's way into a seat in the darkness and settling down for an experience of sights and sounds. Only here, in search of old machines, the projectors, I had walked up a flight of stairs in darkness to encounter other *matériel* of the cinema in a naturally lit room. It was as if the cinematic experience had been given architectural form in broad daylight, as it were, or turned inside out to reveal its tangible components, its flip side. This book has sought the many origins of the cinema that have supplied the mise-en-scène to this room.

NOTES

INTRODUCTION

1. For a critique of modernity theory's tendency to treat the cinema as "ready-made stimuli" experienced by the individual subject in urban space that is likewise often imagined as a pre-"given entity," see Braester 2010, 9–13.

2. In her discussion of the Internet, Wendy Chun (2008) observes that the ideology of the personal computer and the Internet is predicated on a techno-utopianism that conflates storage capacity with memory, emptying our understanding of the past of its constructedness. I borrow the title of my chapter on archives from Chun's essay.

3. See as well James Moran (2002) for a cogent summary of the various fallacies of medium-specificity theories. Rather than understanding video through essential technical features that in turn entail specific and exclusive aesthetic norms, Moran proposes that we see video as defined via its use within specific fields of practice and ranges of possibilities.

4. I am paraphrasing my colleague Marshall Brown, to whom I'm grateful for this formulation.

5. Musser (1990, 18) defines screen practices as "a set of practices that utilized images, voice, sound effects and music for the purpose of projection on to a screen." See also André Gaudreault's contention that "pre-cinema" and "early cinema" were "proto-" and "multiform" phenomena. Any coherence and unity conferred on these phenomena assumes a "panoramic" position exterior to these areas of enquiry (8–9).

6. For two theoretically innovative discussions of this aspect of the cinema and the sensorium, see Rai (2009) and Basu (2012).

7. Art historian Chaitanya Sambrani (2005) and artists such as Atul Dodiya see this recycling as part of India's historical condition, a necessary reflection of socioeconomic issues: "Crafting wings from chopped arms is the prerogative of a despairing artist-citizen," observes Dodiya. "Rogier van der Wyden and Picasso could paint tears. I can only go about circumambulating ladders, sliding down, looking up, and knocking against skulls and bellies. In the final countdown it is all skulls and bellies" (125).

8. For a discussion of mainstream Bollywood's representation of itself as a "retro" pleasure, one that repackages film history as nostalgia within the diegetic and non-diegetic worlds of contemporary mainstream cinema see Walia (2013) and Wilkinson-Weber (2010).

9. For a rich sampling of essays in this vein, see Sundaram (2013).

10. And this is precisely the question posed by Elsaesser as well. He too proposes that if we replace "what" with "when," we will find not one cinema but many.

11. Christian Metz uses the word in two senses (I paraphrase here): as the technological precondition for the cinema (which he identifies as photography and phonography), and in the psychoanalytical sense of the imaginary as a presymbolic stage in the etiology of the self that is opposed to but inevitably tied to the symbolic, or to language. It is this latter sense that has informed screen theory's formulations regarding the pleasures and identifications afforded by the act of seeing, on which the cinema depends. Metz prefaces these definitions of the imaginary with the assertion that any conscious reflection on the cinema along the lines of the imaginary is an attempt to wrest the cinema from the imaginary, to induct it into the symbolic thereby proving that "the field of film . . . is from the outset a semiological one" (Metz 1982, 3–4), that is to say, it is an experience that can be given meaning.

For other uses of the word *imaginary*, see the collection of essays in *Future Cinema* (Shaw and Weibel, 2003), which variously define the imaginary of the cinema as a function of medium specificity, as residing in cinema as technology, as an idea and (platonic) ideal about what the cinema is, and as what emerges in certain reflexive historiographical gestures by artists whose work centers around the cinema.

CHAPTER 1. THE NINETEENTH-CENTURY INDIAN TECHNO-BAZAAR

1. Innovators developed various versions of the processing camera in Europe and America until the 1950s, although they fell out of widespread commercial use by the 1870s. These processing cameras failed to win mass markets, such as the "Photo-See" camera, invented by film pioneer Herman Casler in New York in 1936, or the Aptus Automatic Minute Camera of 1956, the last version of a model that first appeared in 1913 (Coe 1978, 177–88).

2. This is indeed one famous anthropological understanding of what constitutes a bazaar economy offered up by Clifford Geertz that Rajat Kanta Ray has criticized.

3. *Bengal Hurkaru*, Jan. 25, 1841.

4. Asa Briggs devotes an entire chapter to spectacles and photographic cameras in his book *Victorian Things*, the third installment of his magisterial cultural history of Victorian Britain, and for good reason. By spectacles, Briggs refers literally, to eyeglasses, but as in Bengal, there was a relationship between optical products and the newly emerging technologies of mechanical reproduction. The first consequence of Daguerre's announcement in 1839, Briggs tells us, was that people besieged opticians' stores in London with inquiries (1998, 121).

5. Clive Dewey's observations about European artists in India between 1770 and 1830 holds relevance for a historical sociology of a new technological object such as photography:

> [European] expatriate taste was not much inferior to taste in England. Given the constant movement of artists and patrons between England and India, the only enduring difference tended to be one of price. Otherwise, it was a question of lagging and leading: short lags behind the most radical innovators at home; short leads over English taste as a whole. The dominant patrons in India, the nabobs, may well have been in advance of the dominant patrons in England, the gentry. . . . The dead weight of tradition was a less formidable barrier to novelty; and what Anglo-India borrowed from home tended to be what metropolitan fashions presented most prominently to the outside world. The nabobs imitated an image of society in England, rather than society itself; and in that image, as in the press, the contemporaneous loomed disproportionately large. The imitators, also, were especially sensitive to fashion. (1982, 688)

6. A 1913 account describing European life noted that "an up-country cantonment, or for that matter a sudder township [administrative center] would have been atypical indeed had it not included a Cutfisher & Co. dealing in wines, mineral waters, provisions and tobacco; a Huckaback & Co., booksellers, printers, publishers and stationers; a Tusk and Podgett, milliners, tailors and outfitters; Herr Blitzen, the German photographer and portrait painter; Foldy, Riddle & Co., the piano, band instrument and music warehouse; Linseed the chemist, and Signor Campobasso the Italian confectioner. There would, in addition, have been the boot and shoe maker, the art & furniture dealers, the ladies' dressmaker, the hairdresser, and kindred others of this class" (Hervey 1913, 65–66; Renford 1976, 143).

7. One such firm, Smith Stanistreet and Company, established in 1810, entered the photographic supply business very early, and by the turn of the twentieth century became one of the biggest photography studios, developers, and suppliers in South Asia. "Smith, Stanistreet and Company, Industrial and Commercial Bengal, Part 1." Special Issue of *The Englishman*, 1903, 60–62.

8. Bathgate and Co., the other supplier of photo chemicals, was in a similar position and like Smith, Stanistreet & Company, continues to exist to this day in Calcutta.

9. C. Lazarus, a furniture maker, entered the photo-materials business and eventually became a major patron of the Bengal Photographic Society Today, Lazarus's armoires and cabinets go for tens of thousands of dollars in the American antiques market. See for instance the online catalog of Executive Antiques, Albany, New York. antiques-internet.com/new-york/executiveantiques/dynapage/IP379.htm; last accessed Feb. 6, 2007.

10. By 1851, S & B Solomons, opticians with offices in London and Calcutta, were promoting an extensive line of optical and philosophical instruments that included both daguerreotype and calotype instruments.

11. Peliti (born in 1844) had arrived in India from Italy in 1869 after winning a competition to become the house confectioner for the Viceroy of the Government of India, Lord Mayo. His confectionary shop, which sold French, Italian, and English products, was enormously popular. Peliti also owned a bungalow in Simla and as an amateur photographer his skill and expertise gained him the patronage of touring Viceregal and Royal parties. A website, ostensibly by his great-grandson Luca Peliti, includes an undated posed photograph of a European group in front of the Elephanta caves near Bombay, taken, we assume, by Peliti. The group includes two men happily holding up spaghetti in their hand, serving as a starch-laden index of the early history of vernacular or tourist photography, a proud culinary response to the grandiose photographic documentation of Indian archaeology by the colonial state, if ever there was one. "A trip to Elephanta." www.geocities.com/lupeliti/index.html; last accessed Feb. 4, 2007.

12. For example, galleries became a site for the display of photographs and the sale of materials. In 1851, A. W. Roghe a photographer from Frankfurt, visited Calcutta, where he kept many specimen images on hand for those who might have been interested in his photographic portraits on paper in his temporary gallery in the city. Like Roghe, in 1859 other traveling and amateur photographers such as F. Beato and Robert and Harriet Tytler too, held "viewings" of their photographs in Calcutta.

13. *Bengal Hurkaru*, Sept. 24, 1849.

14. *Bengal Hurkaru*, May 9, 1855.

15. Identifying himself only as "C."

16. This particular example also suggests the proximity between photography and print culture. J. L. Belnos, the painter mentioned in the editor's response, may have in fact been Jean-Jacques Belnos, a French miniature artist residing in India. The latter, along with fellow Frenchman M. de Savinghac, introduced lithography to India in 1822 for the purpose of reproducing paintings and prints. This was only one of many intersections between print and photography that we will explore in greater detail in subsequent chapters. Jean-Jacques Belnos arrived in Calcutta around 1807. Although earlier accounts of the origins of lithography in India credit James Nathaniel Rind, Rind's proposal to the East India Company to set up a government printing press was presented only in 1823. Rind also stuck to reproducing maps and documents rather than lithographs of artistic portraits and sketches, which Belnos and Savighnac were said to have produced (Shaw 1998, 92–94).

17. *Bengal Hurkaru*, March 1, 1841, 225.

18. The extent of commercial and private photographic activity is difficult to pin down empirically in these early decades, but in 1841 there are at least ten instances of photographic instruments being advertised for sale in the *Bengal Hurkaru*.

19. Seen historically, ambrotypes and ferrotypes were intermediate processes between the daguerreotype process, and the glass wet-collodion negative. Unlike the daguerreotype process, which provided a one-off direct positive image on copper plates, the wet-collodion process, which supplanted daguerreotypes in the 1850s, was a negative-positive process. Collodion, a viscous liquid, served as the binding agent for the light-sensitive silver nitrates, or emulsion, on the glass plate. The nitrates were the equivalent of what would later be the film on which the image was produced. The result was a glass negative, which yielded, through contact exposure to photographic paper, a positive image. Ambrotypes and ferrotypes did away with the need for the extra step of producing paper positives. They were one-time direct positive images, like the daguerreotype images, but duller and nonreflective, unlike the fine, sparkling quality of the daguerreotype image. They were also produced with the wet-collodion process. In the ambrotype process, the glass plate was backed with black varnish so that the negative image on the plate would appear as a positive image when held up to reflected light. Ferrotypes (also known as tintypes) also relied on wet-collodion negatives, but instead of glass they relied on thin, black lacquered or japanned iron sheets. Once again, held against the light, the negative image appeared positive. Tintypes were the cheapest to produce since the metal plates were a lot cheaper than glass, but both ambrotypes and tintypes were cheap alternatives to daguerreotypes (Jenkins 1975, 41–42).

20. In one of the lists of East India Railway Company rates I found, Class 1 goods were the cheapest to transport, whereas Class 5 goods were the most expensive:

> Class 1—Red earth, fine wood, seeds of all kinds, manure, wooden or iron sleepers.
>
> Class 2—Plans and maps, stationary paper, pewter, steel, starch, telegraphic tripods, nonperishable vegetables, urinals.
>
> Class 3—Tent equipages, ivory combs, scales, locks, woolens, cartridge paper, cheese.
>
> Class 4—Surveying, drawing, and mathematical instruments; lithographic stone, chandeliers, glass and glassware, unpolished furniture, guns and pistols, fishing tackle, japanned ware, lace, lamps, silk umbrellas.
>
> Class 5—Clocks and watches, paintings, drawings, perfumery, photographic apparatus and chemicals, surgical and philosophical instruments, engravings, polished and carved, writings. (*Thacker's Bengal and Agra Directory* 1870, 63)

21. *Thacker's Bengal and Agra Directory*, 1879, Appendix, 151.

22. The earliest form of the "daguerreotype kit came with a box for carrying silver-copper plates, a box for iodizing the silver-copper plates, and a mercury vapor box for developing the exposed plates. In addition to these bulky items, buffers and powders for polishing and bottles of the requisite chemicals completed the kit." The whole kit weighed upward of one hundred pounds (Jenkins 1966, 271). For a detailed and long-spanning history of the design of photographic cameras, see Coe (1978).

23. *Bengal Hurkaru*, Nov. 7, 1849.

24. An important exception here is the pioneer of telegraphy in India, William Brooke O'Shaughnessy, of the Bengal Medical Service (and later responsible for the establishment of British India's telegraphic network) whose experiments in photogenic impressions had occurred as early as 1839 and were described by him in correspondence to the Asiatic Society of Bengal. See Thomas (1986) and Falconer (2001).

25. This aspect of photography, its function in producing a body of knowledge, has received the most scholarly attention. The work of Chris Pinney (1998), who names and formulates the aforementioned two paradigms, is exemplary. See also Pelizzari (2003) and Chaudhary (2012).

26. Each of the photographic societies published journals that exchanged information on fine chemicals and their proportions, adequate light, exposure times, suitable cameras for tropical conditions, suitable genres of representation, the latest manuals and guidebooks, equipment, and even the possibility of locally manufacturing chemicals and supplies for photographers based in India. The apparatus and the science of handling it dominated resident European discourse on the mastery of the photographic process.

27. Needless to add, these worlds overlapped. Official photography relied on the commercial retailers to supply it materials, and employed commercial photographers as well as its own employees who were amateur practitioners to execute its projects. These amateur practitioners were also members of the private societies that, in return, relied on government for patronage. And the commercial trade too, patronized the societies in an effort to encourage more serious amateur engagements with photography to keep the demand for materials growing.

28. One of the most prominent and successful Indian photographers of the nineteenth century, Deen Dayal (1844–1905) was official photographer to the Nizam of the princely state of Hyderabad and to Viceroy Lord Dufferin. He opened studios in Hyderabd and Bombay, and succeeding generations of his family have been particularly effective in preserving his work, including a website operated by his great-granddaughter Hemlata Jain, dedicated to his work and catering to collectors and researchers. The website can be found at www.deendayal.com.

29. A mass market for images centered on the printed chromolithographed image, rather than the individualized consumption of photographic images. Photography played a vital role in the multiplication of printed images as well as in the eventual possibility of mass-produced printed photographic images in newspapers and illustrated books. I elaborate on this in the next chapter.

30. Some photographers proposed albumen, that is, egg white, as a binding agent for the silver salts on glass plates before the photographers as a whole settled

on collodion as a preferable binding agent. They did find use for albumen to coat paper used to produce positive prints off wet-collodion glass negatives. There was a disadvantage in Talbot's calotype process as the image it produced on paper tended to also reveal the fibrous composition of the paper itself; the paper absorbed the silver salts, resulting in a grainy image. For those seeking to produce images with less grain, a coating of albumen on the photographic paper before being sensitized ensured that the image would stay on the surface of the paper as opposed to seeping into the grain. See the web resource by John Burke, Walter Henry, John Burke, Paul Messier, Timothy Vitale (2000).

31. See the volumes produced by Sepia International and The Alkazi Collection of Photography (1999 and 2000). Platinum prints were expensive because the sensitizing salts contained a platinum compound.

32. A rupee was sixteen annas, so two annas would be one-eighth of a rupee and four annas would be one-quarter of a rupee.

33. The advertisement is originally from the second edition of Adeshwar Ghatak's Bangla-language handbook *Photography Shikkha* (trans. *Photography Education*), which was first published in 1903, and reproduced in Siddhartha Ghosh's work.

34. Reprinted in the *Journal of the Photographic Society of India*, March 1895, 50.

35. *The Statesman*, Jan. 1, 1915, 4.

36. *The Statesman*, June 1, 1915, 2. At twelve rupees to the pound, that would be a little more than four pounds.

37. Thanks to Anand Yang for directing me to the relevant sources of information regarding income levels.

38. I am grateful to Nitin Govil for directing me to this argument.

39. Pinney's (1997) study of photographic culture in Central India in the recent postcolonial past, bears this out, as does McDougall's work.

40. Personal correspondence with Peeyush Sekhsaria, and Sekhsaria (2012).

CHAPTER 2 TRAVELING SHOWMEN, MAKESHIFT CINEMAS

1. Salim's projector in Calcutta is of uncertain but probably more recent provenance than its improbable attribution as a 105-year-old Japanese movie projector in a news report suggests (Biswas 2004). The other projector in Ahmedabad carries the metal-embossed rooster trademark of the Pathé film company, thus situating it in the early twentieth century.

2. Bangle makers also rely on discarded film stock for melted celluloid to produce bangles.

3. *The Ramayan* was a seventy-eight-episode televised adaptation of the Indian religious epic of the same name, aired between January 1987 and July 1988 on India's state-run—and at the time only—TV network, Doordarshan. *Chitrahaar* is a film song program, which began airing in 1982, also on Doordarshan. Both

programs were spectacularly successful in the decade prior to the advent of satellite and cable television in the 1990s.

4. The phrase belongs to Bronislaw Manilowski (Cohn 1987, 55).

5. *Bengal Hurkaru*, Feb. 19, 1845.

6. Phantasmagoria also referred to the magic lantern projection adapted for rear projection and included a moveable carriage for the slides so the images projected could increase or diminish in size.

7. *Bengal Hurkaru*, Feb. 19, 1845.

8. Weekly Supplement. *Bengal Hurkaru*, Sept. 13, 1845, 303.

9. *Bengal Hurkaru*, Feb. 12, 1851.

10. *Bengal Hurkaru*, June 23, 1845.

11. *Bengal Hurkaru*, March 15, 1853.

12. The zoetrope and praxinoscope however, used a cylinder, whereas this roll-holding mechanism was more akin to a panorama that unrolled from one spindle to another. Many thanks to Antonia Lant for this clarification.

13. James Waterhouse, "By-ways of Photography," *The Photographic Journal*, Nov. 1905, 351–58.

14. For serious amateurs such as Waterhouse, the shift to dry plates, rather than the later shift to roll films and Kodak, was the definitive index of change, hence the total absence of reference to the Kodak camera in this article. But the absence of reference to Kodak was also due to the fact that the roll film and Kodak camera simply did not catch on in India or in the UK in the way they did in the United States, an aspect I discussed in chapter 2 of this dissertation.

15. *Journal of the Photographic Society of India*, July 1896, 110–11.

16. The journal was published in Calcutta. The editor mentions watching Edison's Kinetoscope "last cold weather" which would ostensibly mean 1895, the year before the Lumière's first screenings in Bombay. The description is equally remarkable as it so closely aligns with the 1903 Edison/Porter film. Were there earlier "kinetoscoped" versions of the Porter film? This is certainly probable given that Edison employed Porter and had overseen the development of the Kinetoscope in his laboratory. Given, however, that journals frequently went into press much later than the date of the issue itself, it is quite possible that the editor's viewing occurred at a much later date.

17. *Journal of the Photographic Society of India*, July 1896, 110–11.

18. Evidence. Report of the Indian Cinematograph Committee, vol.1, 28–29 [henceforth ICCE].

19. A 1908 advertisement reveals that Pathé was also selling phonograph discs and boasted its own "head office and wholesale firm" in Calcutta for discs and "talking machines" (gramophones). Pathé's background in the gramophone industry, and its early ability to appoint subsidiary agents in distant markets would also explain its head start, ahead of all the foreign film companies that would eventually come to India, in cornering the market for the supply of film titles (Ray Choudhury 1991, 14).

20. *The Statesman*, Jan. 16, 1915. 4.

21. In Madras, a similar picture emerges. In 1905, S. Vincent in Madras purchased films and projection equipment from a French touring cinema operator who had fallen ill and wished to return to Europe, and upgraded to a "chronomegophone" in 1909, which allowed for the synchronization of gramophone records with the film. His contemporary Venkiah ordered a chronophone set in 1909 that included a projector, a program of twelve or so single-reel shorts (three hundred to four hundred feet), and synchronized gramophone recordings on large eighteen and twenty-four-inch plates, the whole package costing an astronomical three hundred thousand rupees (Hughes 1996, 41–43).

22. See Bhaumik (2002) for an excellent and detailed account of the emergence of the cinema in Bombay.

23. ICCE, 182.

24. ICCE, 179.

25. ICCR, 182. I do not mean to suggest that Calcutta did not possess a vibrant, thriving urban film culture. Ranita Chatterjee's (2012) recent work sheds considerable light for the first time on Calcutta's film culture. Chatterjee's emphasis on urban Calcutta is also a cautionary reminder for the current work. It is possible to confuse the preponderance of traveling cinemas with the question of whether the cinema thrived in urban Calcutta or not. Based on Chatterjee's work, I would argue that the two are not mutually exclusive.

26. This was cited repeatedly as a problem by those testifying before the ICCE, vol. 2, 668, 675, 688, 695, 762, 869.

27. As we learn from the ICCE reports, firms such as the Eastern Films Syndicate had been formed with capital infusion from the hair oil business run by one of the partners. An earlier version of the firm had failed when a partner's jute profits had fallen along with the falling world prices. ICCE, vol. 2. 692.

28. Priya Jaikumar notes that "the consensus was that an 8000-foot film cost approximately Rs. 2000 to import, including Rs. 300 in customs tax. A film of similar length in India cost about Rs. 20,000 to produce. The cost of renting these films varied proportionately for the exhibitor" (2006, 262, fn. 48).

29. ICCE, vol. 2, 619. See also pages 609, 772.

30. In a useful elaboration and historicization of the phrase "junk films," Kaveh Askari notes the phrase's initial usage to indicate decrepit prints of Hollywood films that arrived in Iran much later than their first release and routed via the Soviet Union, or Baghdad, London, or Paris. These were prints that had already undergone an extensive exhibition cycle and had arrived "out of date, out of place," and as "nonsynchronous material." Askari's evocative phrasing reads the delay (and reuse) of the "junk" print as evidence of a different temporality that upsets progressivist narratives of film history, testifying instead to the "longevity and adaptability" of film prints' "after-lives" (Askari 2014: 101–02). Furthermore, unlike in India, in Iran, the delay in the arrival of films meant that these junk prints were presented to audiences as "classics." Belatedness thus functioned as a marketing strategy.

31. ICCE, vol.1, 105–11.

32. Ibid. 106.

33. See also, in this regard, the emerging work on nontheatrical cinemas in other locations, as well as the possibility of seeing Foucaultian governmentality as a discourse for which the cinema, including nontheatrical cinema, serves as a node. On the former, see for instance, Acland and Wasson (2011), and on the latter, see Grieveson (2009).

34. Government of the Central Provinces and Berar. Report of the Visual Education Committee. Nagpur: Government Printing Press, 1938. Government of India Information Department. India Office Records (British Library).

35. Compared, for instance, to the UK (thirty screens per million) and the U.S (117 screens per million). For an estimated five billion–strong annual moviegoing audience, India has 12,900 movie screens (Ganti 2004, 25).

36. The percentage of touring cinemas to the total number of cinemas in India breaks down as follows. 1950: 26%; 1960–61: 29%; 1970–71: 35%; 1980–81: 38%; 1985–86: 37.5%. The figures from which the above calculations are made are available in Pendakur (2003, 18).

37. See here Uli Gaulke's documentary *Comrades in Dreams* (2006) for its depiction of a young traveling film exhibitor in Maharashtra, juxtaposed with his counterparts in North Korea, the United States and Burkina Faso, for an instance of precisely such sophistication.

38. *Journal of the Photographic Society of India*, July 1896, 110–11.

39. This logic can yoke aesthetic criteria to artisanal practice as well. In Megha Lakhani's film, Feroze and Hanif Bhai describe how they fashion the items in their screening program through a process of economical editing that trims irrelevant scenes and frames from the scraps. Bemoaning the loss of quality in "today's films" they argue that "every scene was useful" in earlier movies, unlike today, when all the scenes are so "wasteful" (Lakhani 2006).

CHAPTER 3. COPYRIGHT AND CULTURAL AUTHENTICITY

1. Subject: Advertisement relating to the exhibition of little girls etc at the cinema.

Home Department, Delhi, The 1st February, 1919

My dear Barron, The accompanying advertisement has been distributed in Delhi and its terms suggest that the exhibition may be open to objection. I am to ask that you will let me know whether this is so and if so whether anything can be done to stop it. Yours sincerely, Sd. J. H. DuBoulay.

Handwritten note in reply:

To: The Hon Mr. C. A. Barron, C.I.E, Chief Commissioner of the Delhi Province

Somebody from the Police Station enquired on the telephone as to the subject matter of the advertisement which was sent as an accompaniment to our letter No. 816c dated the 1st February 1919 to the Commissioner of Delhi. The advertisement related to the exhibition of little girls, middle-size girls, big girls, chubby girls, pretty girls, etc. etc. at the cinema. Sd. A.S 22.2.19. Simla (Police).

Home (Police), 12 February 1919, no. 12 (B), Proceeding, National Archives of India (NAI).

2. The chromolithograph also included everyday iconography. This iconography has through the years comprised nationalist heroes of the independence movement, icons of science and technology, such as dams and factories, which defined the newly independent India, cherubic babies, famous monuments, tourist landscapes, and Bollywood stars. These images are now the kitsch of hipster artifacts in the West—embossed on shopping bags, T-shirts, and lunch boxes—and ubiquitous in India's visual culture.

3. Kriegel's discussion pertains to the consequences of the import, copy, and sale of the wildly popular Indian printed textiles known as calicos by London merchants. Their further imitation by provincial textile merchants beyond London provoked debate over whether these designs could be copyrighted in order to protect London merchants from their provincial counterparts. One of the many arguments made in favor of offering copyright protection to London calicos claimed a distinction between the British "patterns" and an Indian "national style," and claimed the latter as a more general un-copyrightable aesthetic expression. The argument implicitly claimed that the British patterns were "inspired" by an Indian national style but were also clearly distinct from it, and therefore deserving of protection. For opponents, the hierarchy between copy and original made little sense and, if anything, the hundreds of copies churned out in London and elsewhere had added value to the distant Indian originals, and therefore should have no restrictions on their production.

4. 22 October, 1883, no. 38, NAI. GOI Home Department (Judicial).

5. Memo from "D.F.P," 17 July 1884, 22 October, 1883, no. 38, NAI, GOI Home Department (Judicial).

6. It would be useful at this juncture to assess the technological preconditions for these disputes. Photography and printing technology intersected in three ways. The first involved the combination of photography and lithography in the form of photo-chromolithography, an offshoot of chromolithography. In this case, photography became a function of photomechanical printing technologies. Although photography played an important part in Birdwood's project to salvage India's threatened past, by the late nineteenth century its initial utility as a stand-alone mode of documentation was supplanted by its function in augmenting and amplifying the scale of methods to produce printed images. A second interface involved the ability to print photographs in large quantities for newspaper publication. Subsequent

chapters in this book explore this interface in some detail. A third interface involved using photographs for the unauthorized duplication of chromolithographs produced by the Indian lithographic printing presses, contemporary to the heyday of this process, whose chromolithographs became phenomenally popular from the 1880s onward and underwent unauthorized duplication precisely by being photographed, a third use of photography in relation to print culture.

7. Ibid, 34–44.

8. Oleography was a process that duplicated chromolithographs in the printing press using oil paints to give them a glossy sheen.

9. Numerous scholars have noted that this popular visual print capitalism, one that used mythic cosmologies and messianic time, can be considered "neo-traditionalist" in its mode of picturing a nation. The mode is quite at variance with the harsh rupture between cosmology and history that has underscored elsewhere the theorization of the origins of the nation-form (Rajadhyaksha 1993; Pinney 1997).

10. On a more practical level, these petitions brought the hidden practices of these presses and their competitors into the juridical space of colonial law, the very law that also sought to unsuccessfully regulate the semantics of these images.

11. Baboo Kristo Chunder Pal, letter to the Secretary, Legislative Department, 30 April 1883, August 1884, nos. 143–45, National Archives of India (NAI), Government of India (GOI) Home Department (Judicial).

12. Ibid.

13. Ibid., Appendix C.

14. Ibid., Appendix G.

15. Ibid., Appendix A.

16. It is not clear to me whether the 1862 Fine Arts Copyright Act did in fact afford protection to the dominions, even in theory. Was this Act an imperial or a national act? As Professor Lionel Bently has noted in correspondence on the subject, "The fact that the 1862 Act protected artistic works, including photographs, only within the UK, was made clear in 1903 by the Canadian case of Graves v. Corrie" (Email from Prof. Bently, October 9, 2006). If this is so, then the plaintiffs in the Calcutta Art Studio case, and indeed the judge as well, misunderstood the extent of protection the Act afforded.

17. The names of these presses themselves indicate the brush of mechanical reproduction with norms of artistic value. The Art Studio and the Steam Press.

18. Vasudeo G. Goshi, letter to the Secretary, Legislative Department, 17 June 1883, Aug. 1884, nos. 143–45, NAI, GOI Home Department (Judicial).

19. January 1910, nos. 179–90 (A), NAI, GOI Home Department (Books and Publications).

20. It was not a coincidence that the manager of Ravi Varma's press was German. Germany dominated the trade in trivial pictures or mass-produced oleographs of scenes from classical European literature. Ravi Varma's work was stylistically very close to its German forerunners with Indianized stage workers in front of mildly

Orientalized backdrops. Fritz Schleizer was crucial for the cutting-edge printing technology in the Ravi Varma Press. P. Gephardt, another German, assisted him as the master lithographer in the press. Germany also dominated the production of picture postcards. Photographs were sent to Germany to be transformed into postcards before being sent back to India (Varma, Neumayer, and Schelberger, 2005).

21. The Ravi Varma enquiry came in 1903. In 1908, Ashutosh Dutt, a sub-inspector of schools in Ranchi and an amateur photographer, wanted to know if he could register his photographs for copyright. In 1910, C. S. Sundaram Brothers, photographers in Tinnelvely wanted a response on their enquiry regarding copyright of photographs. January 1903, nos. 138–39 (A), NAI, GOI Home (Books and Publications); May 1908, nos. 15–16 (B), NAI, GOI Home Department (Books); October 1910, nos. 40–41 (B), NAI, GOI Home Department (Books).

22. Calcutta Trades Association to the Government of Bengal, 18 Feb. 1907, January 1910, nos. 179–90 (A), NAI, GOI Home Department (Books and Publications).

23. H. Adamson, memo 11 Oct. 1907, January 1910, nos. 179–90 (A), NAI, GOI Home Department (Books and Publications).

24. This blurring of the distinction between reproduction and original was not exclusive to India. Stephen Bann's study of the relation between painters, printmakers, and photographers in nineteenth-century France uncovers similarly fine gradations between the original and the copy, particularly with regard to reproductive engravings that painters understood to enhance the permanence and value of paintings. Repetitions or replicas of paintings executed by the painter himself for patrons, as well as the widely recognized possibility that a translation by engraving or by repetition could be superior to the "original," compromised the original/copy distinction even further. Both original and copy were subject to internal differentiations. The prominent printmakers who emerged in the nineteenth century contemporaneously with the photographers and painters in France adhered to "a distinctive new philosophy of visual communication—developing simultaneously with, though in some ways antithetical to, the modernist aesthetic—that places the concept of reproducibility to the forefront" (Bann 2001, 28). As Bann notes, even setting aside the religious question in the Benjaminian distinction between exhibition and cult value, there is no denying that the "fecundity" of the methods of image making resulted in a "reinvestment" of the image with potency (30).

25. Appelate Civil. Vasudeo Ganesh Joshi v. Anupram Haribhai Trivadi, December 18, 1919. Dec. 18, 1919. *Indian Law Reports (Bombay)* vol. 44. 724.

26. Goshi was in all probability a misspelling of Joshi and Travedi of Trivedi. I am retaining the misspellings in my discussion.

27. Indian Law Reports (Bombay), 1919, vol. 44: 724.

28. Act XX of 1847 (The Indian Copyright Act, 1847), the first copyright act in British India, made no mention of images and defined a book to include "any encyclopedia, Review, Magazine, Periodical Work or work published in a series of books or parts . . . or volumes, parts, essay, articles or portions thereof" (Government of India 1898, 54). Twenty years later, Act XXV of 1867 (The Press and Registration

of Books Act) required all newspapers, periodicals, and books to be registered and considered such registration to be the same as a registration for copyright purposes under Act 20 of 1847. This act now defined the book to include "every volume, part, or division, of a volume or pamphlet in any language, and every sheet of music, map, chart or plan separately printed or lithographed" (635). Clearly, this act improved on the 1847 act insofar as it acknowledged certain kinds of graphic and printed matter but there was still no mention of pictures (photographed or otherwise), paintings, sculptures, and engravings. In other words, an entire category of works that would under later legislation be considered artistic works were still missing. There was, however, one acknowledgment of engravings, but only in a section detailing the requirements of submitting new edition(s) of the published book to the local government for their records (639).

29. In 1864, the Secretary of State of the British government urged the Government of India to take steps for the improvement and extension of copyright. A bill was drawn up proposing "that facilities be given for the protection of copyright in pictures, engravings, prints and other similar productions," but this bill was not adopted (Bently 2006). In 1877, the Home Office in London sent a memo to the various presidencies and provinces regarding amending the existing copyright act and extending copyright protection to photographs, sculptures, engravings, paintings, and lectures. The response was divided: some provinces reported that the instances of the above were so few that no legislation was necessary at the time. Others noted that enquiries had either come in regarding the copyright in photographs, or that there was no harm in advance legislation. The matter ended with the Imperial government noting that no bill would be drafted, and no legislation enacted, until such time that the Royal Commission, which was considering changes to International and Colonial copyright law that year (1877), had published its report and findings. The Royal Commission report was published but no action was taken to amend copyright law in the UK, let alone in the colonies.

30. Following on the heels of the Berne Convention of 1886, the International and Colonial Copyright Bill of 1886 proposed that new classes of artistic works (including prints, paintings, and photographs) be included in copyright law "as the case requires." March 1886, nos. 176–77 (A), NAI, GOI, Home (Judicial).

31. In 1910, faced with a barrage of requests, the Home and Legislative departments of the government of India drafted a bill specifically accounting for copyright in photographs that vested value in the photograph's negative and conferred rights to the owner of the negative. January 1910, nos. 179–90 (A), NAI, GOI Home (Books & Publications). I have not been able to locate disputes over photographs produced by studios or paid photographers in colonial India, although in the British context this was clearly a bone of contention, for example in Nottage and Another v. Jackson (Law Reports (London), 1882–83, IX: 627–38).

32. The 1914 Act defined four main classes of work: the literary, dramatic, musical, and artistic works. Engravings and photographs were placed under the category of artistic works, along with paintings, drawings, sculptures, artistic craftsmanship, and architectural works of art. Engravings included "etchings, lithographs,

wood-cuts, prints and other similar works, not being photographs" and photographs included "photo-lithographs and any other work produced by any process analogous to photography" (III, 35 (i) (Law Reports, 1911: 201).

33. The first copyright Act in India passed in 1847, whereas photographs were covered as worthy of copyright protection only in 1914.

34. Reuters Telegram Company, letter to GOI, 17 April, 1878, Home (Publications), June 1878 nos. 36–39, NAI, GOI.

35. Letter No. 1053, Home (Publications), June 1878 nos. 36–39, NAI, GOI.

36. C.B. 14-5-78; A.J.A., 20-5-78, Home (Publications), June 1878 nos. 36–39, NAI, GOI.

CHAPTER 4. THE CINEMA AS MASS CULTURE

1. The hypocritical gathering organized by Vijay's brothers and the rich publisher is meant to commemorate and remember Vijay, after the poems have achieved wild success.

2. *Ji* is an honorific in Hindi, appended as a sign of respect.

3. This idea of the author as genius was influential enough, for instance, to inform decades of historiography on the literatures of Bengal. Literary historians prioritized themes of transcendence and visionary experience over themes that were more mundanely material and sociohistorical in nature. The literary canons that these historians constructed saw the encounter with European Romanticism as a turning point for the emergence of a legitimate Bengali literature. Thus, the encounter with English poets, for instance, marked the "before" and "after" of Bengali literature's ignobility and its legitimacy, respectively (Sengupta 1995).

4. My translation.

5. For summarizing accounts of Phalke's life and career, see Barnuow and Krishnaswamy 1980; Rajadhyaksa and Willemen 1994; and Watwe 2004.

6. Phalke was no different from discursive efforts elsewhere, such as the Pure Film Movement in Japan around the same time (Gerow 2010), to extricate the cinema from its moorings as a "filmed play" and to assert its medium specificity, as he indeed did.

7. See Watwe (2004) and Paresh Mokashi's 2009 Marathi-language feature film (and India's entry for the foreign language film category of the Academy Awards), *Harishchandrachi Factory* (*Harishchandra's Factory*). The latter inexplicably turns Phalke into a lovable Chaplinesque figure and paints the period via a slapdash mise-en-scène in broad brushstrokes with a strong emphasis on Phalke's family life.

8. Every indexical image is also an iconic one demanding recognition of the depicted person's similitude to a real-life counterpart. That iconicity, in the context of a preexisting system of classification or meaning, seeks to fix the potential of excess that always accompanies the photographic image as index (Gunning 1995, 2007).

9. "The concept of aura which was proposed above with reference to historical objects may usefully be illustrated with reference to the aura of natural ones. We define the aura of the latter as the unique phenomenon of a distance, however close it may be. If, while resting on a summer afternoon, you follow with your eyes a mountain range on the horizon or a branch which casts its shadow over you, you experience the aura of those mountains, of that branch. This image makes it easy to comprehend the social bases of the contemporary decay of the aura" (Benjamin 1985, 222–23).

10. "We define the aura . . . as the unique phenomenon of a distance, however close it may be" (222).

CHAPTER 5. THE EMERGENCE OF TOPICALITY

1. There's a technological context for this. "While photography seemed the ultimate in the mechanization of visual information, it could not itself be easily mechanized," wrote Estelle Jussim (1983, 2) with regard to the printing of photographs prior to the 1880s. Even as the photograph was alienable from its base (the negative image) and duplicable, it was not amenable to rapid duplication at the same scale as the lithographic image till the late 1880s. The arrival of halftone amplified and made ubiquitous the presence of the photographic image, in illustrated books, in family albums, and in newspapers. Compared to this ubiquity, the official grand photographic projects required a formal framing of subjects that, when studied, offers a rich glimpse into the official colonial intellectual framework in ways that amateur photography cannot.

2. In Ben Singer's study of modernity and the cinema, the innumerable images of disastrous street accidents, dismemberments, and bodily damage represented in the American illustrated press are part sensationalism, part social critique directed at the effects of modernity. They are also examples of the "hyperstimulus" and stress of modern urban life. What is noteworthy though, is that the vast majority of images Singer considers are not halftones; they are wood and line engravings, watercolors, paintings (Singer 2001, 89).

3. Editorial Comments, *Journal of the Photographic Society of India (JPSI)* (May 1899): 82.

4. George Ewing, "The Indian Amateur Photographer," *JPSI* 5 (1892): 101; emphasis in original.

5. Ewing, 101–102.

6. While bicycle photography refers to photographers on bicycles, snapshot photography specifies the nature of the cameras used (portable hand cameras) and the nature of the images produced this way ("instantaneous" snapshots), but also encompasses bicycle photography.

7. Later analogies would extend Kodak's simplicity of use to the mechanized scooter, arguing for the latter's speed as a matter of convenience. *Times of India*, "The Future of Scooters," Sept. 9, 1919, A5.

8. Editorial Comments, *JPSI* (Sept.1897): 196.

9. James Waterhouse, "Photography and the Bicycle," *JPSI* (Sept. 1896): 146–48.

10. Author unknown, *JPSI* 16 (March 1902): 83.

11. W. A. B., "Some snapshots of an Indian Bazaar," *JPSI* 17 (1903). Photo spread, not paginated, and p. 395.

12. When, in 1907, the *JPSI* published an article regarding ideal snapshots for newspaper illustration, it listed what were by now mantras: the chance event whose randomness was only matched by the randomness of the mass and what photo might strike its fancy, timeliness, which meant the photo needed to keep pace with the telegraphing of news events that made their reception near-simultaneous with their occurrence, and a certain roughness and imperfection of quality over the perfectly composed picture, especially if the former possessed a detail of great emotional or affective relevance for the public. Florence Donaldson, "The Increasing Demand for Journalistic Illustration," *JPSI* 21(238) (Oct. 1907): 327–29.

13. As we have seen in chapter 4 as well.

14. Donaldson, "The Increasing Demand."

15. Gaudreault's word, to refer to an uninterrupted series of images on screen.

16. Plates 15 and 16 are titled "Massed bands (close view)" and "Massed bands (distant view)." Plates 19 and 20 are titled "Review of British Troops" and "Review of Native Troops." The album comprises a total of thirty-one numbered plates.

17. I have referenced this particular essay by Ravi Vasudevan (2011) in chapter 2 as well in the context of discussing official attitudes to decrepit film prints. I find my arguments regarding formal aspects of particular films closely mirroring Vasudevan's in some instances (as we will see in chapter 7 when I discuss the found footage and compilation film), and benefiting greatly from his careful mapping of the links between official film initiatives and the commercial film industry.

18. For a detailed account of the role of photography with regard to crime, see Clare Anderson's work (2004). For an account of the relation of photography, crime, and early cinema, including a detailed discussion of Bertillon's anthropometry, see Gunning (1995).

19. "Committed for Trial," *Times of India*, July 4, 1903, 5. Where numerous items had been stolen in one instance, as was the case in a Bombay-bound steamer from England, the exclusivity of ownership of the Kodak, valued in 1912 at Rs. 75, ensured that when discovered in the suspect's possessions, it would be among the clinchers for assigning guilt beyond doubt ("Mail Boat Thefts," *Times of India*, Nov. 2, 1912, 10). The Kodak company itself became the victim of theft, when one of its employees siphoned Rs. 4,000 of customer receipts for drinking and gambling ("Bombay Police Courts," *Times of India*, Dec. 20, 1916).

20. *Illustrated Weekly*, Jan. 8 1913, 17.

21. For example, movie records of the "insurrectionary districts" in Bengal were asked to be suppressed by the government when the war correspondent who

had recorded the films sought to screen them. "The position in India: Recent Visitor's Views," *Times of India*, Feb. 6, 1909, 14.

22. Incidentally, the use of the cinema for solving crime, in itself, was not new. ICC reports contain numerous occasions when officials ask if the cinema might be used as a tool for police instruction in solving crimes, or to show the ingenious methods of pickpockets so crowds are better informed, or to teach the police how to handle crowds. (ICCR 1927–28, Bombay/Sind: 711; ICCR 1927–28, Calcutta: 525–26).

CHAPTER 6. POLITICS ACROSS MEDIA.

1. *Times of India*, Feb. 17, 1900, page number unavailable.

2. A. O. Thompson, "The Recent Disturbances, Seismic and Social in Bengal," *JPSI* (Aug. 1897): 353.

3. A vest pocket–sized twin-lens camera (hence, jumelle, French for twin) that tapered toward the front and looked like opera glasses. This camera had been patented by Jules Carpentier in 1892 and was extremely popular for snapshot photography. Carpentier, a Frenchman, went on to patent the Cinematographe and designed cinematographic camera-projectors for the Lumières (Coe 1978, 148, 150).

4. For an account of the importance of the railway in the colonial imagination, and a description of its various representations in India, British as well as Indian, see Kerr (2003).

5. Thompson, "The Recent Disturbances": 353.

6. Ibid., 354.

7. Ibid.

8. For a detailed discussion of the partition, its circumstances and consequences for political action, see Johnson (1973). The Swadeshi agitations also produced secret anarchist societies with avowed aims of armed political action, ranging from thefts and picketing to planned assassinations. I discuss the coverage of these agitations separately.

9. "Calcutta Letter: Hustling the Port Trust," *Times of India*, Nov. 13, 1913, 6.

10. *Illustrated Weekly of India*, Sept. 7, 1912, 9. See also Aug. 9, 1912, 7.

11. "City of Palaces," *Illustrated Weekly of India*, April 3, 1912, 2; see also "Rebuilding of Calcutta," ibid., 3.

12. "Curious Calcutta Story," *Illustrated Weekly*, April 10, 1912, 16.

13. *Times of India*, Sept. 12,1907, 6.

14. Ibid.

15. *The Bengalee*, Feb. 21, 1902, 2; See also the *Classic Theater* notice on May 10, 1902, 2.

16. *Bengalee*, Feb. 23, 1902.

17. The historiographical issues here are not perhaps restricted to the cinema in India. Nicholas Hiley reminds us that while the 1980s "historical turn" since

the Brighton Conference, has resulted in meticulous attention to paper prints and surviving negatives, in the early decades of the cinema the individual film was not the unit of exhibition. The program and access to time in the auditorium were the draw of the cinema. An emphasis on textual analysis fails to capture the gap between production and reception (Hiley 2012).

18. *The Bengalee*, Feb. 21, 1902, 2.

19. "The Position in India: Recent Visitor's Views," *Times of India*, Feb. 6, 1909, 14.

20. *The Bengalee*, Jan. 17, 1907.

21. *Times of India*, June 21, 1928, 13.

22. The documentary narrates the story of the indiscriminate shooting by British forces, in April 1919, on peaceful congregants in a park called Jalianwala Bagh in the city of Amritsar in Punjab. The event is an iconic one in the history of the nationalist movement.

23. The reuse of footage from earlier films was widespread in the information films about India that were produced by the British and Americans alike. Richard Osborne (2011) discusses the changing agendas that framed the same footage differently in different films.

24. *Times of India*, Nov. 13, 1918, 11.

25. *Times of India Illustrated Weekly of India*, Supplement, Oct. 3, 1906, 1.

26. *Times of India Illustrated Weekly of India*, Supplement, Oct. 31, 1906, 3.

27. *The Illustrated London News* regularly published photographs of riots and clashes with the police on full-page spreads. It is not clear why copies of these broadsheets were retained at the Nehru Memorial, given that these images were published in a London newspaper. If the aim is to archive images of mass mobilization, there isn't much of a difference in function between the original unpublished snapshots and those snapshots that appeared in *The Illustrated London News*. There isn't much of a difference in contextualization of news images in *London News* and *The Illustrated Weekly of India*, for instance. In both, full-page spreads veered between a focus on rioting or violence (much more frequently so in London), a continuing supply of interesting tourist sights in India, including its people, as well as an insistent fascination with huge bodies of the mangled metal of train wrecks. In these images of train wrecks, we ought to consider the density and volume of mangled metal as symbolic currency attesting to the weighty achievements of empire, as well as of a public sphere that encompasses animate people as well as inanimate objects.

28. My notes list the image's title as "Home Rule Movement: A Procession, 1916." This image is not a procession. Unfortunately, in the process of acquiring copies of snapshots, I found I had received many I had never ordered, did not receive a few that I did order, and received quite a few whose numbers did not correspond to the numbers assigned to it in the album, and for which I have titles.

29. Movie audiences can be imagined or statistical. They are imagined to the extent that they are projections of the filmmaker's imperatives and statistical in the sense of being an actual massing of people who were photographed. Our

snapshots, however, lie somewhere in between that of a discursive construction and a visual registration, caught between state discourses and the orphaned snapshot. For a discussion of the difference between statistical and imagined audiences, see Christie (2012).

30. For an insightful discussion of *Kismet*, see Vasudevan (1991).

CHAPTER 7. THE ABUNDANT EPHEMERAL

1. Anand Holla, "Born-Again Cinema," *Mumbai Mirror*, Dec. 9, 2012, 12.

2. Dinyar Patel, "India's Archives: How Did Things Get This Bad?" India Ink, *New York Times*, March 22, 2012. http://india.blogs.nytimes.com/2012/03/22/indias-archives-how-did-things-get-this-bad/; accessed July 1, 2013.

3. Sometime between 1991 and 1994, as a student of Fergusson College, Pune, I made an appointment at the National Film Archive of India (which was located not very far from my college campus) to view Phalke's films. If my memory serves me right, I was given a TV monitor and a video cassette recorder and I watched the extant early Phalke films on that monitor. In the course of my viewing, a gentleman came and introduced himself to me as Kamal Swaroop and said he noticed I was viewing Phalke's films and that he was working on a biography of Phalke. That was my only encounter with Swaroop's work (and him), till now. At the time of this writing, I have not yet seen the movie that accompanies the volume: *Rangabhoomi* (2014), Swaroop's film on Phalke's life (or rather his translation of his own research into Phalke's life, into images).

4. The name of Phalke's mother.

5. An actress who appeared in Phalke's films.

6. Ravi Verma is the painter-printer discussed in chapters 3 and 4, whose mass-reproduced prints of his own paintings of mythological subject matter (such as "Sarasvati" in Swaroop's comments) became ubiquitous. As also mentioned in those two chapters, Phalke trained as a printer at one point, including a stint in Ravi Verma's press.

7. Tehelka TV. *Cinema and Me: Episode 9 Kamal Swaroop*. YouTube. Published March 22, 2012. www.youtube.com/watch?v=RtxboGynvhM; accessed Jan. 24, 2014.

8. The phrase is Bob Stam and Randal Johnson's (1995, 124).

9. For a superb discussion of the film, see Beugnet and Ezra (2009).

10. The "golden age" also emerges in contrast to what Rajadhyaksha calls "statist-internationalist" histories of Indian cinema. These were histories periodized by Satyajit Ray's art film classic *Pather Panchali* (1955) and in which nothing of value seemingly existed before Ray, which essentially meant giving short shrift to the entire preindependence era of Indian cinema (2009, 78). The result is the construction of a national cinema tradition while also celebrating Indian cinema's relevance for the

history of the art film as a transnational genre (or even narrating that relevance as an implicit precondition for the definition of Indian cinema as a national cinema).

11. Rajadhyaksha terms this uneasy relationship "an unresolved dispute over what [the cinema] was doing, as against what the state thought it was doing (resolved it seems, only in the 200s, with the onset of globalization)" (2009, 82).

12. See also Stringer (2003) for the various functions of classical Hollywood programming at the London Film Festival over two decades. Stringer makes note of the myriad functions and challenges of film retrospectives—from fetishizing technology (those originally behind the movie and behind its later restoration) to a fairly traditional understanding and celebration of authorship, to balancing the imperative of redeeming the lowbrow in the context of a festival of otherwise difficult, highbrow art films. In the process, alliances are formed between existing archives, film industries, and commercial and corporate film institutions. On the positive side, Stringer sees retrospectives as contributing to a "decentered, deterritorialized view of Hollywood's reception history." This view exposes the context-specific concerns that inform what I would consider to be not just classical Hollywood's recommodification that Stringer notes, but also its reentry into the realm of popular history (95).

13. Mainstream newspapers such as *The Times of India* carried reviews of these movies in the pre-DVD (and a still early VHS) era that indicates theatrical release.

14. An international co-production, *Shalimar* starred Dharmendra, Zeenat Aman, and Shammi Kapoor, all well-known actors and stars in the Bombay film industry. Rex Harrison and Sylvia Miles rounded the cast in a movie that tries to appeal to two audiences at once. There was the audience familiar with Hollywood conventions (and therefore the songs in the film were removed for the international release, and the title changed to *Raiders of the Lost Stone*—a shameless take on *Raiders of the Lost Ark* (1981). Then there was the audience in India that expected some of the amplified emotional intrigue of the melodramatic mode. The movie did well with neither audience.

15. For a review that lambasted the movie see Dileep Padgaonkar, "Bhelpuri and Ketchup," *Times of India*, Sept. 10, 1978, 10.

16. For example, an eighteen million dollar animation film on Lord Krishna was part of Shah's 2003 plans. *Times of India*, Aug. 5, 2003, B1.

17. The article titled "Piracy, Piracy" (playing on the title of the movie), described Shah pretending to be a disinterested customer, listening incredulously and with horror as the London grocery store owner boasts of having already circulated five hundred tapes of *Cinema Cinema*. In the ensuing confrontation the shopkeeper observes that he has provided the filmmaker with free publicity and physically removes Shah from his premises. The report goes on to describe the UK's woefully inadequate piracy laws, and Shah's now destroyed hopes of collecting between thirty and forty thousand pounds in box office receipts for the movie. The movie ran, Shah claims, to packed houses for the first three weeks, and the report ends with Shah's decision to not pursue legal remedies against the shopkeeper because the

British cops were already possessed of "strong anti-Asian feeling." (*Times of India,* Aug. 17, 1980, 5).

18. Stephen Hughes proposes that we see such forms of access as part of a "living archive" of private collections, state archives, as well as private institutions formed in the public trust specifically in order to collect materials, to acquire film related collections, and to make these accessible to the public (Hughes 2013).

19. On the relation between social memory and site specificity, see Atkinson (2007).

20. *Shalimar,* which I saw as a child in Calcutta (Kolkata), seems to have become a cult classic among "Bollywood-o-philes." But the movie itself is overshadowed by its soundtrack, which has also become iconic as an example of "Bollywood Funk," music that emerged from Bombay cinema soundtracks between the 1960s and 1980s. The background scores of many of the movies from this period veered close to the style of funk music in the United States, for example in Blaxploitation films. R. D. Burman was a key composer who drew especially on the orchestral arrangements of funk for the soundtrack as well as for songs that emblematized youth and modernity in Bombay cinema. His music has now become part of a connoisseur-driven and targeted promotion of a distant pop culture by specialty record labels.

21. For a discussion that compares the digital QuickTime movie to a Joseph Cornell box, see Sobchack (2003). For a discussion of miniaturization, see Stewart (1993).

22. For a discussion of microhistory, including in relation to Siegfried Kracauer's writing, see Ginzburg (2012).

23. For a review of *Cinema Cinema,* see Khalid Mohammed, "Film Hi . . . Valentine to Show Biz Old Days," *Times of India,* May 15, 1983, 5.

24. In this aspect, the movie differs from films such as Mark Rappaport's *Rock Hudson's Home Movies,* which Jonathan Rosenbaum reads as a response to the age of video, or to a crisis in the medium of film (Rosenbaum, "Rock Criticism"). See also Philip Rosen's (1993) discussion of the crisis of confidence in the photographic image, induced by a combination of new media (television) and postmodern theory.

25. "An archival orphan is like an answer to which the scholar has yet to find the question," notes Frank Kessler (2013, 127), an observation that applies with regard to the footage utilized by *Cinema Cinema,* provided we acknowledge that the "answer" here already knows its question, or context. We do know, after all, where these incomplete scenes come from and where they ought to belong. As such these aren't enigmatic scenes; they are transparent but incomplete ones.

26. See Wees (2002, 4) for a taxonomy of how found footage can be used: in the realist mode of literal referentiality, modernist mode of critical interrogation, detournement or tangentializing the footage's original meanings, and in the postmodern mode as in music videos and without an explicit agenda.

27. My argument here closely mirrors that of Ravi Vasudevan (2011) who proposes that the frequent reuse and recycling of stock footage in the information films served generic and iconic functions as much as they may be seen as indexical records of the profilmic arena.

WORKS CITED

1879. *Acts Passed by the Governor-General in Council in the Year 1878*. Calcutta: Superintendent of Government Printing.

1882–83. *Law Reports. Queens Bench Division*. Vol. IX. London: Eyre and Spottiswoode.

1911. *Law Reports. The Public General Statutes*. London: Eyre and Spottiswoode.

"A Trip to Elephanta." www.geocities.com/lupeliti/index.html; accessed February 4, 2007.

Abbas, Ackbar. 1988. "Walter Benjamin's Collector: The Fate of Modern Experience." *New Literary History* 20(1): 217–37.

Acland, C. R. 2003. *Screen Traffic: Movies, Multiplexes, and Global Culture*. Durham: Duke University Press.

———, and Haidee Wasson. 2011. *Useful Cinema*. Durham: Duke University Press.

Agnew, Jean-Christophe. 1993. "Coming up for Air: Consumer Culture in Historical Perspective." In *Consumption and the World of Goods*, edited by John Brewer and Roy Porter. London and New York: Routledge.

Altick, Richard Daniel. 1978. *The Shows of London*. Cambridge: Belknap Press of Harvard University Press.

Amad, Paula. 2012. "From God's-eye to Camera-eye: Aerial Photography's Post-humanist and Neo-humanist Visions of the World." *History of Photography* 36(1): 66–86.

———. 2010. *Counter-Archive: Film, the Everyday, and Albert Kahn's Archives de la Planète*. New York: Columbia University Press.

Anderson, Clare. 2004. *Legible Bodies: Race, Criminality, and Colonialism in South Asia*. New York and Oxford: Berg.

Anderson, Steve. 2011. *Technologies of History: Visual Media and the Eccentricity of the Past*. Hanover, NH: University of Dartmouth Press.

Appadurai, A. 1986. "Introduction: Commodities and the Politics of Value." In *The Social Life of Things: Commodities in Cultural Perspective*, edited by A. Appadurai, 3–63, Cambridge and New York: Cambridge University Press.

Appadurai, Arjun. 1996. *Modernity at Large: Cultural Dimensions of Globalization*. Minneapolis: University of Minnesota Press.

Archer, M., and W. G. Archer. 1955. *Indian Painting for the British, 1770–1880; An Essay by Mildred and W. G. Archer*. London: Oxford University Press.

Armitage, Kay. 2008. "Traveling Projectionist Films." *Film International* 6(4): 41–43.

Askari, Kaveh. 2014. "An Afterlife for 'Junk Prints': Serials and Other Classics in Late-1920s Tehran." In *Silent Cinema and the Politics of Space*, edited by Jennifer Bean, Anupama Kapse, and Laura Horak, 99–120. Bloomington: Indiana University Press.

Atkinson, David. 2007. "Kitsch Geographies and the Everyday Spaces of Social Memory." *Environment and Planning* 39: 527–40.

Azoulay, Ariela. 2008. *The Civil Contract of Photography*. New York: Zone Books.

———. 2010. "Getting Rid of the Distinction between the Aesthetic and the Political." *Theory, Culture & Society* 27(7–8): 239–62.

Banerjee, Sumanta. 1989. *The Parlour and the Streets: Elite and Popular Culture in Nineteenth Century Calcutta*. Calcutta: Seagull Books.

———. 2006. *Crime and Urbanization in Urban India: Calcutta in the Nineteenth Century*. Kolkata: Tulika Books.

Bann, Stephen. 1984. *The Clothing of Clio: A Study of the Representation of History in Nineteenth Century Britain and France*. New York, Cambridge: Cambridge University Press.

Barnouw, Erik, and Subrahmanyam Krishnaswamy. 1980. *Indian Film*. 2nd edition. New York: Oxford University Press.

Barron, A. 2004. "The Legal Properties of Film." *Modern Law Review* 67: 177–208.

Basu, Anustup. 2012. *Bollywood in the Age of New Media: The Geo-Televisual Aesthetic*. Reprint edition. Edinburgh: Edinburgh University Press.

Batchen, G. 1997. *Burning with Desire: The Conception of Photography*. Cambridge: The MIT Press.

Bayly, C. A. 1996. *Empire and Information: Intelligence Gathering and Social Communication in India, 1780–1870*. Cambridge and New York: Cambridge University Press.

Beaster Jones, Jason. 2009. "Evergreens to Remixes: Hindi Film Songs and India's Popular Music Heritage." *Ethnomusicology* 53(3): 425–48.

Beegan, Gerry. 2008. *The Mass Image: A Social History of Photomechanical Reproduction in Victorian London*. Basingstoke and New York: Palgrave Macmillan.

Benjamin, Walter. 1969. *Illuminations*. Translated by Harry Zohn. Edited by Hannah Arendt. New York: Schocken Books.

Bently, L. 1994. "Copyright and the Death of the Author in Literature and Law." *The Modern Law Review* 57: 973–86.

———. 2006. "Trade, Development, and Multiple Layers of Lawmaking: Copyright, Translations and Relations between Britain and India, 1880–1914." Paper presented at Chicago Kent College of Law, October 13, 2006.

Beugnet, M., and Elizabeth Ezra. 2009. "A Portrait of the Twenty-First Century." *Screen* 50(1) (Spring): 77–85.

Bhaskar, Ira, and Richard Allen. 2009. *The Islamicate Cultures of Indian Cinema.* New Delhi: Tulika Books.

Bhaumik, K. 2002. "The Emergence of the Bombay Film Industry, 1913–1936." PhD diss., Oxford University.

———. 2010. "A Significant Absence: the Colonial State and the Globalization of Mass Entertainment in Early 20th Century South Asia." *Marg* 61(3): 48–61.

Biswas, Soutik. 2004. "Calcutta Cart Keeps Film Rolling." *BBC News*, January 12. news.bbc.co.uk/2/hi/south_asia/3389067.stm; accessed September 30, 2007.

Blees, John. 1877. *Photography in Hindostan; or Reminiscences of a Travelling Photographer.* Bombay: Education Society's Press.

Bolter, J., and Richard Grusin. 1999. *Remediation: Understanding New Media.* Cambridge: MIT Press.

Bottomore, S. 1995. "'An Amazing Quarter Mile of Moving Gold, Gems and Genealogy': Filming India's 1902/03 Delhi Durbar." *Historical Journal of Film Radio and Television* 15(4): 495–515.

Braester, Y. 2010. *Painting the City Red: Chinese Cinema and the Urban Contract.* Durham: Duke University Press.

Briggs, Asa. 1988. *Victorian Things.* London: Batsford.

Brill, Leslie. 2006. *Crowds, Power, and Transformation in Cinema.* Detroit: Wayne State University Press.

Burch, Noël. 1978–79. "Porter or Ambivalence." *Screen* 19: 91–105.

———. 1990. *Life to Those Shadows.* Berkeley: University of California Press.

Burgoyne, Robert. 2003. "Memory, History, and Digital Imagery in Contemporary Film." In *Memory and Popular Film*, edited by Paul Grainge. Manchester: Manchester University Press.

Burke, John, Walter Henry, Paul Messier, and Timothy Vitale. 2000. Albumen. albumen.conservation-us.org; accessed May 26, 2013.

Burke, Peter. 1997. *Varieties of Cultural History.* Ithaca: Cornell University Press.

Campagnoni, Donata. 2006. "The Preservation, Care and Exploitation of Documentation Related to the Cinema." *Film History: An International Journal* 18(3): 306–18.

Chakrabarty, Dipesh. 1996. "Remembered Villages: Representation of Hindu-Bengali Memories in the Aftermath of the Partition." *Economic and Political Weekly* 31/32: 2143–51.

———. 2004. "Romantic Archives: Literature and the Politics of Identity in Bengal." *Critical Inquiry* 30: 654–82.

Chakravarty, Sharmila. 2012. "Lights, Camera . . . Awesomeness!" *Indian Architect and Builder* 25(5): 82–85.

Chanan, Michael. 1980. *The Dream That Kicks: The Prehistory and Early Years of Cinema in Britain.* London and Boston: Routledge and Kegan Paul.

Chatterjee, P. 1995. *The Nation and Its Fragments: Colonial and Postcolonial Histories.* 1st Indian edition. Delhi: Oxford University Press.

———. "Bengal Politics and the Muslim Masses, 1920–47." In *India's Partition: Process, Strategy, and Mobilization*, edited by Mushirul Hasan. Delhi: Oxford University Press.

Chatterjee, Ranita. 2011. "Journeys In and Beyond the City: Cinema in Calcutta, 1897–1939." PhD Diss. University of Westminster, London.

———. 2012. "Cinema in the Colonial City: Early Film Audiences in Calcutta." In *Audiences: Defining and Researching Screen Entertainment Reception*, edited by Ian Christie. Amsterdam: Amsterdam University Press.

Chattopadhyay, Swati. 2002. "'Goods, Chattels, and Sundry Items': Constructing 19th-Century Anglo-Indian Domestic Life." *Journal of Material Culture* 7(3): 243–71.

———. 2005. *Representing Calcutta: Modernity, Nationalism, and the Colonial Uncanny, Asia's Great Cities*. London and New York: Routledge.

Chaudhary, Zahid R. 2012. *Afterimage of Empire: Photography in Nineteenth-Century India*. Minneapolis and London: University of Minnesota Press.

Chaudhuri, Sukanta. 1990. *Calcutta, the Living City*. Calcutta and New York: Oxford University Press.

Christie, Ian. 2012. "Introduction: In Search of Audiences." In *Audiences: Defining and Researching Screen Entertainment Reception*, edited by Ian Christie. Amsterdam: Amsterdam University Press.

Chun, Wendy Hui Kyong. 2008. "The Enduring Ephemeral, or the Future Is a Memory." *Critical Inquiry* 35(1): 148–71.

Coe, Brian. 1978. *Cameras*. New York: Crown.

Cohn, Bernard S. 1996. *Colonialism and Its Forms of Knowledge: The British in India. Princeton Studies in Culture/Power/History*. Princeton: Princeton University Press.

Crary, Jonathan. 1999. *Suspensions of Perception: Attention, Spectacle, and Modern Culture*. Cambridge: MIT Press.

Creekmur, C. nd. "The Devdas Phenomenon." *philip's filums*, May 2012: www.uiowa.edu/~incinema/DEVDAS.html.

Cubitt, S. 2004. *The Cinema Effect*. Cambridge: MIT Press.

Danks, Adrian. 2006. "The Global Art of Found Footage Cinema in Traditions of World Cinema." In *Traditions in Global Cinema*, edited by Linda Badley et al., 241–53. New Brunswick: Rutgers University Press.

Dass, Manishita. 2004. "Outside the Lettered City: Cinema, Modernity, and Nation in India." PhD diss, Stanford University.

———. 2009. "The Crowd outside the Lettered City: Imagining the Mass Audience in 1920s India." *Cinema Journal* 48:4: 77–98.

Dewan, D. 2001. "Crafting Knowledge and Knowledge of Crafts: Art Education, Colonialism, and the Madras School of Arts in Nineteenth-Century South Asia." PhD diss. University of Minnesota.

———. 2003. "Scripting South Asia's Visual Past: *The Journal of Indian Art and Industry* and the Production of Knowledge in the Late Nineteenth Century." In *Imperial Co-Histories: National Identities and the British and Colonial Press*, edited by J. Codell, 29–44, Madison, NJ: Fairleigh Dickinson University Press.

Dewey, Clive. 1982. "Figures in a Landscape: Anglo-Indian Art." *Modern Asian Studies* 16(4): 683–97.

Doane, Mary Ann. 2007. "Imaging Contingency: An Interview with Mary Ann Doane." *Parallax* 13(4): 16–25.

Edwards, Elizabeth, Chris Gosden, and Ruth B. Phillips. 2006. "Introduction." In *Sensible Objects: Colonialism, Museums, and Material Culture*, edited by Elizabeth Edwards, Chris Gosden, and Ruth B. Phillips. Oxford and New York: Berg.

Elsaesser, T. 2008. "Afterword—Digital Cinema and the Apparatus: Archaeologies, Epistemologies, Ontologies." In *Cinema and Technology: Cultures, Theories, Practices*, edited by Bruce Bennett, M. Fustenau, and A. Mackenzie. London: Palgrave Macmillan.

Ernst, Wolfgang. 2011. "Media Archaeography—Method and Machine Versus History and Narrative of Media." In *Media Archaeology: Approaches, Applications, and Implications*, edited by Erkki Huhtamo and Jussi Parikka. Berkeley: University of California Press.

Ewing, George. 1895. *A Handbook of Photography for Amateurs in India*. Calcutta: Thacker, Spink.

Falconer, John. 2001. *India: Pioneering Photographers 1850–1900*. London: British Library and Howard and Jane Ricketts Collection.

———. 2002. "'A Pure Labor of Love': A Publishing History of The People of India." In *Colonialist Photography: Imag(in)ing Race and Place*, edited by Eleanore Hight and Gary D. Samson. London: Routledge.

Field, C. 1878. *Law of Evidence in British India*. 3rd edition. Calcutta: Thacker, Spink.

Freitag, Sandria. 2002. "Visions of the Nation: Theorizing the Nexus between Creation, Consumption, and Participation in the Public Sphere." In *Pleasure and the Nation. The History, Politics, and Consumption of Public Culture in India*, edited by Rachel Dwyer and Christopher Pinney. New Delhi: Oxford University Press.

Furedy, Christine. 1981. "British Tradesmen of Calcutta 1830–1900: A Preliminary Study of Their Economic and Political Roles." In *Women, Politics, and Literature in Bengal*, edited by C. B. Sealy. East Lansing: Asian Studies Center, Michigan State University.

Ganti, Tejaswini. 2004. *Bollywood: A Guidebook to Popular Hindi Cinema*. Routledge Film Guidebooks. New York: Routledge.

Garga, B. D. 1996. *So Many Cinemas: The Motion Picture in India*. Mumbai: Eminence Designs.

———. 2007. *From Raj to Swaraj: the Non-Fiction Film in India*. New Delhi: Penguin Books.

Gaudreault, André. 2000. "The Diversity of Cinematographic Connections in the Intermedial Context of the Turn of the 20th Century." In *Visual Delights: Essays on the Popular and Projected Image in the 19th Century*, edited by Simon Popple and Vanessa Toulmin Trowbridge. Wiltshire, UK: Flicks Books.

———. 2001. "Fragmentation and Assemblage in the Lumière Animated Pictures." *Film History* 13(1): 76–88.

Geary, P. 1986. "Sacred Commodities: The Circulation of Medieval Relics." In *The Social Life of Things: Commodities in Cultural Perspective*, edited by A. Appadurai, 169–93. Cambridge: Cambridge University Press.

Ghosh, Siddhartha. 1998. *Chobi Tola: Bangalir Photography Charcha*. Calcutta: Ananda.

Ginzburg, Carlo. 2012. *Threads and Traces: True, False, Fictive*. Berkeley: University of California Press.

Gordon, Eric. 2010. *The Urban Spectator: American Concept Cities from Kodak to Google*. Hanover, NH: Dartmouth College Press.

Goswami, Omkar. 1992. "*Sahibs, Babus,* and *Banias*: Changes in Industrial Control in Eastern India, 1918–50." In *Entrepreneurship and Industry in India, 1800–1947*, edited by Rajat Kanta Ray. Delhi and New York: Oxford University Press.

Government of India. 1898. *The Un-repealed Acts of the Governor General in Council, 1834 to 1867*. Vol. 1. Calcutta: Superintendent of Government Printing.

Govil, Nitin. 2005. "Something to Declare: Trading Culture, Trafficking Hollywood and Textual Travel." PhD diss. New York University.

———. 2006. "Bollywood and the Frictions of Global Mobility." In *Media on the Move: Global Flow and Contra-Flow*, edited by Daya Kishan Thussu, 84–98. London and New York: Routledge.

Grainge, P. 2008. *Brand Hollywood: Selling Entertainment in a Global Media Age*. London, Routledge.

Grieveson, Lee. 2009. "On Governmentality and Screens." *Screen* 50(1): 180–87.

Griffiths, Alison. 2013. *Shivers Down Your Spine: Cinema, Museums, and the Immersive View*. New York: Columbia University Press.

Grimaud, E. 2002. "La projection morcelée: Fragments de films, intermédiares et public dans un cinéma de Bombay." *L'Homme* 164: 81–104.

Guha-Thakurta, Tapati. 1992. *The Making of a New "Indian" Art: Artists, Aesthetics, and Nationalism in Bengal, C. 1850–1920*. Cambridge and New York: Cambridge University Press.

———. 2006. *The Aesthetics of the Popular Print. Lithographs and Oleographs from 19th and 20th Century India: An Exhibition of Prints from the Collection of Sanjeet Chowdhury, March 11-15, 2006*. Kolkata [Calcutta]: Birla Academy of Art and Culture.

Gunning. Tom. 1983. "An Unseen Energy Swallows Space: The Space in Early Film and Its Relation to American Avant-Garde Film." In *Film Before Griffith*, edited by John Fell, 355–66. Berkeley: University of California Press.

———. 1995. "Tracing the Individual Body: Photography, Detectives, and Early Cinema." In *Cinema and the Invention of Modern Life*, edited by Vanessa Schwarz and Leo Charney, 15–45. Berkeley: University of California Press.

———. 2002. "Bodies in Motion: The Pas De Deux of the Ideal and the Material at the Fin-de-Siècle." In *Arret sur image, fragmentation du temps/Stop Motion, Fragmentation of Time*. Nadir: Editions Payot Lausanne.

———. 2007. "Moving Away From the Index: Cinema and the Impression of Reality." *Differences* 18(1): 29–52.

———. 2008. *The Films of Fritz Lang: Allegories of Vision and Modernity*. London: British Film Institute.

Gupta, Akhil. 1992. "The Reincarnation of Souls and the Rebirth of Commodities: Representations of Time in "East" and "West." *Cultural Critique* 22: 187–211.

Gutman, Judith Mara. 1982. *Through Indian Eyes*. New York: Oxford University Press: International Center of Photography.

Haggard, S. 1987–88. "Indian Film Posters." *Sight and Sound* 57(1): 62.

Hansen, Miriam. 1999. "The Mass Production of the Senses: Classical Cinema as Vernacular Modernism." *Modernism/modernity* 6(2): 59–77.

Hardt, Michael. 2006. "Bathing in the Multitude." In *Crowds*, edited by Jeffrey T. Schnapp and Matthew Tiews. Stanford: Stanford University Press.

Harris, Neil. 1979. "Iconography and Intellectual History: The Half-Tone Effect." In *New Directions in American Intellectual History*, edited by Paul Keith Conkin and John Higham. Baltimore: Johns Hopkins University Press.

Hervey, H. 1913. *The European in India*. London: Stanley Paul.

Hiley, Nicholas. 2012. "At the Picture Palace: the British Cinema Audience, 1895–1920." In *Audiences: Defining and Researching Screen Entertainment Reception*. Amsterdam: Amsterdam University Press.

Hobsbawm, E. J., and C. Wrigley. 1999. *Industry and Empire: From 1750 to the Present Day*. New York: The New Press.

Horak, Jan-Christophe. 2001. "The Hollywood History Business." In *The End of Cinema As We Know It* edited by Jon Lewis, 33–42. New York: New York University Press.

Hughes, Stephen. 1996. "Is There Anyone Out There? Exhibition and the Formation of Silent Film Audiences in South India." PhD diss., University of Chicago.

———. 2005. "Mythologicals and Modernity: Contesting Silent Cinema in South India." *Postscripts* 1.2/1.3: 207–35.

———. 2013. "The Production of the Past: Early Tamil Film History as a Living Archive." *Bioscope: South Asian Screen Studies* 4(1): 71–80.

Hutchens, B. C. 2007. "Techniques of Forgetting? Hypo-Amnesic History and the An-Archive." *SubStance* 36(2): 37–55.

Indian Cinematograph Committee. 1928. *Indian Cinematograph Committee, 1927–28: Evidence*. 5 volumes. Calcutta: Government of India Central Publication Branch.

Indian Law Reports. 1919. Indian Law Reports (Bombay Series), 44.

Inglis, S. 1999. "Master, Machine, and Meaning: Printed Images in Twentieth-Century India." In *Unpacking Culture. Art and Commodity in Colonial and Postcolonial Worlds*, edited by R. B. Phillips and C. B. Steiner, 122–39. Berkeley and Los Angeles: University of California Press.

Israel, M. 1994. *Communications and Power: Propaganda and the Press in the Indian Nationalist Struggle, 1920–1947*. Cambridge South Asian Studies; 56. Cambridge and New York: Cambridge University Press.

Jaikumar, Priya. 2006. *Cinema at the End of Empire: A Politics of Transition in Britain and India*. Durham: Duke University Press.

Jain, K. 2001. "Muscularity and Its Ramifications: Mimetic Male Bodies in Indian Mass Culture." *South Asia: Journal of South Asian Studies* 24: 197–224.

———. 2003. "More Than Meets the Eye: The Circulation of Images and the Embodiment of Value." In *Beyond Appearances? Visual Practices and Ideologies in Modern India*, edited by S. Ramaswamy, 33–70. New Delhi: Sage.

———. 2005. "India's Modern Vernacular: On the Edge." In *Edge of Desire: Recent Art in India*. London: Philip Wilson.

———. 2007. *Gods in the Bazaar: The Economies of Indian Calendar Art*. Durham: Duke University Press.

———. 2009. "Archive, Repertoire, or Warehouse? Producers of Indian Popular Images as Stakeholders in a Virtual Database." *South Asian Visual Culture Series* 3: 1–14.

Jenkins, John. 1981. "Camera Collecting—Tropical Cameras." *The Photographic Collector* 2(2): 70–75.

Jenkins, R. V. 1975. "Technology and the Market—George Eastman and the Origins of Mass Amateur Photography." *Technology and Culture* 16(1): 1–19.

Jenkins, Reese. 1966. "Some Interrelations of Science, Technology and the Photographic Industry in the Nineteenth Century." PhD diss., University of Wisconsin.

Johnson, Gordon. 1973. "Partition, Agitation, and Congress, Bengal, 1904–1908." *Modern Asian Studies* 7(3): 533–88.

Joshi, Priya. 2002. *In Another Country: Colonialism, Culture, and the English Novel in India*. New York: Columbia University Press.

Jussim, E. 1974. *Visual Communication and the Graphic Arts; Photographic Technologies in the Nineteenth Century*. New York: R. R. Bowker.

Kagal, Ayesha. 1980. "Opening up Pandora's Box: The Video Wave." *Times of India*, August 17, 1980.

Kalyan, Rohan. 2011. "Fragmentation by Design: Architecture, Finance, and Identity." *The Grey Room* 44: 26–53.

Kapur, Anuradha. 1993. "The Representation of Gods and Heroes: Parsi Mythological Drama of the Early Twentieth Century." *Journal of Arts and Ideas* 23/24.

Kapur, Gita. 1988. "Ravi Varma: Representational Dilemmas of a Nineteenth Century Indian Painter." *Journal of Arts and Ideas* 23/24.

Karlekar, Malavika. 2005. *Re-Visioning the Past: Early Photography in Bengal 1875–1915*. New Delhi, Oxford, and New York: Oxford University Press.

Kerr, Ian. 2003. "Representation and Representations of the Railways of Colonial and Post-Colonial South Asia." *Modern Asian Studies* 37(2): 287–326.

Kessler, Frank. 2013. "Pathé versus Pathé, Exhibit A: Reading an Archival Document." *Film History: An International Journal* 25(1): 118–29.

Kriegel, L. 2004. "Culture and the Copy: Calico, Capitalism, and Design Copyright in Early Victorian Britain." *Journal of British Studies* 43: 233–65.

Krishen, P. 1991. "Knocking on the Doors of Public Culture: India's Parallel Cinema." *Public Culture* 4(1): 23–41.

Lala Deen Dayal. www.deendayal.com; accessed May 26, 2013.

Larkin, Brian. 2008. *Signal and Noise: Media, Infrastructure and Urban Culture in Nigeria*. Durham: Duke University Press.

Legg, S. 2007. "Beyond the European Province: Foucault and Postcolonialism." In *Space, Knowledge, and Power: Foucault and Geography*, edited by J. W. Crampton and S. Elden, 265–90. Aldershot, Hampshire: Ashgate.

Lipkin, Steven, Derek Paget, and Jane Roscoe. 2005. "Docudrama and Mock Documentary: Defining Terms, Proposing Canons." In *Docufictions: Essays on the Intersection of Documentary and Fiction Filmmaking*, edited by Gary Rhodes and John Springer. Jefferson, NC: Macfarland.

Lister, Martin, Jon Dovey, Seth Giddings, Iain Grant, and Kieran Kelly. 2009. *New Media: A Critical Introduction*. 2nd edition. Milton Park, Abingdon and New York: Routledge.

Lobato, Ramon. 2012. *Shadow Economies of the Cinema: Mapping Informal Film Distribution*. London: Palgrave Macmillan on behalf of the BFI.

MacDougall, David. 2006. *The Corporeal Image: Film, Ethnography, and the Senses.* Princeton: Princeton University Press.

Mace, O. Henry. 1999. *Collector's Guide to Early Photographs.* 2nd edition. Iola, WI: Krause Publications.

Maddison, Angus, and Organisation for Economic Co-operation and Development. Development Centre. 2003. *The World Economy: Historical Statistics*, Development Centre Studies. Paris, France: Development Centre of the Organisation for Economic Co-operation and Development, 2003.

Majumdar, Neepa. 2009. *Wanted Cultured Ladies Only! Female Stardom and Cinema in India, 1930s–1950s.* Chicago: University of Illinois Press.

Margulies, Ivone. 2003. "Exemplary Bodies: Reenactment in *Love in the City*, *Sons*, and *Close-Up*." In *Rites of Realism: Essays on Corporeal Cinema*, edited by Ivone Marguies, 217–44. Durham: Duke University Press.

Mazumdar, R. 2013. "Editorial: Celluloid Memories and the Digital 'Present.'" *BioScope: South Asian Screen Studies* 4(2): 93–95.

Mazumdar, Ranjani. 2010. "The Man Who Was Seen Too Much: Amitabh Bachchan on Film Posters." *Tasveer Ghar: A House of Pictures*, September 7. www.tasveergharindia.net/cmsdesk/essay/106/index.html.

Mazzarella, W. 2009. "Making Sense of the Cinema in Late Colonial India." In *Censorship in South Asia: Cultural Regulation from Sedition to Seduction*, edited by R. Kaur and W. Mazzarella, 63–86, Bloomington: Indiana University Press.

Metz, Christian. 1982. *The Imaginary Signifier: Psychoanalysis and the Cinema.* Bloomington. Indiana University Press.

Miller, T. 2005. *Global Hollywood 2.* London: BFI Publishing.

Mitchell, W. J. T. 2005. *What Do Pictures Want? The Lives and Loves of Images.* Chicago: University of Chicago Press.

Mitter, P. 2003. "Mechanical Reproduction and the World of the Colonial Artist." In *Beyond Appearances? Visual Practices and Ideologies in Modern India*, edited by S. Ramaswamy, 1–32, New Delhi: Sage.

Moran, James. 2002. *There's No Place like Home Video.* Minneapolis: University of Minnesota Press.

Moretti, Franco. 2000. "The Slaughterhouse of Literature." *Modern Language Quarterly* 61(1): 207–28.

Mukerji, C. 1983. *From Graven Images: Patterns of Modern Materialism.* New York: Columbia University Press.

Mukherjee, Madhuja. Sarai: Centre for the Study of Developing Studies. 2007. "Looking at the Glasses Darkly: Revisiting Calcutta Studios." mail.sarai.net/pipermail/reader-list/; accessed January 24.

Musser, Charles. 1990. *The Emergence of Cinema: The American Screen to 1907.* New York: Scribner.

Navitski, Rielle. 2013. "Sensationalism, Cinema, and the Popular Press in Mexico and Brazil, 1905–1930." PhD diss. University of California, Berkeley.

Ollman, Arthur. 1983. *Samuel Bourne: Images of India, Untitled. 33.* Carmel, CA: Friends of Photography.

Ong, Aihwa. 2006. *Neoliberalism as Exception: Mutations in Citizenship and Sovereignty.* Durham: Duke University Press.

———, and Stephen J. Collier. 2005. *Global Assemblages: Technology, Politics, and Ethics as Anthropological Problems*. Malden, MA: Blackwell.

Osborne, R. 2011. "India on Film, 1939–47." In *Film and the End of Empire*, edited by C. MacCabe and L. Grieveson. London: Palgrave Macmillan.

Pedulla, Gabriele. 2012. *In Broad Daylight: Movies and Spectators After the Cinema*. 1st edition. Brooklyn: Verso.

Pelizzari, Maria Antonella, ed. 2003. *Traces of India: Photography, Architecture, and the Politics of Representation, 1850–1900*. Montreal and New Haven: Canadian Centre for Architecture; Yale Center for British Art: Yale University Press.

Phalke, D. G. 1987. "Dossier." *Continuum* 2.1.

Pinney, Christopher. 1997. *Camera Indica: The Social Life of Indian Photographs*. Chicago: University of Chicago Press.

———. 2004. *"Photos of the Gods": The Printed Image and Political Struggle in India*. London: Reaktion.

———. 2004. "The Nation (Un)Pictured? Chromolithography and 'Popular' Politics in India, 1878–1995." *Critical Inquiry* 23: 834–67.

———. 2008. *The Coming of Photography in India*. London: British Library.

———. 2009. "Iatrogenic Religion and Politics." In *Censorship in South Asia: Cultural Regulation from Sedition to Seduction*, edited by R. Kaur and W. Mazzarella, 29–62. Bloomington: Indiana University Press.

Prasad, Ritika. 2013. "'Time-Sense': Railways and Temporality in Colonial India." *Modern Asian Studies* 47(4): 1252–82.

Punathambekar, A. 2010. "Ameen Sayani and Radio Ceylon: Notes towards a History of Broadcasting and Bombay Cinema." *BioScope: South Asian Screen Studies* 1(2): 189–97.

———. 2013. *From Bombay to Bollywood: The Making of a Global Media Industry*. New York: NYU Press.

Rai, Amit S. 2009. *Untimely Bollywood: Globalization and India's New Media Assemblage*. Durham: Duke University Press.

Rajadhyaksha, R. 1986. "Neo-Traditionalism: Film as Popular Art in India." *Framework* 32/33: 20–67.

———. 1993. "The Phalke Era: Conflict of Traditional Form and Modern Technology." In *Interrogating Modernity: Culture and Colonialism in India*, edited by P. Sudhir and T. Niranjana, 47–82. Calcutta: Seagull Books, 1993.

———. 2004. "The 'Bollywoodization' of Indian Cinema: Cultural Nationalism in a Global Arena." In *City Flicks: Indian Cinema and the Urban Experience*, edited by Preben Karrsholm, 113–39. Kolkata: Seagull Books.

———. 2005. "Visuality and Visual Art. Speculating on a Link." In *Edge of Desire: Recent Art in India*. London: Philip Wilson.

———. 2009. *Indian Cinema in the Time of Celluloid: From Bollywood to the Emergency*. Bloomington: Indiana University Press.

———, and Paul Willemen. 1994. *Encyclopaedia of Indian Cinema*. London and New Delhi: British Film Institute; Oxford University Press.

Rajan, Gita. 2012. "Evidence of Another Modernity: Lala Deen Dayal's 1903 Durbar Photographs." In *Power and Resistance: The Delhi Coronation Durbar*, edited by

Julie Codell. Ahmedabad, India: Mapin Publishing, The Alkazi Collection of Photography; U.S.: Grantha Corporation.

Ramaswamy, S. 2003. *Beyond Appearances? Visual Practices and Ideologies in Modern India*. New Delhi: Sage.

Ray, Rajat Kanta. 1995. "Asian Capital in the Age of European Domination: The Rise of the Bazaar, 1800–1914." *Modern Asian Studies* 29(3): 449–554.

Ray Choudhury, Ranabir. 1992. "Early Calcutta Advertisements, 1875–1925" (a selection from *The Statesman*).

Renford, Raymond K. 1987. *The Non-Official British in India to 1920*. Delhi: Oxford University Press.

Ricoeur, Paul. 1995. *Figuring the Sacred: Religion, Narrative, and Imagination*. Minneapolis: Augsburg Fortress.

Rodowick, David Norman. 2007. *The Virtual Life of Film*. Cambridge: Harvard University Press.

Rose, M. 1988. "The Author as Proprietor: Donaldson v. Becket and the Genealogy of Modern Authorship." *Representations* 23: 51–85.

Rosenbaum, Jonathan. nd. "Rock Criticism." www.jonathanrosenbaum.com/?p=7158; accessed July 4, 2013.

———. nd. "The Seberg We Missed: Interview with Mark Rappaport." www.jonathanrosenbaum.com/?p=19905; accessed July 4, 2013.

Rosenstone, Robert. nd. "From the Film and Media Column in the November 1999 *Perspectives*: Reel History with Missing Reels?" American Historical Association. www.historians.org/perspectives/issues/1999/9911/9911fil1.cfm; accessed July 6, 2013.

Roy, Srirupa. 2007. *Beyond Belief: India and the Politics of Postcolonial Nationalism*. Durham: Duke University Press.

Sambrani, Chaitanya. 2005. "On the Double Edge of Desire." In *Edge of Desire: Recent Art in India*. London: Philip Wilson.

Sampson, Gary D. 1992. "The Success of Samuel Bourne in India." *History of Photography* 16(4): 336–47.

Sarkar, J. 1954. "A Century of Historic Prints." *Bengal Past and Present* LXXIII(136–37).

Sarkar, Sumit. 1989. *Modern India: 1885–1947*. Basingstoke: Macmillan.

Savras, R., and David Frohlick. 2011. *From Snapshots to Social Media: the Changing Picture of Domestic Photography*. London and Heidelberg: Springer.

Schaffer, Simon. 1996. "Babbage's Dancer and the Impresarios of Mechanism." In *Cultural Babbage: Technology, Time, and Invention*, edited by Francis Spufford and Jennifer S. Uglow. London: Faber.

Schulze, B. 2003. *Humanist and Emotional Beginnings of a Nationalist Indian Cinema in Bombay: With Kracauer in the Footsteps of Phalke*. Berlin: Avinus.

Sengupta, M. 1995. "Constructing the Canon: Problems in Bengali Literary Historiography." *Social Scientist* 23(10/12): 56–69.

Shaw, Graham. 1998. "Calcutta: Birthplace of the Indian Lithographed Book." *Journal of the Printing Historical Society* 27: 89–112.

Shaw, Jeffrey, and Peter Weibel. 2003. *Future Cinema: The Cinematic Imaginary after Film*. Cambridge and London: MIT Press.

Simon, Jane. 2006. "Recycling Home Movies." *Continuum* 20(2): 189–99.

Simone, N. 2012. "Photography and Communication Media in the Nineteenth Century." *History of Photography* 36(4): 451–56.

Singer, Ben. 2001. *Melodrama and Modernity: Early Sensational Cinema and Its Contexts*. New York: Columbia University Press.

Sinha, Pradip. 1990. "Calcutta and the Currents of History, 1690–1912." In *Calcutta, the Living City, Vol. 1*, edited by Sukanta Chaudhuri. Calcutta and New York: Oxford University Press.

Sobchack, Vivian. 2003. "Nostalgia for a Digital Object: Regrets on the Quickening of QuickTime." In *Future Cinema: The Cinematic Imaginary after Film*, edited by Jeffrey Shaw and Peter Weibel. Cambridge and London: MIT Press.

Srinivas, S. V. 2000. "Is There a Public in the Cinema Hall?" *Framework: The Journal of Cinema and Media*. www.frameworkonline.com/42index.htm; accessed January 30, 2008.

Stam, Robert, and Randall Johnson. 1995. "The Cinema of Hunger: Nelson Pereira Dos Santos' *Vidas Secas*." In *Brazilian Cinema, Expanded Edition*, edited by Robert Stam and Randall Johnson. New York: Columbia University Press.

Stein, Deborah. 2011. "To Curate in the Field: Archaeological Privatization and the Aesthetic 'Legislation' of Antiquity in India." *Contemporary South Asia* 19(1): 25–47.

Steiner, C. B. 1999. "Authenticity, Repetition, and the Aesthetics of Seriality: The Work of Tourist Art in the Age of Mechanical Reproduction." In *Unpacking Culture. Art and Commodity in Colonial and Postcolonial Worlds*, edited by R. B. Phillips and C. B. Steiner, 87–103. Berkeley and Los Angeles: University of California Press.

Sternberger, Paul Spencer. 2001. *Between Amateur and Aesthete: The Legitimization of Photography as Art in America, 1880–1900*. Albuquerque: University of New Mexico Press.

Stewart, Susan. 1993. *On Longing: Narratives of the Miniature, the Gigantic, the Souvenir, the Collection*. Durham: Duke University Press.

Stoler, Ann. 2002. "Colonial Archives and the Arts of Governance." *Archival Science* 2: 10.

Strauven, Wanda. 2011. "The Observer's Dilemma: To Play or Not to Play." In *Media Archaeology: Approaches, Applications, and Implications*, edited by Erkki Huhtammo and Jussi Parika. Berkeley: University of California Press.

Stringer, Julian. 2003. "Raiding the Archive: Film Festivals and the Revival of Classic Hollywood." In *Memory and Popular Film*, edited by Paul Grainge. Manchester: Manchester University Press.

Sundar, P. 1995. *Patrons and Philistines: Arts and the State in British India, 1773–1947*. Delhi: Oxford University Press.

Sundaram, Ravi. 2013. *No Limits: Media Studies from India*. New Delhi: Oxford University Press.

———. 2001. "Recycling Modernity: Pirate Electronic Cultures in India." In *Sarai Reader 1: The Public Domain*. New Delhi: Sarai/CSDS/Society for Old and New Media.

Swaroop, Kamal. 2013. *Tracing Phalke: the Man and His Times, 1840–1944*. Limited Edition. National Film Development Corporation, India.

Tanvir, K. 2013. "Pirate Histories: Rethinking the Indian Film Archive." *BioScope: South Asian Screen Studies* 4(2): 115–36.

Taylor, Charles. 2004. *Modern Social Imaginaries*. Durham: Duke University Press.

Thakurta, T. G. 1988. "Artists, Artisans, and Mass Picture Production in Late Nineteenth- and Early Twentieth-Century Calcutta: The Changing Iconography of Popular Prints." *South Asia Research* 8: 3–45.

———. 2006. *The Aesthetics of the Popular Print. Lithographs and Oleographs from 19th and 20th Century India: An Exhibition of Prints from the Collection of Sanjeet Chowdhury*, March 11–15, 2006, Kolkata: Birla Academy of Art and Culture.

Thissen, Judith. 2012. "Beyond the Nickelodeon: Cinemagoing, Everyday Life, and Identity Politics." In *Audiences: Defining and Researching Screen Entertainment Reception*, edited by Ian Christie, 45–65. Amsterdam: Amsterdam University Press.

Thomas, G. 1979. "The First Four Decades of Photography in India." *History of Photography* 3(3): 215–21.

———. 1986. "O'Shaughnessy's Experiments in Colour Photography." *History of Photography* 10: 175.

Thomas, R. 1985. "Indian Cinema: Pleasures and Popularity." *Screen* 26(3): 116–31.

Thompson, Kristin. 1985. *Exporting Entertainment: America in the World Film Market 1907–34*. London: BFI.

Thorburn, David, and Henry Jenkins. 2004. "Introduction: Toward an Aesthetics of Transition." In *Rethinking Media Change: The Aesthetics of Transition*, edited by David Thorburn, Henry Jenkins, and Brad Seawell. Cambridge: MIT Press.

Trope, Alison. 2001. "Le Cinéma pour le Cinéma: Making a Museum of the Moving Image." *The Moving Image* 1(1): 30–67.

Tsivian, Yuri. 2008. "What Is Cinema? An Agnostic Answer." *Critical Inquiry* 34(4): 754–76.

Tweedie, James. 2010. "Delirious Cities and their Cinema: On Koolhaas and Film Studies." *Public Culture* 22(2): 369–97.

Uroskie, Andrew V. 2014. *Between the Black Box and the White Cube: Expanded Cinema and Postwar Art*. Chicago and London: University Of Chicago Press.

Varma, R. R, E. Neumayer, and C. Schelberger. 2005. *Raja Ravi Varma: Portrait of an Artist: The Diary of C. Raja Raja Varma*. Delhi and New York: Oxford University Press.

Vasudevan, Ravi. 1991. "The Cultural Space of a Film Narrative: Interpreting *Kismet* (Bombay Talkies, 1943)." *The Indian Economic and Social History Review* 28(2): 171–85.

———. 1995. "Film Studies, New Cultural History, and the Experience of Modernity." *Economic and Political Weekly*, November 4, 2809–14.

———. 1996. "Shifting Codes, Dissolving Identities: the Hindi Social Film of the 1950s as Popular Culture." *Third Text* 10(34): 59–77.

———. 2000. "The Politics of Cultural Address in a 'Transitional' Cinema: A Case Study of Indian Popular Cinema." In *Rethinking Film Studies*, edited by C. Gledhill and L. Williams, 130–31. London: Arnold.

———. 2011. "Official and Amateur: Exploring Information Film in India, 1920s–40s." In *Film and the End of Empire*, edited by C. MacCabe and L. Grieveson. London: Palgrave Macmillan.

Walia, R. 2013. "Techno-Nostalgia: Colorization of K. Asif's Mughal-E-Azam." *BioScope: South Asian Screen Studies* 4(2): 137–58.

Watwe, Bapu. 2004. *Dadasaheb Phalke. The Father of Indian Cinema*. Translated by S. A. Virkar. New Delhi: National Trust of India.

Wees, William. 2002. "The Ambiguous Aura of Hollywood Stars in Avant-Garde Found-Footage Films." *Cinema Journal* 41(2): 3–18.

Wilkinson-Weber, C. M. 2010. "A Need for Redress: Costume in Some Recent Hindi Film Remakes." *BioScope: South Asian Screen Studies* 1(2): 125–45.

Zryd, Michael. 2003. "Found Footage Film as Discursive Metahistory: Craig Baldwin's Tribulation 99." *The Moving Image* 3(2): 40–61.

FILMOGRAPHY

"An Affair to Remember." Series. 2012–15. *Headlines Today*. Living Media TV.

"Bhavnani, M. and Films Division of India. 1953. *Black Sheep*."

"Dutt, Guru. 1957. *Pyaasa*. Guru Dutt Films Private Limited."

Jain, Nishta. 2005. *City of Photos*. Bangalore: India Foundation for the Arts and the Jan Vrijman Fund.

Kadam, Prashant, 2006. *The Bioscopewallah*. India: Prashant Kadam.

Krishnaswamay, S., and Films Division of India. 1980. *Through a Different Lens*.

Lakhani, Megha. 2006. "Prakash Traveling Cinema." India: National Institute of Design.

MacDougall, David, and Judith MacDougall. 1991. *Photo Wallahs: An Encounter with Photography in Mussoorie, a North Indian Hill Station*. DVD. Berkeley: Oxnard Film Productions., SEPT (Television station: France), and University of California Berkeley, Extension Center for Media and Independent Learning.

"Mukherjee, Gyan. 1943. *Kismat*. Bombay Talkies.

Nag, Hiren. 1983. *Film Hi Film*. Shabab International Production Associates. www.youtube.com/watch?v=iy6dpib2YbY; accessed July 21, 2013.

Shah, Krishna. 1979. *Cinema Cinema*. Shabab International Production Associates. www.youtube.com/watch?v=pwt0DCpPuLQ; accessed July 21, 2013.

Sternberg, Tim. 2007. *Salim Baba*. DVD. USA: HBO.